Strindberg's *The Ghost Sonata*

Strindberg's *The Ghost Sonata*
From Text to Performance

Egil Törnqvist

Amsterdam University Press

Cover illustration: Elin Klinga as the Young Lady and Jonas Malmsjö as the Student in Ingmar Bergman's 2000 production of *The Ghost Sonata* at Dramaten in Stockholm. Photo: Bengt Wanselius.

Cover design: Kok Korpershoek [KO], Amsterdam

Lay-out: JAPES, Amsterdam

NUGI 925
ISBN 90 5356 435 7 (paperback)
ISBN 90 5356 454 3 (hardcover)

Table of contents

Preface

Some thirty years ago I followed the rehearsals of Ingmar Bergman's production of *The Ghost Sonata* at the Royal Dramatic Theatre (Dramaten) in Stockholm. This resulted the following year in a book in Swedish.

The present book, though partly based on the former one, has a broader scope. Its main purpose is to illuminate the Strindbergian source text both as a text for the reader and as an embedded text for the spectator, that is, as a text – whether in source or target form – transposed to and received via audiovisual or aural media: stage, screen, air.

The book is divided into four chapters. The first is devoted to an analysis of the source text, the second to various translation problems related to English and American renderings of the play, the third to some significant stage productions, and the fourth to some adaptations of it for radio and television. Special attention is given to Ingmar Bergman's highly successful 1973 production. The four chapters are framed by a Prologue and an Epilogue. In the former, I elucidate the biographical and literary background. In the latter, I discuss the impact of the play, both as a text and as a production, on dramatists and directors. Four appendices provide detailed information about the drama text and about Bergman's 1973 production, a complete transcription of which is found in the last appendix. At the end of the book, there is a select, annotated list of productions, intended to supplement the discussion in chapters Three and Four and to stimulate further research.

Unless otherwise indicated, all quotations from non-English sources, including Strindberg's source text, are in my own rendering, although I naturally owe much to existing translations of *Spöksonaten*, the Swedish title of the play that concerns us.

I use the past tense for non-durative modes (stage) and the present tense for durative (repeatable) modes (text, screen, air). The existence of a taped, i.e. durative recording of a stage presentation cannot change the fundamental fact that such a recording can never correspond completely to the intended live performance, the non-repeatable theatrical event.

'Recipient' is used as an umbrella term for the reader, the spectator and the listener.

The typography of drama texts varies somewhat. Since such variation seems rather irrelevant, I have deemed it desirable to standardize the typography as follows: For stage and acting directions, I use italics throughout. The same principle is applied in my transcriptions of performance passages. Speaker-labels are put in low-case capitals and printed in roman.

Titles of non-English works are usually given in English translation. The original titles are added in the index. The following abbreviations are used:

SS   *Samlade Skrifter av August Strindberg*, ed. John Landquist, Stockholm: Bonniers, 1912-1921.

SV   *August Strindbergs Samlade Verk*, chief ed. Lars Dahlbäck, Stockholm: Almqvist & Wiksell / Norstedts, 1981- .

The figures following the abbreviations indicate volume and page(s).

Three dots within quotations indicate either a pause or an interrupted speech. Omissions within quotations are indicated by a hyphen within square brackets: [-].

In the transcription of stage and TV presentations, the following abbreviations are used:

BG   Background

FG   Foreground

L   Left

R   Right

A substantial part of this book has appeared earlier in the following publications: "Ingmar Bergman Directs Strindberg's *Ghost Sonata*," *Theatre Quarterly*, Vol. III, No. 11, July-Sep., 1973; *Bergman och Strindberg*: Spöksonaten – drama och iscensättning, Dramaten 1973, Stockholm: Prisma, 1973; *Strindbergian Drama: Themes and Structure*, Stockholm: Almqvist & Wiksell International / Atlantic Highlands, N.J.: Humanities Press Inc., 1982; *Transposing Drama: Studies in Representation*, London: Macmillan, 1991; and *Between Stage and Screen: Ingmar Bergman Directs*, Amsterdam: Amsterdam University Press, 1995. All articles/chapters have been thoroughly revised for this book.

For their helpful assistance I wish to thank the respective staff of the Strindberg Museum, the Strindberg archive of the Royal Library, the Royal Dramatic Theatre, the Drottningholm Theatre Museum, the National Archive of Recorded Sound and Moving Images, and the Photographic Archive of the Swedish Television, all in Stockholm, as well as Theaterinstituut Nederland in Amsterdam.

The illustrations have been made possible thanks to a generous grant from the Swedish Institute in Stockholm.

Prologue

An important event in theatre history occurred in late autumn 1906 when the young actor and theatre manager August Falck met the elderly writer August Strindberg. It was then that the idea of founding an intimate theatre in Stockholm, solely devoted to Strindberg's plays, arose. A year later the idea had become reality.

Strindberg had several times earlier tried to set up a theatre of his own, notably in 1888 when he founded his shortlived Scandinavian Experimental Theatre in Copenhagen. Now, after the emergence of intimate stages in Paris (Antoine), Berlin (Brahm), and London (Grein), and encouraged by Falck's successful tour with *Miss Julie*, the situation seemed more favourable. Precisely in 1906 Max Reinhardt, influenced by the Preface of *Miss Julie*, had opened his Kammerspiel-Haus in Berlin.

Inspired by the new theatre plans, Strindberg quickly wrote his four chamber plays, each of them characterized, as he puts it, by

> the intimate in form, a restricted subject, treated in depth, few characters, large points of view, free imagination, but based on observation, experience, carefully studied; simple, but not too simple; no great apparatus, no superfluous minor roles, no regular five-acters or "old machines," no long-drawn-out whole evenings.[1]

According to his *Occult Diary*, the first chamber play, *Thunder in the Air*, was finished already on 25 January. By 6 March, Strindberg was at work on the second one, *The Burned Site*. And two days later, *The Ghost Sonata* or "The Ghost Supper" as it was then alternatively called was completed. Apparently the last two were written very quickly and more or less simultaneously. Falck informs us:

> I was allowed to sit in the room outside and steal in on my toes to fetch a few manuscript pages. He wrote with whizzing speed, pulled away the completed pages and threw them unblotted on the floor, where I collected them, carried them away and sat down to read them. [-] After dinner, he 'loaded' himself, you actually saw how his thoughts were working; above the eyes appeared what looked like thick calluses, and the forehead and the temples seemed to grow, enlarge from the strain of finding concise expressions. Short notes, difficult to grasp, were strown around him on the table, in the drawers, in his pockets. The chamber plays arose like a jigsaw puzzle from these fragments.[2]

A couple of weeks after *The Ghost Sonata* was finished, Strindberg sent the play to his German translator, Emil Schering, along with a letter in which he clarified the play's religious nature:

> By today's post I am sending you a Second Chamber Play (Opus 3), called *A Ghost Sonata* (with the subtitle Kama Loka,[3] though this ought not to be included). It is *schauderhaft* [horrible] like life, when the scales fall from our eyes and we see *Das Ding an Sich* [The Thing-in-itself]. It has form and content: the Wisdom that comes with the years when our knowledge of life has accumulated and we have acquired the ability to comprehend it. That is how "The World Weaver" weaves men's destinies; secrets like these are to be found in *every* home. People are too proud to admit it; most of them boast about their imaginary happiness, and generally hide their misery. The Colonel plays his auto-comedy to the end; illusion (Maya) [the veil of illusion] has become reality to him – the Mummy wakes up first, but cannot wake others....
>
> I have suffered as though in Kama Loka (Scheol) [the realm of death] while writing it, and my hands have bled (literally).
>
> What has saved my soul from darkness during this work is my Religion (=*Anschluss med Jenseits*) [contact with the beyond]. The hope of a better life to come, and the firm conviction that we live in a world of folly and delusion (illusion), from which we must struggle to free ourselves.
>
> For me, however, things have grown brighter, and I have written with the feeling that these are my "Last Sonatas."[4]

After he had received an enthusiastic answer from Schering, Strindberg wrote him a new letter, in which he says:

> It was a great and novel pleasure for me in my Easter suffering to find you so quickly taken by *The* Gespenster *Sonata* (that's what it should be called, both after Beethoven's Ghost Sonata in D minor and his Ghost Trio, not 'Spuk' therefore).[5] And you are the first to read it! I hardly knew myself what I had done, but sensed it was something sublime, which made me shudder [-].[6]

A week later he suggested to Schering that

> the following could be inserted into the last scene of *The Ghost Sonata*, or made visible in letters of fire above *Toten-Insel*: "And God shall wipe away all tears from their eyes; and there shall be no more death, neither sorrow, nor crying, neither shall there be any more pain: for the former things are passed away." (Rev. 21:4)[7]

These suggestions were, however, never effectuated.
A few weeks later he wrote to Schering that he

had begun a major Chamber Play with *"Toten-Insel"* (Böcklin's) as a setting. The beginning was good (Kama-Loka) but I lost interest, as though I'd lost interest in life, and had a presentiment of the end. For ten years I have been preparing myself for death and have lived, as it were, "on the other side."

In a postscript he added that in the chamber plays "one lives in a world of Intimations, where people speak in half tones, mutedly, because they are ashamed of being human!"[8]

When Strindberg wrote his chamber plays, he still did not know how intimate the theatre would be where they were to be performed – luckily, for had he known, these plays may well have turned out differently.[9] He and Falck played with different alternatives. Not until June 1907 did they settle for the locality at Norra Bantorget. The theatre opened with *The Pelican* on 26 November 1907.

In the three years that Strindberg was attached to the Intimate Theatre, he provided Falck and the actors with a stream of directorial information in the form of notes and letters. He even published a *Memorandum to the Members of the Intimate Theatre*, in which he described what he meant by a chamber play:

> in drama we seek the strong, highly significant motif, but with limitations. We try to avoid in the treatment all frivolity, all calculated effects, places for applause, star roles, solo numbers. No predetermined form is to limit the author, because the motif determines the form. Consequently: freedom in treatment, which is limited only by the unity of the concept and the feeling for style.[10]

Although the first edition of *The Ghost Sonata* carries the date 1907, the play was not available in bookshops until 23 January (*SV* 58:395), two days after the opening at the Intimate Theatre.

Less than a month after the play was completed, Strindberg wrote to Schering:

> Now I beg you, read my new dramas only as that; they are mosaic work as usual, from my own and other people's lives, but please don't take them as autobiography or confessions. Whatever doesn't correspond with facts is fiction, not lies.[11]

Although he here guards himself against a biographical reading, he is at the same time anxious to point out that the play is grounded in reality.

When Strindberg wrote *The Ghost Sonata* he had been divorced from his third wife, the actress Harriet Bosse, for close to two and a half years. They stayed in touch, however, until she remarried in 1908. Strindberg, filled with an intense longing for his beautiful young ex-wife, remained in the apartment, Karlavägen 40, located in the well-to-do part of Stockholm called Östermalm, where he and Harriet had moved in as a newly married couple and where their daughter Anne-Marie was born in 1902. On 11 July 1908 Strindberg moved into a newly built apartment block, Drottninggatan 85, in another, more central part of Stockholm. Here, in what he called the Blue Tower, now accommodating the Strindberg Museum, he was to stay until his death on 14 May 1912.

Despite Strindberg's warning not to read the play as autobiography, scholars have been eager to point out biographical elements in it. The Student, Martin Lamm declares with his usual inclination to identify the protagonists of the plays with the author, "is Strindberg himself," and Act I creates a mood typical of Östermalm.[12] Olof Molander even claims that the house in *The Ghost Sonata* corresponds to the one in which Strindberg lived when writing the play.[13] There are indeed references to Strindberg's apartment in the drama. The palms surrounding the marble statue resemble the "laurel grove" that he had arranged there. In a room next to the library, there was a Buddha on the mantlepiece.[14] The "death screen" belonged to Strindberg's sister Anna and his brother-in-law Hugo Philp; Strindberg linked it with a hospital in Stockholm, where his niece worked as a nurse.[15]

Both the dead Consul and the crippled Old Man, Jacob Hummel, have been connected with Isaac Hirsch, a well-known Jewish wholesale dealer who began his day by handing out money to a crowd of beggars gathered outside his front door.[16] The love duet between the Young Lady and the Student was inspired by the couple Märta Philp (one of Strindberg's daughters) and Hugo Fröding, and perhaps also by the couple Greta Strindberg (another daughter) and Henry Philp who got engaged in 1906. The Mummy and the Colonel have borrowed traits from Strindberg's sister Anna and her husband Hugo Philp, who had put 'von' in front of his surname.[17] The Young Lady also has something in common with Anna, who resembled Harriet and who "was bored with everyday matters and loved lofty music."[18] The idea of mummification appears in Strindberg's novella *Alone*, in which three old "mummies" and a young man are playing cards in a beautiful corner apartment. The fictional I comments: "Never did I see [-] the tiredness of life so condensed as in this room." This seems to anticipate the ghost supper in the Colonel's round salon. Even the Milkmaid has a counterpart in reality. In an open letter, "Mrs Therese" relates that when she was twelve, she was employed as a milkmaid and that she delivered milk to Strindberg for quite some time.[19]

When he was writing *The Ghost Sonata*, Strindberg went through a crisis:

> My servant left, the house stood on end; I had to change servants six times in 40 days, one [servant] worse than the other. Finally I had to tidy up myself, lay the table and light

the fire; I ate black pig's food from a carrier – in one word, I had to suffer all the bitterness of life without understanding the reason. (*SV* 65:430)

Here we find the background for the Young Lady's household problems in Act III. If we take into account that Strindberg at this time suffered from psoriasis,[20] it is understandable that, like the Young Lady, he experienced the household duties as repulsive.

The most important autobiographical aspect, perhaps, concerns the feeling of unreality which we come across in the drama and which mirrors Strindberg's own experience of life in this period. In the section entitled "A whole life in an hour" – a fitting title for *The Ghost Sonata* – he relates in *A Blue Book I* how he, during a morning walk in the city, visits various places connected with his own past. "In one hour I had passed through my whole life in living pictures; only three years remained and I would reach the present. It was like an agony or moment of death, when all of life passes by." (*SV* 65:161)

Here we have a counterpart, in a way, to the "living pictures" the Old Man, who is soon to die, shows the Student in Act I. At the same time, the beginning of the section shows something of the Student's lust for life. The connection between youth (the Student) and old age (Hummel) is latent in the piece, which indicates that Strindberg could identify himself with both characters.

Strindberg's mosaics relate not only to his life but also to his reading. When he calls *The Ghost Sonata* "a fairy- or fantasy-tale in the present," he indicates the play's connection with E.T.A. Hoffmann's *Fantasy Pieces in the Style of Callot*.[21] From Hoffmann Strindberg borrowed the device of mixing the natural with the supernatural, to take "what is supernatural quite naturally, thereby saving the poetry (the mood)"[22] – his characterization of Hoffmann's stories. As Lindström points out, he also borrowed part of the plot from Hoffmann's short story "The Empty House," which relates how the chief character, a student, is tempted by a mysterious power to visit a house located in a prestigious street. After he has fallen in love with the young woman he has seen in the windows of the house, he enters the house and discovers what is hidden behind the façade: how an old aristocratic lady has gone mad after an unhappy love affair; how she now hides to the world, cared for by a servant with a mummy-like face; and how the affair has resulted in a child who has grown up as someone else's daughter.[23]

Another important source of inspiration, Lindström demonstrates,[24] was Alain-René Lesage's novel *The Devil upon Two Sticks*. In the early years of the century, Strindberg gathered material for a drama dealing with Asmodeus, a demon originally appearing in the apocryphic Book of Tobit in the Old Testament, where the angel Raphael binds his feet together – hence the name "diable boiteux." In Lesage's novel a young student saves a demon, Asmodée, from imprisonment. To divert his benefactor, Asmodée lifts the roofs off the houses of Madrid and shows the student the perversity passing within. The student concludes: human beings are not what they seem to be.

Shortly after *The Ghost Sonata*, Strindberg published a number of essays on Shakesperean drama addressed to the members of the Intimate Theatre. It is therefore not surprising to find correspondences between plays like *Hamlet* and *Macbeth*, each granted a separate essay, on the one hand and *The Ghost Sonata* on the other.

"Who is Hamlet?" Strindberg asks in the *Hamlet* essay, and he answers his own question:

> He is Shakespeare; he is man when he leaves childhood, enters life, and finds everything is quite different from what he had imagined it. Hamlet is the awakened youngster, who discovers that the world is out of joint and feels called upon to set it right, and becomes desperate when he puts his shoulder to the stone and finds it immovable.[25]

This characterization fits the Student. When we first see him he appears full of idealistic innocence. As the play progresses he grows desperate at his own inability to change the world.

When conceiving the two visions in *The Ghost Sonata*, Strindberg was undoubtedly inspired by the Shakesperean ghost scenes. The dramaturgic function of the visions is the same as that of the ghosts in *Hamlet* and *Macbeth*: they bear witness to secret crimes. Hummel's last confrontation with the Milkmaid recalls Macbeth's confrontation with the ghost of Banquo. In *Macbeth* too we may talk about a ghost supper and there too it is a ghost conjured up by a sick conscience: only Macbeth sees it.

When Hamlet describes his mother's vices, she complains: "These words like daggers enter in my ears." In one of the notes for *The Ghost Sonata*, it says, presumably with a reference to the Student and the Young Lady: "He murders her with words."[26]

Goethe's *Faust*, which Strindberg calls "man's greatest poem,"[27] was another source of inspiration. As already indicated, *The Ghost Sonata* deals, among other things, with the relationship between an old man, Hummel, and a young man, the student Arkenholz. The basic identity between the two, each representing a phase in life, recalls the rejuvenation motif in *Faust*; in Buchwald's words:

> While we get to know Faust as a *man*, the pupil is a *youngster*, and certainly a youngster whom we trust will once become a Faust.[28]

Both Shakespeare's Ophelia and Goethe's Gretchen have undoubtedly served as models for Strindberg's Young Lady, Adèle. When Faust first sees Gretchen in the street he bursts out:

> Beim Himmel, dieses Kind ist schön!
> So etwas hab ich nie gesehn.

> By heaven, this child is beautiful!
> Never have I seen anything like it.

When the Student sees the Young Lady in the street he bursts out: "I've never seen such a woman of woman born." As soon as Mephistopheles, diabolic like Hummel, notes Faust's interest in Gretchen, he assures him that he will find her for him; and he adds:

> Und selig, wer das gute Schicksal hat,
> Als Bräutigam sie heimzuführen!

> And blessed he whose good fate it is
> To bring her home as a bridegroom!

As Sprinchorn has observed,[29] these lines seem paraphrased by Strindberg's Student when he says: "Happy the man who may lead her to altar and home." After which the Student calls his agreement with Hummel "a pact" and wonders: "Must I sell my soul?" Gretchen dwells in "a small, clean room," Adèle in a beautiful little room which she is anxious to keep clean. Both women are connected with flowers – as is Ophelia – and their windows are filled with flower pots. The flower-woman connection is explicitly stated in both plays. *Faust I* ends with Gretchen's death, *The Ghost Sonata* with Adèle's. A voice from above tells us that Gretchen, despite her sins, "is saved." Similarly, the Student's final prayer for Adèle combined with the angelic music coming from the Isle of the Dead suggests that she is saved.[30]

An obvious loan is "The Song of the Sun," twice recited by the Student. This is a fragment, adapted by Strindberg, from the Old Icelandic poem *Sólarljóð*, dating back to the 12th or 13th century. This visionary poem, though metrically and to some extent mythologically related to the poems of the *Elder Edda*,[31] is conceptually Christian.[32]

Other works that may have had an impact on *The Ghost Sonata* include Charlotte Brontë's *Jane Eyre*, Balzac's *Séraphita*, several works by Dickens, one of Strindberg's favourite authors,[33] and Erckmann's and Chatrian's popular melodrama *The Polish Jew*.[34]

One: Source text

Several of the motifs dealt with in *The Ghost Sonata* can be traced back to Strindberg's jottings from around the turn of the century. Consider, for example, the following title suggestions: "The Last Sonata," "Sunday Morning," "The Vampire," "The Ghost House," "The Ghost Hour," "The House of Babel."[1] Among the outlines for plays from around this time, mostly consisting of brief, often cryptic notations, many links with *The Ghost Sonata* can be found. One of them carries the title "The Sleeping City." The protagonist is a "young student," who "grows older during his journey [through life]":

> He gets to see the reverse side of life; all the falsehood and wretchedness – But the knot is this: despite all the wretchedness, one must have forbearance and train oneself in indulgence. This he does not learn until he visits his own dwelling and sees himself. *The world of illusions. Life a dream, a prison. The world of folly.*[2]

The expression "the world of illusions" returns in another outline, called "*The Old Ones*," here with the addition: "nothing holds when grasped; everything vanishes: set carpets etc."[3] Compare the play where the Old Man states that he owns "everything to be seen here – furniture, curtains, china, linen cupboard...etcetera." Under the heading "*Scenes*," Strindberg notes among other things: "They read the newspaper. / The beggars arrive. / The party. The ghost supper. / Old Lies and New." The outline begins: "The wife at the gossip mirror. Half blind: about to be operated."[4]

In a third outline, entitled "Chamber play," the collapse of a house is indicated:

> A Street corner; and across it a big house. A man, standing at the street corner, is looking upwards at the house, where people are sitting reading newspapers. [-] A servant comes out of the house and asks the man to leave, gives him money; but he does not want to leave. -What are you waiting for? – For the house to tumble down...[5]

In the outline entitled "Sunday Morning" there is a setting which points forward both to the opening and ending of *The Ghost Sonata*:

> The background, a narrow street in the shade leading inwards, opens up across a stretch of water; behind the water a green isle with a small Gothic church bedded in leaves; above it in the distance a church with a cupola up above. The golden crosses of the two churches as well as the globes below them are strongly lit by the sun.[6]

The isle recalls both Strindberg's own "verdant isle"[7] – a recurrent motif both in his writing and in his paintings – and Böcklin's *Die Toteninsel* (The Isle of the Dead) or, as Strindberg wrote it, *Toten-Insel*. But the Christian aspect made visible in the outline is in the play reduced to sound effects (organ music, church bells) in the beginning and replaced by Böcklin's confessionally more neutral Isle of the Dead at the end. It is tempting to see an associative development from the church cupolas in the outline to the bulb in Buddha's lap, an image of the world, at the end of the play. Clearly, Strindberg has striven to replace Christianity with syncretism.

"Sunday Morning" also contains a list of factors creating "Sunday mood": "The Guardsman on Parade / the Milkmaid, free and in her Sunday best / Silence on the streets / Finally the church bells are heard." The outline begins:

> The Milkmaid by the fountain. Sunday morning. A half drunk night-watcher discovers that it is Sunday; asks for a drink – from the girl; his burst eye and that of the horse. [-] The girl removes the stains from his coat.[8]

Here we are close to the opening of the play. But the Milkmaid still appears very real. This is true also of an outline consisting of one long acting direction, ending:

> At the fountain two little milkmaids in summer dress. They have hung their white berets on the fountain. Ärla pulls up her stockings and adjusts her suspenders; Anna arranges her hair, replaits her plait while mirroring herself in the fountain.
>
> It is a warm Sunday morning, the first of August. (*SS* 45:344-45)

As appears from the changes in the manuscript, Strindberg decided fairly late to turn the Milkmaid into a vision.

Apart from the original 1907 edition, the important Swedish editions of *The Ghost Sonata* are those of *SS* 45 (1921), edited by John Landquist, and *SV* 58 (1991), edited by Gunnar Ollén. Although the play in all three editions is entitled *Spök-sonaten*, the hyphen is usually dropped in comments on the play, even by Strindberg himself (*SV* 58:395). Both editors assume that Strindberg read and made some corrections in the proofs. A comparison between the original manuscript, now in the Strindberg Archive of the Royal Library in Stockholm, the first edition and *SS* 45 reveals a number of differences, mostly concerning punctuation and spelling.[9] In the same way, there are a number of minor differences between *SS* 45 and *SV* 58.[10]

With regard to punctuation, Robinson observes:

> In the later plays, and most particularly in *The Ghost Sonata*, Strindberg employed an idiosyncratic system of *points suspensifs*, asterisks, single and triple dashes, semicolons

and colons in the manner of musical notation to indicate shifts in tone and rhythm, pauses, or changes of focus in a character's thought pattern."

Outwardly, *The Ghost Sonata* consists of three parts, lacking dramaturgic designations in *SS* and *SV* but provided with numbers in the latter edition. The three parts have variously been termed 'acts,' 'scenes' or – when the sonata form is stressed – 'movements.'"

Despite the play's title, there is no reason to replace the dramaturgic terms 'act' and 'scene' by the vaguer musical term 'movement.' But which of the two should we prefer? 'Act' implies that *The Ghost Sonata* is a three-act play, 'scene' that it is a one-acter. In a one-act play we expect the three unities to be adhered to and the play to be presented without any intermission. According to these criteria, *The Ghost Sonata* is a three-act play and I shall therefore use the term 'act' in the following. This term also agrees with Strindberg's indication of a curtain at the end of parts 1 and 2.

Within the three acts we can distinguish forty-nine configurations." This term delineates a unit whose beginning and end from the recipient's point of view is determined by

1. one or more entrances/exits (change of character constellation)

2. change of place

3. curtain or blackout (change of time).

As appears from the configuration chart in Appendix 1, Strindberg has not always indicated the presence of the characters clearly. This is especially remarkable at the end of the play where the solution suggested in the chart is only one of three possibilities. As an alternative to what is suggested there, the Student may be thought to remain on the stage also during conf. 49. More awkward but formally possible is it to have Bengtsson remain during this configuration. The question of whether or not the Student should be visible when *Toten-Insel* is reproduced depends on whether we regard the final vision as an expression of his subjective experience. The alternative I have selected emphasizes the universal significance of the final tableau and testifies to the playwright's endeavour to influence the audience directly. This alternative was, arguably, so obvious to Strindberg that he forgot to make it explicit.

There are other inconsistencies which can best be accounted for as carelessness resulting from Strindberg's fast way of writing" and his negligence as a proof-reader. The Caretaker, for example, is mentioned in the list of dramatis personae although he does not appear in the play, whereas, on the other hand, the Cook, the Maid and the Beggars appear in the play but not in the list of characters. It is also remarkable how little attention Strindberg pays to the

Dark Lady, considering the fact that she is on the stage throughout Act I. Why does he not let her and the Posh Man take part in the homage paid to the Student in conf. 20? Has he forgotten to indicate an exit on their part after conf. 18? Or do they continue their conversation in whispers while the rest hail the Student? Does the Caretaker's Wife remain on the stage until the end of the act or does she exit shortly after the conversation with the Young Lady in conf. 11? We may also wonder whether the guests at the ghost supper remain on the stage when the Student recites "The Song of the Sun" at the end of Act II (conf. 39) or whether an asterisk in the middle of this configuration indicates their exit. Strindberg does not clarify these matters and it is evident that the chart in these cases mirrors my own choices.

Of the play's fifteen individual characters only three – the Student, the Young Lady, and the Colonel – appear in all the three acts. It is also noteworthy that the number of characters diminishes with each act. If we exclude the Beggars of Act I, there are twelve characters in this act, nine in Act II, and six in Act III. The gradual reduction harmonizes with the shrinking space indicated in the series street-round room-hyacinth room.

Of great interest is the frequent use of mute configurations and characters. No less than ten of the forty-nine configurations depend on pantomime. In Act I seven of the characters (plus the Beggars) are mute, while two only have a few lines to speak. In fact, there are only three proper speaking parts: the Old Man, the Student and Johansson. In Act II five of the characters are mute, or nearly so, while five have speaking parts. In Act III there are three speaking parts against three mute ones. A glance at the distribution of silent/spoken configurations with regard to the different characters reveals that several of the speaking parts have long moments of silence. Thus the Colonel speaks only in 6 configurations, while he remains mute in 36. For the Young Lady the corresponding figures are 5-31, for the Mummy 6-10.

The unity of time and place is loosely adhered to in the play. The place of action is "an anonymous city."[15] Every act is spatially linked to the next one. Along with the Student, we move from the street (Act I) through the round drawing-room (Act II) to the hyacinth room (Act III), from wider to narrower space, a Dantean journey in reverse. By synchronizing this inward movement with the Student's increasingly negative view of life, Strindberg indicates a connection between life experience and denial of life. Not until the end of the play is this unity destroyed through the introduction of Böcklin's *Toten-Insel*. It will appear that Strindberg's use of space is quite cinematic. "The gradual revelation of the rotten foundations of the house [-] is presented visually by a zoom from act to act towards the center of the house."[16] The spatial 'turn-around' in Act III has its counterpart in a reversed point of view, the young couple now appearing in the foreground, the old couple in the background.

Also with regard to time, the three acts are kept together. The action takes place some time between 1898 and 1907, that is, between the Spanish-American war, referred to in the play, and the year of publication.[17] Since the hyacinths are in bloom and the Opera is playing, the season seems to be late spring.[18] Act I opens on a Sunday morning, Act II plays in the afternoon and evening of the same day, Act III a few days after Hummel's funeral about a week later. Again the introduction of *Toten-Insel* means a disruption of the temporal unity. However, through the spatial arrangement of Acts II and III – we see just about the same people from opposite directions – Strindberg creates the illusion that hardly any time at all has passed between these acts. Also in other parts of the play an uncertain sense of time is created. Thus the ticking of the clock and the many pauses during the ghost supper contribute to the impression that the fictive time is much longer than the playing time. Parabolically, the drama covers a whole life or even, in a sense, the history of mankind. We can thus speak of no less than three time levels in *The Ghost Sonata*.

It is a matter of dispute whether the play has a unity of action or not. Usually the Old Man, being the most active character, has been considered the protagonist. But his disappearance at the end of Act II then becomes a problem. Those who adhere to this view are forced to conclude that Act III signifies a superfluous repetition of what we have already witnessed. Szondi argues that it fails, "because, with no epic support, it could not generate dialogue of its own."[19] This argument, which neatly places *The Ghost Sonata* where Szondi wants to have it – in the transitional period he terms "the drama in crisis" – actually suits his thesis better than the play.

It is in this context noteworthy that the vampiric Old Man of Acts I-II has a counterpart in the Cook of Act III. This character was significantly added at a late stage, presumably to strengthen the unity of the play. The connection between Hummel and the Cook could be interpreted in different ways. It stresses, we could argue, the idea that evil is an inextricable part of life. We could even, in this play about spectres, see the Cook as a reincarnation of Hummel or, at least, as an avenger of him.

Focusing on the Young Lady, the play deals with the possibility of saving her from the symbolic collapse of the house. In the first two acts the Old Man tries to save her, in the last one the Student.

But it is the Student who has the truly unifying function in the play as the outsider learning about the house and its inhabitants.[20] Schematically, the action is then as follows:

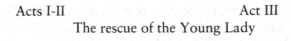

Acts I-II   Act III

The rescue of the Young Lady

Rescue attempt by the Old Man   Rescue attempt by the Student
Revenge attempt by the Old Man   Revenge attempt by the Cook

The Student's experience of life

In *The Ghost Sonata* Strindberg resorts to several well-known types of exposition.[21] In Act I he lets the Student, who knows nothing about the house, be informed by the Old Man; we get a dialogue of questions and answers. At the beginning of Act II this type of exposition is repeated in the gossip between the two servants. Here Bengtsson informs the new-comer Johansson, who functions as a kind of stand-in for the Student ("it was always my dream to enter this house"). The ghost supper may be seen as a parody of another classical type of exposition: the meeting of old acquaintances. In Act III we find yet another kind: two people in love who have recently met.

It is the first of these types – the conversation between the Old Man and the Student – which Strindberg handles in an unconventional way, by sometimes providing "questions without answers"[22] and by letting Hummel's description of the people in the house be supplemented by dumb shows of the characters he is commenting on.

According to Szondi, the development of modern drama is characterized by an increasing resort to epic devices as a result of the fact that interest in interpersonal relations has been replaced by concern for intrapersonal aspects. In *The Ghost Sonata* – so runs his argument – people need "an epic narrator" since their own versions are altogether subjective and unreliable.[23] As the Colonel puts it: "What's the point of talking – we can't fool each other anyway." More than anyone else the Old Man illustrates the deceit referred to by the Colonel. It is true that Hummel's speeches carry a strong epic note. But since he has close, guilty relations to the people he is commenting on, he is not an impartial, reliable narrator. In retrospect, his presentation of the inhabitants of the house has rather the characteristics of self-justification.

While Strindberg himself has referred to *The Ghost Sonata* as "a fairy- or fantasy-tale in the present with modern houses,"[24] the play has been read as a "parodied fairy tale."[25] Here is the courageous young hero who can see what others cannot see because he is a Sunday child. He falls in love with a beautiful

young lady who lives in a castle which seems paradisaic to him. A benevolent
magician helps him to find his way into the castle. In the second act, he discovers that there are trolls inside who keep the young princess prisoner. The magician is prepared to fight with them. In the last act hero and princess seem
happily united. But the play does not end the way we expect. The hero is disillusioned: "Where are faith and honour? In fairy tales and children's plays!"
However, the paradise of the fairy tale can be reached just the same – beyond
life. That is where the stable values lacking in life are to be found, the hero
hopes. And there the play ends.

The bold knight of the fairy tale who saves the princess from the dragon
has his counterpart in *The Ghost Sonata* in the young man who saves the
young woman from the hell of life to a heavenly paradise. The immanent happiness of the fairy tale ("and they lived happily ever after") is replaced by a
subjective, transcendent happy ending for one of the two. But since the Student's hope, visualizing a blessed existence after death, is shared by us all, the
concluding tableau expresses what we might term a subjective universalism.

The play title has both an exoteric and an esoteric meaning. The exoteric
meaning is that since life on earth is a shadow life, a mirage, it follows that we
are all ghosts – whereas those who appear as ghosts in the play, although
dead, are the truly living. To the late Strindberg life was synonymous with
death, death with life.

Esoterically, the title alludes to Beethoven's Piano Sonata No. 17 in D minor (Op. 31 No. 2), usually called The Tempest. In his letter to Schering on 27
March 1907, Strindberg refers to it as the *Gespenster* (Ghost) sonata. He had
used it in an earlier play, *Crimes and Crimes*, to indicate the pangs of conscience afflicting the protagonist.

Strindberg presumably also wished to indicate in the title that the structure
of the play is somehow akin to that of music.[26] The subtitle – "Chamber Play
Opus III" – suggests this, especially when combined with Strindberg's own
definition of the term 'chamber play': "the concept of chamber music transferred to drama. The intimate action, the highly significant motif, the sophisti-
cated treatment."[27] Thus Steene finds that the play is

> divided into three movements (Scenes) according to the musical form ABA. Scenes 1
> and 3 concern the Student's confrontation with the world of the play; scene 2 in which
> the Student takes no active part deals with the guests at the ghost supper and their un-
> masking. Finally, the Student brings the play to a close by a restatement and summing-
> up ("the coda") of its major themes [-].[28]

In this general sense, the analogy seems convincing, although it does not carry very far. Going one step further, other critics have tried to specify the tempi of the three 'movements.' According to Sprinchorn

> The first and longest scene [-] is a brisk allegro, its mood sustained by the youthful buoyancy of the Student and by the grasping eagerness of the Old Man as they lay their plans for entering the house of elegance. In sharp contrast is the second scene or movement, the largo. To its slow tempo and its long silences the ghost supper takes place. The final scene is a quiet andante, which stresses the principal theme of the sonata and brings it to a close with a brilliant coda that restates all themes.[29]

How personal this interpretation of the three 'movements' is appears from the fact that Berendsohn has used quite different designations for the last two parts – allegro furioso, largo[30] – whereas Vowles identifies the whole play with the second movement of the Piano Trio: largo assai ed espressivo.[31]

In a sonata we find an expository part, presenting the theme, an executive part and a repetitive part similar to the expository one and ending in a coda which often, particularly with Beethoven, grows into a second execution. This arrangement bears a certain kinship to that of *The Ghost Sonata*. Thus Act III opens in a light and hopeful mood, recalling the situation at the beginning of Act I, while the second part of Act III, the coda, signifies a furious repetition of what has earlier taken place – the 'murder' of the Young Lady corresponding to the drowning of the Milkmaid – and an execution, since the Student, not Hummel, is now the agent. But the musical parallel is hardly striking.

More rewarding, perhaps, would be to apply Strindberg's description of the dialogue of *Miss Julie* to that of *The Ghost Sonata*. In the Preface of the former play he writes that the dialogue "wanders, providing itself in the opening scenes with material that is later reworked, picked up, repeated, expanded, and added to, like the theme in a musical composition" (*SV* 27:109). Going on the idea that the play title provides a key to the play's composition, even in details, Jarvi has made an heroic attempt to demonstrate the play's essentially musical structure by dividing it up into a number of smaller segments: introduction, statement of first theme, bridge passage, repetition of first theme, episode A, episode B, etc.[32] But here again, one can't help feeling that the thematic web of the play is too complex and too wandering to allow for such a strict compartmentalization. The analogy fails to convince.

When Strindberg notes that "the significant motif" forms an important part of what he means by "the concept of chamber music transferred to drama," he seems to be saying much the same as Hummel, when he states that "though the tales are different, they all hang together on a thread, and the theme recurs regularly." The recurring theme is the antithesis between being and seeming, between *Sein* and *Schein*. The events which take place, the activities of the characters, their existence shown to us – all are but variations, concretizations of this basic theme. In this arrangement we find the essential reason why we may figuratively speak of a musical structure in *The Ghost Sonata* – as we may in any strongly theme-oriented drama.

In a Prologue written for the opening of his own Intimate Theatre, Strindberg refers to the journey that mankind must undertake "from the Isle of the Living to the Isle of the Dead." He alludes to Arnold Böcklin's famous paintings. At his request, copies of these by the prominent Swedish painter Carl Kylberg had been placed at either side of the stage in the Intimate Theatre.[33]

In *The Ghost Sonata* we witness a similar journey. The house we see on the stage represents the House of Life which at the end vanishes and is replaced by the Isle of the Dead. In the course of the play we journey to another reality. Along with the Student, we gradually discover that the house which on the outside looks so attractive (Act I), has a much less appealing interior (Act II). Life may not be what we had expected but, like the Officer in *A Dream Play*, the Student believes that *amor vincit omnia* (Act III). Yet even this proves to be an illusion. Like everyone else, the beloved Young Lady is tainted by Original Sin ("sick at the source of life"). The stable, attractive house proves to be a mirage. The true reality – this is what Strindberg wants us to experience – is to be found in the afterlife.

The fundamental idea of the play, then, is that life on earth is painful and illusory and that when we die we are saved from this pseudo-existence (back) to the original one. Only by hoping for this can we endure this life. This ties in with the idea that the living are actually ghosts – as indicated by the speaker-label "The Mummy" and the reference to the "ghost supper" in Act II.[34]

The Student is "a Sunday child" who "can see what others cannot see." Believing in the value of verbal communication, he studies languages, also in an endeavour to find the unity behind and beyond the linguistic tower of Babel mankind has erected "to keep the secrets of the tribe." (Hummel, by contrast, prefers silence.) The Student is the only one who sings in the play, "matching human language with the 'universal language' of music."[35] Above all he is Everyman, starting out in life enthusiastically but ending it in disillusion. His hope for a better existence hereafter, justifying the pain of this life, is therefore not just an individual hope but, as in *A Dream Play*, a universal one, the hope of mankind.

As we have already noted, the fundamental theme is found in the conflict between illusion and reality, *Schein* and *Sein*. In the antithesis between mask and face, façade and interior, word and deed, and in the depiction of the dead as living, the living as dead – everywhere we are confronted with the fundamental idea that the world is not what it looks like and mankind not what it seems to be.[36] To make this basic idea dramatically effective Strindberg turns his protagonist, the Student, into an outsider who only gradually gains insight into the true state of things. Originally influenced by the character who incarnates the materialistic *Schein*, Hummel, the Student eventually comes to see reality as it is. From another point of view, the Student represents an earlier stage in Hummel's life, while his development suggests that he will eventually turn into another Hummel. Together the Student and Hummel, the young man and the old man, give a picture of Man, of the fate of Man.

In the last instance, therefore, *The Ghost Sonata* is an allegorical drama, a parable, depicting the pilgrimage of Man, a station drama, in which each station (act) corresponds to an inner state of mind. After the three earthly stations, which may well be connected with youth, middle age and old age – each characterized by what Strindberg in the notes for *A Dream Play* calls "the treacherous hope" – a fourth station, "the station of rest," awaits us: *Toten-Insel* – where "hope maketh not ashamed" (Rom. 5:5).

The pre-scenic action in *The Ghost Sonata* – the action preceding the opening of the play – is complicated and, on several points, obscure. It therefore seems legitimate to attempt an unravelling of the various human destinies with which we are confronted. The following presentation of the characters – in the order found in the list of dramatis personae – based on a combination of the facts given in the text, may prove helpful.

THE OLD MAN. Company director Jacob Hummel – the name is false – who is a little over 80 became engaged to Beate von Holsteinkrona when he was twenty, but when she allowed herself to be seduced by the Colonel, the engagement was broken off. To avenge himself Hummel seduces the Colonel's wife Amalia. She gives birth to their daughter Adèle. When the Colonel learns about what has happened, he beats his wife. Amalia leaves him, perhaps in the hope that Hummel will marry her and take care of their daughter. But Hummel "gets the women to leave when he's tired of them." And Amalia returns to the Colonel.

Among the many women with whom Hummel has had a liaison, Bengtsson's cook is one. For two years Hummel was a sponger in Bengtsson's kitchen. When he was living in Hamburg as a usurer and "bloodsucker" he was responsible for the drowning of the little Milkmaid. He ruined his former friend, the merchant Arkenholz, a circumstance which seems to have led to Arkenholz' insanity and premature death. He caused the death of the Consul by running him into debt, literally and figuratively. He turned Johansson, chief servant among the servants (the Beggars) with whom he surrounds himself, into a "slave."

Hummel has a son, "a scoundrel" who tortures the life out of him. (We never learn who the mother is.) At the end of the drama, we get to know that this son has had a homosexual relationship with the man who carried the mace at Hummel's funeral and that Hummel had borrowed money "from his son's admirer." The courageous Student appears to be a healthy contrast to Hummel's own son.[37] By offering the Student his possessions, while he is still alive, Hummel deprives his own son of his inheritance.

Hummel claims that he is "very rich," and Johansson describes him as a powerful man: "he looks at houses, tears them down, opens up streets, settles squares" and "he always keeps in with the police."

As we have seen, Hummel has much on his conscience. He is a hardened liar, a Don Juan, a tyrant, a usurer, a "horse thief in the human market," a "vampire" and a murderer. All in all, his crimes indicate his recklessness towards his fellow-men. Indeed, Hummel bears a certain kinship to the Devil himself.

Is Hummel, then, altogether evil? His assurance that he has not "always been like this" and that "you're always related to them [people] in some way" suggest that he is not. Although he is the most guilty character in the play – he is presumably also the oldest and the connection does not seem coincidental – it is not he but the Colonel who has initiated the chain of crimes. Nothing prevents us from seeing Hummel as a once innocent young man, who has gradually lost faith in his fellow-men after the Fiancée and the Colonel have deceived him. Viewed in this light, his brutality against the Colonel becomes more understandable.

However, Hummel is not always negative about others. He admits that the Consul could be compassionate, and that the Fiancée, once beautiful, is still attractive. And his comment on the Young Lady is *con amore*. "Have you ever seen such a masterpiece?", he rhetorically asks the Student. Hummel, in fact, claims that his recklessness is determined by his concern for the youth: "That was my mission in this house: to root out the weeds, expose the crimes, settle past accounts, so that the young people may have a fresh start in this home, which I have given them!"

But his way of acting may also have other reasons. Confronted with the Student and the Young Lady, Hummel may well relive his own youthful self and that of the Fiancée in them – just as he recalls the Mummy as a young woman when he regards the marble statue of her. From a quite different angle, his altruism vis-à-vis the young couple may be seen as resulting from his pangs of conscience. "You see, I have taken all my life. Now I have a longing to give, give," he confesses to the Student. The demand for the good deed that will wipe out old crimes and reconcile the Powers feels urgent for the aging man. He now wants to play the role of benefactor to the son of the man against whom he has trespassed: "before I die, I want to see you happy...Our destinies are entwined through your father." But Hummel does not see, or want to see, that the means he employs – the one-sided unmasking of others – is a new crime, hubris, which is punished according to the law of retribution.

THE STUDENT. Young Arkenholz, we have already noted, occupies a special place in the play: that of observer, interlocutor, catalyst.[38] Assisted by the Old Man, he regards the house and its inhabitants from the outside in Act I. In Act II he enters the house. In Act III he learns about its many deficiencies. Not until all this has happened, does he take a vigorous part in the action.

The Student represents man(kind). Innocent and hopeful, he enters life (the stage), different from those who have done so before him and who are marked by it. The contrast is strengthened by the fact that the Student is the only character who, initially, is independent of the house and its inhabitants. Gradually he gets to know life, outwardly and inwardly. On the basis of his experience he makes up the balance.

The Student's experience of the house – of life – is partly synchronized with that of the recipient. Thus at the beginning of Act III, both he and we can still be optimistic, since he regards the Young Lady as untainted by the duplicity characterizing humanity at large.

The Student is surprisingly versatile. He is interested in sports and music, sings, writes poetry, studies languages. The last has a symbolic meaning, for "languages are [-] codes and he who finds the key understands all the languages of the world." Arkenholz seeks the meaning beyond the words or, to put it differently, he seeks a language which expresses thoughts instead of disguising them. Like most young men, he dreams of a beautiful wife, pretty children and wealth. But he also harbours more unusual qualities. He showed courage when the house collapsed the night before, and being a Sunday child he is provided with second sight.

His unusual surname, Arkenholz – we never learn his Christian name – has been explained in different ways.[39] Quite suggestive is Sprinchorn's idea that the name refers to the biblical ark made of wood (Germ. Holz),[40] indicating that the Student is another Noah trying to save people from catastrophes. It is indeed a kind of deluge that we witness at the end of the play. "Alas for us all, alas! Saviour of the World, save us; we perish," the Student exclaims after he has declared that a curse rests on all creation.

At the very beginning of the play, the Student is linked with two other biblical figures. When he says that he has "bandaged up injured people and kept watch over the sick all night," we associate him both with Jesus and with the compassionate Samaritan – especially since he refers to the Milkmaid as the "good Samaritan." The expression is a key to the whole configuration which recalls the passage in John 4:7-14, where Jesus meets a woman from Samaria at Jacob's well.[41] "Give me to drink," he asks her. "Give me a drink of water," the Student asks the Milkmaid. When he begs her to bathe his poor eyes with the "fresh water," it is an allusion to the following words by the Samaritan woman:

> from whence then hast thou that living water? Art thou greater than our father Jacob, which gave us the well, and drank thereof himself, and his children, and his cattle? (John 4:11-12)

The 'conversation' between the Student and the Milkmaid takes place next to the street drinking fountain. Close by it we see 'father Jacob' Hummel, seated in his wheelchair. The antithesis in the biblical text between Jacob's earthly water, which only temporarily quenches the thirst, and Jesus' living water which does so eternally, is here latently present in the contrast between earthly existence on which Hummel's power rests and the afterlife for which the Student finally hopes.

THE MILKMAID's fate is linked with that of Hummel, as Bengtsson informs us:

> Later I came across this man [Hummel] in Hamburg under another name. He was then a usurer, a bloodsucker. But he was also accused there of having lured a girl out on to the ice to drown her, because she had witnessed a crime he feared would be discovered...

That Hummel managed to get the Milkmaid to drown appears from the fact that when she appears for the second time, "*she raises her arms as if she were drowning, and stares at the* OLD MAN."

What kind of crime, witnessed by the Milkmaid, had the Old Man committed? Why a milkmaid? And why does she wear summer clothes if she was drowned in the winter?

What we would expect is that Hummel, who "has been a Don Juan" and who gets the women "to leave when he's got tired of them," has seduced the girl, and that this has led to undesirable consequences.[42] But Bengtsson's way of expressing himself is in that case a bit strange. It indicates rather that the Milkmaid has witnessed how Hummel has seduced, or raped, another woman. Hummel himself significantly declares: "in the kind of errand I have in mind, one does not take any witnesses along. Nature itself has endowed man with a kind of shame, which tries to conceal what should be concealed." Bengtsson's vague way of expressing himself is possibly determined by the fact that it underlines the parallel between the relationships Milkmaid-Hummel and Hummel-Johansson. The latter has committed an error which only Hummel knows about.

The theme of food takes a prominent place in Strindberg's writings. In a very fundamental sense, food to him means life. "Scarce or spoilt food is a threat to life. To feed at the breast or to hand out food is a holy, life-giving act of love."[43] The sucking vampire has her antipode in the suckling mother. Hummel and the Cook are the vampires of the play. In the Milkmaid we find the opposite, nourishing character. When Strindberg provides the Cook with a "colouring bottle with scorpion letters on it," he gives her an attribute which blatantly contrasts with the Milkmaid's white bottles.

THE CARETAKER'S WIFE. Her husband has received his post as caretaker of the house in 'payment' for the Consul's sleeping with his wife. The Dark Lady is the result of this adultery.

THE DEAD MAN. Vainglorious and charitable, he has become indebted to the usurer Hummel. In vain he tries to repay his debts by cheating the state. When he does not succeed, he commits suicide. This is why the Mummy can tell Hummel: "you murdered the Consul [-], you strangled him with notes of hand." We even get an indication of how the Consul has died. When the Mummy sends Hummel away to the closet, she does it with the words: "There's a rope hanging in there that can represent the one you strangled the consul with up there."

THE DARK LADY is an illegitimate daughter of the dead Consul and the Caretaker's Wife.[44] The following line by Hummel indicates that she knows who her real father is: "now his daughter's involved in another man's marriage and is wondering about the inheritance." In the short, cryptic conversation between her and the Posh Man, the nature of their relationship is indicated. He has obviously made her pregnant. She wants to marry him before this becomes visible. But since he is not divorced from his wife, he cannot remarry. The recent death of the Consul also makes marriage inappropriate at this time. Not prepared to marry a servant's daughter or even to acknowledge his paternity, he suggests that she goes away to give birth to the child secretly. His attitude is similar to that of the Consul and Hummel.

THE COLONEL incarnates duplicity. He has deceived his wife – provided they were married at the time – with Hummel's fiancée. He has had the Young Lady grow up in the belief that she is his own daughter. Like Hummel, he has once been a servant and a sponger but an aristocratic mask – moustache, false teeth, wig, corset and uniform, a dubious title which is no longer valid and a false noble name – has disguised this circumstance. The Colonel has so long cherished false ideas about himself that role-playing has become second nature to him. This appears when he complains to Hummel that the Student is not "a nobleman and our equal" after Hummel has demonstrated that the Colonel is merely "footman XYZ."

THE MUMMY. Nobody knows how old she is. She must be at least 55 and may be 75. She apparently did not marry the Colonel until she was 35 – although she made him believe that she was 19. Both Hummel and the Posh Man have been her lovers. With the former she has a daughter, the Young Lady, named Adèle. The Colonel seems to have believed for quite some time that he is Adèle's father (which explains the choice of her name) – until the Mummy told him of the true situation in a fit of anger.

The Mummy has tried to leave her husband but she has always returned to him; once she even divorced him only to remarry him. What is true about the people in the house generally, is true of her marriage to the Colonel: "We have broken up and left and gone our ways infinitely many times, but we're drawn together again," for "crimes and secrets and guilt bind us together." None of the characters is so guilt-ridden as the Mummy, who has virtually ceased to live after her adultery with Hummel. Since then she hides in the dark closet, repenting her sin. She "can't stand cripples" (Hummel) and "sick people" (Adèle), because they remind her of what she has done. Imagining that she is a parrot, she even denies her human nature.

With the parrot we associate three qualities: vanity, speaking ability and imprisonment. Representing deformed, encaged human life – the closet is clearly the Mummy's cage – the "talkative bird" points to language as a dubious means of communication.

According to Bengtsson, the Mummy is crazy because "when people sit together for a long time tormenting each other, they go crazy." Bengtsson here refers not so much to matrimonial monotony as to the tendency to remind one another of errors in the past. The Mummy tries to escape from all this. Isolating herself and imagining, or simulating,[45] that she is either a parrot or that she is dead, she feels too guilty to accept being human.

But not even as a parrot can she completely forget the past. Polly's "Is Jacob there?" prepares us for Amalia's "Is it you, Jacob?", the first words spoken by the Mummy "*in her normal voice.*" Having repented for twenty years, she finally recovers or drops her mask. The parrot sickness is transferred to the unrepentant cripple.

Apart from the crazy Polly and the sensible Amalia, the Mummy appears in the form of the beautiful marble statue, her youthful, innocent self.

One more aspect of the parrot language should be noted. There is an old Swedish game known as "Jacob, where are you?", in which a blindfolded person (the master) has to catch the other (the servant Jacob), assisted by the sounds he receives in answer to his question "Jacob, where are you?" When the servant is caught, the roles are reversed.

When we first hear the Mummy ask "Is Jacob there?", she finds herself in the closet. It is a hide-and-seek situation hinting at the hide-and-seek between master and servant, innocent and guilty, which stands central in *The Ghost Sonata* with its surprising reversal of roles. When the Old Man finally answers the Mummy's question with his "Jacob is there," it indicates that he acknowledges that he is caught. The game has come to an end.

THE YOUNG LADY. "A victim of the discord which a mother's 'crime' has implanted in a family, a victim of the errors of an age, of circumstances, of her own deficient constitution" – thus Strindberg characterizes Miss Julie.[46] The description admirably fits Miss Adèle. Remarkably passive, Adèle does not perform any actions which contribute to a profound characterization of herself. The most enigmatic character in the play, she is primarily delineated by what others have to say about her.

The Young Lady is ignorant of the fact that Hummel is her father. This is at any rate the conclusion we must draw when she refers to "company director Hummel's" funeral at which she has evidently not been present. She has not heard Hummel's revelations in Act II. And the Colonel who is anxious to keep up appearances has never told her the truth. The Young Lady, we must conclude, dies without having learnt about her own identity.

At the beginning of the play her aristocratic pastime is emphasized. She rides on horseback, cares for hyacinths, goes to the Opera, reads books, plays the harp. At the end of Act III, on the other hand, we learn that she serves the servants, carrying out all the dirty chores they refuse to do or do carelessly. The Young Lady's life, in other words, is not what it seems to be.

THE POSH MAN. In the list of characters, it says: "called Baron Skanskorg" – a subtle hint that his nobility is as illegitimate as that of the Colonel and that his name, with its military associations, is as false as Hummel's. In view of this, the designation "Posh Man" indicates his façade mentality.

The Posh Man, who has been the Mummy's lover, is the recently dead Consul's son-in-law. This is why he is dressed in mourning. He is about to get divorced from his wife who "offers him a stone house to get rid of him" – a gift reminding us of the visualized stone house Hummel intends to give to the Young Lady and the Student. The Posh Man has obviously married for money. Hummel seems to refer to this when he metaphorically calls him "the jewel thief." He lives "up above" in the house, and it is his bedclothes which are aired on the balcony. Referring to the Posh Man's divorce, Hummel remarks that the elegant quilt "was meant for two to sleep under, now it's for one."[47]

JOHANSSON. He is "an educated man" and has been a bookseller. He once committed a crime which only Hummel knows about. "Instead of having me locked up, he made me his slave," Johansson tells the Student.

BENGTSSON, for a generation the Colonel's servant, has earlier served Hummel. But Bengtsson, who must be quite old, was once an independent man, and in those days Hummel "for two whole years" was a sponger in his kitchen. Later, Bengtsson met Hummel in Hamburg, where he heard that he was responsible for the Milkmaid's drowning. The reason why Strindberg places the crime abroad is presumably that in this way it seems more plausible that the other characters are ignorant of it. Bengtsson's knowledge of the crime explains Hummel's fear of him. When he reveals the crime, Bengtsson functions as a *deus ex machina*.

Bengtsson is not the man he appears to be. Although he has received a medal "because of his great merits," he has "very great" flaws. The theme of seeming versus being applies to him too.

THE FIANCÉE. The 79-year-old Beate von Holsteinkrona represents the high nobility. She is a secular canoness, a privileged person. Sixty years earlier, when she was 19, she became engaged to Hummel – hence the subjective speaker-label – a circumstance which she seems to have forgotten altogether. While still engaged, she allowed herself to be seduced by the Colonel. A beauty in her youth, she is still "an attractive old woman" although she "*looks crazy.*"

THE COOK is "big and fat" from all the meat-stock she has been drinking – leaving the fibres and the water to the family she is serving. As a result, the Young Lady is pining away.

The Cook has been interpreted in various ways. To Lamm, she is simply an accident, a proof that Strindberg could not keep his own household problems outside his work.[48] It is indeed quite likely that Strindberg added this character to his play as an act of revenge on the housemaid who left him two days before the drama was completed.[49] But this explanation is hardly sufficient. For, as we shall see, Strindberg included the Cook in the play largely because she has a function there. Lamm's biographical motivation signifies a distrust of the playwright's dramaturgic competence. Wilkinson, seeing her as "a caricature both of a nurturing mother and of a loyal servant,"[50] indicates at most that she is part of the grotesque collection of characters inhabiting the house.

More satisfying is Delblanc's suggestion that the Cook is "a punishing representative of the lower classes," who "repays the upper classes with the means at her disposal."[51] The idea of class struggle is, in fact, voiced by the Cook herself, when she tells the Student and the Young Lady, both representatives of the upper classes: "You suck the strength out of us, and we out of you." To Delblanc, the Cook is both a realistic and a symbolic figure; in the latter capacity, she is "a projection of the social guilt weighing on the bourgeois society of *The Ghost Sonata*."[52] The Cook, in other words, has both an objective and a subjective reality. It is a separate problem whether the subjective aspect should be sought within the social or the existential sphere. Leifer leans in the latter direction when seeing the Cook as partly a representative of "the evil of existence," partly of that which is "low and earthbound within the Young Lady."[53] In the latter case, the Cook is again viewed as a projection, this time not as the guilt of a whole social class but of "what is evil" within a representative individual. By combining the Cook with the Young Lady – turning them into a Calibariel – Leifer tries to integrate the Cook in the play and give an explanation for the Young Lady's obscure illness.

The Old Man is past 80, the Fiancée 79. Sixty years ago they got engaged. He was then 20, she 19. About the Mummy we learn that when she was 35 she told the Colonel that she was 19. According to Bengtsson, the Mummy "has been sitting here for forty years" with "the same husband." But the Mummy claims that she has "been sitting for twenty years" in the closet. The seeming contradiction can be solved if we interpret Bengtsson's "here" as referring not to the closet but to the apartment.

Since the Young Lady is the fruit of an adultery on the part of the Mummy, she must be less than 40. We never learn her exact age. When Lindström declares that she is 20,[54] he obviously bases this assumption on the information that the Mummy has repented her adultery "for twenty years." This is reasonable. The young Student, who is himself around 20, is in love with the Young Lady and he finds her very beautiful. Hummel calls her "my little girl." Both he and the Colonel refer to her and the Student as "the young people." The Young Lady seems to be a virgin, etc. Yet, if we accept Bengtsson's information about forty years of married life, the Young Lady cannot be 20, since in that case the Mummy was 55 when she gave birth to her. If, on the other hand, we assume that the Young Lady is 35, then the Mummy was only 40 when Adèle was born. But this alternative has the disadvantage that it leaves unexplained why the Mummy did not withdraw into the closet to repent her sin until fifteen years after the birth of her daughter.

Both alternatives can be further corroborated. Since the Fiancée, who is now 79, was 19 when she and Hummel got engaged, and since the Mummy, presumably when she married the Colonel, told him that she was 19, it seems plausible that the Young Lady is now 19 – especially since it will then be quite logical that the Mummy has repented her sin for twenty years, that is, begun to do so immediately after the adultery was committed or after the pregnancy was discovered. Moreover, we may, as already indicated, assume that the Student is now 20, that is, of exactly the same age as Hummel was when he got engaged to the Fiancée. According to this alternative, the parallel between Hummel-the Fiancée and the Student-the Young Lady is emphasized. The parallel is supported by Hummel's assurance that he, Hummel, has "not always been like this" and that he once swore a woman eternal faithfulness combined with the information that the Fiancée "once was young and beautiful."

But we can also connect the pairings Student-Young Lady and Colonel-Mummy. Like the young Mummy, the Young Lady may be seen as 35, although she looks like 19. With this interpretation, the Student becomes another Colonel who is duped with regard to the age of the adored woman. Hummel's comment when the Student is captivated by the Young Lady's beauty – "You can see it! – Not everyone sees her beauty..." – can be seen as an indication of this.

The correspondences between on the one hand the Old Man-the Colonel-the Student and on the other the Fiancée-the Mummy-the Young Lady are suggestive.[55] They provide the ages of man with a kind of psychological loading. The young and the old mirror each other. In a variation of the medieval dialogue between the living and the dead, Strindberg seems to say: this is what you once were, this is what you will once become. Together the two generations give a picture of every human being's progression from innocence to guilt, from youth to old age, of how the expulsion from Paradise is constantly repeated.

In this context it is important if the Young Lady *is* 19 or merely looks so. According to the former alternative, she *is* pure, according to the latter, she is not what she seems to be, that is, not essentially different from the other deficient characters. When the Student, in his intercession for her, states that she is "innocent," we may regard his characterization as either a factual statement or as an expression of wishful thinking. Our uncertainty concerning the Young Lady's age reflects our uncertainty concerning her nature generally. Strindberg is suggestively evasive – and very realistic, for this is, after all, the way we experience people around us. As Hummel puts it: "We can't judge a human being!"

Strindberg gives very sparse and rather capricious information about the outward appearance of the characters. In Act I we learn indirectly that the Dark Lady carries this speaker-label because she is "*darkly dressed*"; that the Old Man has "*white hair and beard and glasses*"; that the Milkmaid is "*dressed in summer clothes, with brown shoes, black stockings and a white beret*"; that the Student is "*sleepless and unshaven*"; that the Colonel is "*in civilian clothes*"; that the Fiancée is "*white-haired*"; that the Young Lady first wears a "*modern English Amazone dress*," that is, a riding habit, and later changes her clothes; that the Dead Man appears in his "*winding-sheet*"; and that the Posh Man is in "*mourning*." In Act II we are informed that Bengtsson wears a "*livery*," whereas Johansson wears "*tails and white tie*"; that the Old Man wears a "*frock coat*," a "*top hat*" and a wig and that he carries "*crutches*";

that the Colonel has a moustache, false teeth, a wig, a metal corset and wears a signet ring; that the Fiancée "*appears mad*"; and that the Posh Man is still in "*mourning*." In Act III the Cook is described as a "giant woman." That is all.

Consequently, we do not receive any direct information about what the Mummy looks like. However, the Old Man's remark that "she is now sitting in there like a mummy" and Bengtsson's observation that "she thinks she's a parrot," provide indirect information about her appearance. Similarly, we can only indirectly conclude that the Student in Act I may well wear a student's cap,[56] and that his clothes, after his rescue feat the preceding night, are dirty and torn. We lack information about how the Old Man is dressed in Act I and how the Young Lady is costumed in Act III. We may conclude that the Colonel is dressed in a uniform in Act II but since he has been (!) "an acting colonel in the American volunteer force," it is hard to know what it looks like – at least for a non-American audience. How the Fiancée and the Caretaker's Wife are dressed we never learn, and we are never told what kind of clothes the Young Lady changes into in Act I. As appears from this survey, there is no correlation between the importance of the characters in the play and the attention Strindberg bestows on their outward appearance. The only colours indicated are white, black and once – for the Milkmaid's shoes – brown.

The grouping of the characters illustrates a basic theme in the play. In all the acts we find a visualized contrast between the materialism of old age on the one hand and the idealism of youth on the other.

When the curtain rises for Act I we see, in front of the stone house in the background, an advertising column to the left and a street drinking-fountain to the right. Already in these properties we sense a contrast, since "a drinking fountain is so much more important, more elemental, than an advertising column."[57] The play opens with three characters on the stage, all of them positioned to the left. Close to the advertising column we find the Old Man in his wheelchair. Behind him the Caretaker's Wife is sweeping the entrance. And behind her the Dark Lady stands immobile on the stairs of the house. Above her there is an explicit sign of death: the windows on the first floor which are covered by white sheets indicating that the Consul who lived there has just died. Together these three characters represent a dark group, a group signifying death. It is hardly a coincidence that they are all connected with the recently dead Consul, the Caretaker's Wife as his mistress, the Dark Lady as his illegitimate daughter, the Old Man as his 'murderer.'

Contrasting with the trio to the left is a trio to the right: the Milkmaid, "*dressed in summer clothes*" and with a "*white beret*" on her head, close to her the young Student with, we may assume, his white student's cap and, when the blind of the drawing room is raised, "*a white marble statue of a young woman,*" an obvious pendant of the immobile Dark Lady.

We now have two groups on the stage: to the left a dark group connected with the house in the background, to the right two young people in light clothing, concerned with the "fresh water" of the fountain rather than with the massive stone house behind them.

In the second act we have entered the affluent building. In the middle we see the round drawing-room, to the left the hyacinth room, where the Young Lady is sitting reading, to the right the green room with the Colonel behind his mahogany desk – a striking contrast. After a while the Student joins the Young Lady and during the rest of the act the hyacinth room forms a silent, youthful, loving background for the hateful acts of revenge taking place among the old-age people in the drawing-room in the foreground.

In the final act we find ourselves in the hyacinth room, where the Student and the Young Lady in a lyrical 'antiphon' declare their love for one another. Through a door to the right we can see the Colonel and the Mummy sitting silently together, because "they have nothing to say to each other, because neither believes what the other says." In other words: in the foreground loving communication, in the background hateful isolation. A contrast in space and, even more, in time.

Throughout the three acts Strindberg groups his characters so that the thematic conflict of the play – the contrast between youthful optimism, innocence and idealism and the disillusion, materialism and guilt of old age – is clearly visualized.

All Strindberg's chamber plays centre around houses – rotting, burning or burned houses. Although the symbolic significance of the house visualized in *The Ghost Sonata* has long been recognized,[58] this significance is often forgotten when various aspects related to the house are discussed.

Symbolizing earthly existence, the house is inhabited by a varied group of people, representing different ages, social classes and relationships. The house is "*modern*"; it was a contemporary situation Strindberg was describing in 1907.

When we first meet the Student, the house still appears attractive to him and to us. Entering the house, he believes, is like entering Paradise. His innocent faith gains support by the attractive and seemingly stable house front with its paradisaic features:

> *Through the round room's open windows can be seen, when the shades are raised, a white marble statue of a young woman, surrounded by palms, brightly lit by sunlight. In the window to the left pots of hyacinths (blue, white, pink) can be seen.*

But what we and the Student see is merely a façade. Once inside the house, the situation changes. He now experiences the house as "strange," later as "rotten." Finally the realistic fiction is done away with: "Jesus Christ descended into hell – that was his pilgrimage on earth, this madhouse, this prison, this charnel-house, the earth." Similarly, the Student enters 'hell': his moving inwards – from the street through the round room to the hyacinth room – is an inverted pilgrimage from Paradiso via Purgatorio to Inferno. By synchronizing this movement with his increasingly negative attitude to the world, Strindberg implies a relationship between life experience and denial of life. To make sure that the Student's changing view of the house is not interpreted as his individual reaction, Strindberg also has Johansson independently share his experience. The servant first declares that it has always been his "dream to get into this house"; later he is forced to conclude that "it's a terrible house." In Act III this movement is repeated with coda-like swiftness. At the beginning the Student, now in love, believes that although life may be purgatory, love nevertheless ensures exemption. Soon he learns that he is mistaken. The hyacinth room is just another "room of trial": beautiful to look at but full of flaws.[19] He then comes to the conclusion that life is an inferno.

The hyacinth room testifies to the desperate attempts of the Young Lady of "keeping the impurity of life at bay." The attempt proves in vain. The room is located, it seems, between the round room – the disillusioned domain of the aged – and the kitchen, the domain of materialism.[60] Purity – this is the conclusion – cannot be found in this life. It must be sought in the afterlife: "*The room disappears, Böcklin's* Toten-Insel *becomes the backdrop.*"

The destruction of the house at the end is well prepared. The day before, the Student has seen a house falling down:

> STUDENT. [-] I was drawn to that obscure little back street where the house later collapsed...I got there and stopped in front of the building which I had never seen before...Then I noticed a crack in the wall, heard the joints creak; I dashed forward and grabbed hold of a child who was walking right below the wall...The next moment the house collapsed --- I was safe but in my arms, where I thought I had the child, was nothing...

This description should be compared to another. When Hummel asks the Student whether he has noticed the house we see on the stage, the Student answers:

> I've certainly noticed it...I walked by here yesterday when the sun shone in the windows and, imagining all the beauty and luxury inside, I said to my companion: "Fancy having an apartment there four flights up, a beautiful young wife, two pretty little children, and a private income of 20,000 crowns..."

We get the impression that this was the first time the Student saw or paid attention to the house. This is significant, since it is precisely the Student's unfamiliarity with the House of Life that motivates his infatuation with it.

The Student, then, has the previous day discovered two houses: the one we see before us and the one that collapsed. Symbolically, it is one and the same house, representing existence. Strindberg implies this by referring to "that obscure little street" in one case and to "*a side-street running towards the back*" in the other. It is as though one front of the house on the stage has already collapsed, while the other one follows suit at the end of the play.

On closer inspection, it becomes clear that the Student's pre-scenic behaviour corresponds to his scenic one. Thus in Act I we see him admiring the house, dreaming to enter it. In Act II he enters it and discovers the crevices in the walls. And in Act III he tries to save, not a child but a young woman from the symbolic collapse of a house. When the Student towards the end calls the Young Lady a "poor little child, child of this world of illusion, guilt, suffering and death," it is not only to stress the fact that she is a representative of mankind, a child of man. It is also to clarify her identity with the child the Student has earlier tried to save who, "walking right below the wall," corresponds to the Young Lady when she first enters below the wall of the visualized house.[61] The Student's reaction when he first sees the Young Lady is in this context illuminating. He "*covers his eyes with his hand*." It is as though he cannot trust his own eyes after the vision of the child the day before.

The essential connection between the child and the Young Lady does not appear until the end of the play. Northam interprets it as follows: "the young and innocent girl has been rescued from the collapse of the House of Life, but only spiritually; the Student's arms remain empty."[62] There is, of course, a connection between the two manoeuvres of rescue. But what is the nature of this connection? If one does not believe that the Young Lady is innocent, another interpretation seems more relevant. The child the Student thought he had saved did not exist, that is, the innocence ascribed to or symbolized by the child cannot be found in this life, only in our illusory views of it. As the Student puts it: "Where is anything that keeps what it promises? In my imagination." Branded by Original Sin, we are all guilty. The Student discovers that the Young Lady, far from being innocent, is "sick at the source of life." The innocent child he thought he had found in her suddenly disappears. He is left empty-handed, deprived of the illusion that purity is to be found in this life.

What, then, causes the house to collapse? We learn that Hummel demolishes houses. Just as the house is built of stones, so Life consists of individual lives. This is why the house is "full of defects." Hummel's attitude to his fellow-men is succinctly summarized by his servant. The Old Man, Johansson says, "sows a little word, picks out one stone at a time until the house collapses...figuratively speaking." By revealing the shortcomings of the various inhabitants, by demonstrating the rottenness of Life, Hummel indirectly makes the house collapse.

As the materialist of the play, Hummel, not unlike the biblical Tempter, boasts that he owns everything that can be seen. But he is not the only materialist. The wife of the Posh Man, we learn, presents her husband with "a stone house to get rid of him." And both the Student and Johansson dream of material comfort.

Hummel's revelatory eagerness in Act II is repeated by the Student at the end of Act III. When he assumes that "the world would collapse if you were absolutely frank," he actually foreshadows the end, which demonstrates how his candid outburst not only kills the Young Lady but also causes the house – the world – to collapse.

Representing Life, the house reflects the hierarchy characteristic of human society. In *A Blue Book I*, Strindberg writes in a piece entitled "Through constraint to freedom":

> The teacher continued: In this world you are constrained for you are all dependent on each other, press upon each other like the stones of a vault, from above, from below, from the sides; guard each other, spy on each other. Thus freedom does not, may not exist in this building called state and society. Since the foundation-stones must carry the greatest burden, they are of grey stone, while the rest are light bricks. There are also some luxurious bricks, which do not carry anything, just adorn, while they are supported by others; still, they adorn, feel embarrassed and dispensable, but they serve as adornment, and this they get to hear. (SV 65:76)

Here three social classes, appearing also in *The Ghost Sonata*, are metaphorically outlined. Among the luxurious bricks we find the Consul and the Secular Canoness and, at least seemingly, Baron Skanskorg, the Colonel and the Young Lady. Among the light bricks are company director Hummel, merchant Arkenholz and the Student. The grey stones are represented by Johansson, Bengtsson, the Milkmaid, the Cook, the Caretaker's Wife, the Dark Lady, the Maid and the Beggars.

This being the situation, we would expect the class struggle to take a prominent place in the drama. The dependency of the lower classes is indeed indicated in a few places. Thus the Caretaker's Wife seems to have got her husband a job by 'selling' herself to the Consul.[63] Johansson "slaves for [his] food, which isn't the best." And Hummel surrounds himself with beggars who, in return for their pushing his wheelchair, only get "a hint of something nice at his funeral." The last clause may be interpreted figuratively: the death of the bourgeois class means bread for the working class. When the Beggars, admonished by Hummel to pay respect to the Student, *"uncover their heads,"* they significantly do not cheer.

The representatives of the upper classes devote themselves to drinking punch, cultivating hyacinths, horse-riding, playing the harp, visiting the Opera, etc. The Student significantly desires an apartment "four flights up," where the bricks of luxury are found.

But Strindberg has not drawn an altogether black-and-white picture. Moreover, the social status of the characters is at times rather uncertain. Thus Johansson and Bengtsson have fallen down the social ladder, while the opposite is true of Hummel. The Colonel has climbed from lower class to false upper class, and it is likely that the Posh Man has done the same. The Mummy's social status is unclear. The Dark Lady, daughter of the Consul and the Caretaker's Wife, is a social hybrid. And so is, and to an even greater extent, the Young Lady, daughter of a former servant, now company director, brought up by a former servant, now false nobleman and colonel.

It could, of course, be argued that *The Ghost Sonata* is an attack on bourgeois society and that Buddha's dream that "poor earth is to become a heaven" concerns a social utopia. But this idea would only be convincing if it could be demonstrated that the collapse of the house at the end represents the collapse of a socio-economic system. The closing picture of *Toten-Insel* points in quite another direction. And what is emphasized in the play is not what separates characters belonging to different social classes but what unites them as representatives of erring and suffering humanity.[64] Their varying fates form a meaningful backdrop for the Mummy's central line: "We are poor human beings, we know that; we have erred; we have sinned, *like everyone else*" (my italics).

It is significant that at the end of "Through constraint to freedom," the house is given a metaphysical rather than a social significance. Having stated that we may speak of a socially determined longing for freedom and that it is up to "the management" to see to it that the citizens do not carry heavier burdens than they are obliged to, Strindberg continues:

> But behind this general longing for freedom, there is another more profound one, often confused with the former kind. It is the pining of creation for liberation from the shackles of the flesh, most pregnantly expressed by St. Paul: "O wretched man that I am! who shall deliver me from the body of this death?" [Rom. 7:24] But this freedom can be gained only through the patient acceptance of the constraint of this world. Hence, through constraint to freedom! (*SV* 65:76)

There is apparently a conflict within the author himself between his socio-political and his religious conviction. While he feels the need to revolt against earthly authorities, he is inclined to subordinate himself to heavenly ones. The same ambivalence we find in the Student's final monologue.

It is hardly surprising that the social criticism plays a limited role in *The Ghost Sonata*. If each individual has been given a task in life, as Strindberg wished to believe, and if his salvation depends on whether he accepts this task or not, there is no reason to admonish the lower classes to revolt. To the elderly Strindberg religion is no opium for the people.

The Milkmaid and the Dead Man are the two ghosts of the play. Their function is similar to that of the Ghost in *Hamlet*. They bear witness to secret crimes which must be expiated. Shakespeare makes this quite clear by letting his Ghost address Hamlet. Strindberg's ghosts, on the other hand, are mute.

Both plays begin with a ghost scene. The Milkmaid testifies to Hummel's murder just as the Ghost indicates Claudius' secret murder. Both visions appear three times, under different circumstances. The Milkmaid makes her first entrance before the Student just as the Ghost appears to the guards and to the audience before Hamlet sees it. In this way she is experienced as a flesh-and-blood reality by the recipient. The connection with Hummel, who is already on the stage, also becomes more evident.

Between the Milkmaid's first and second appearance, the dead Consul makes his entrance. He too has been 'murdered' by Hummel. At her first appearance, the Milkmaid is seen only by the visionary Student, who is also the only one who sees the Dead Man. (That the audience sees what he sees does not mean that we, like him, are provided with second sight. It is a dramaturgic concession to clarify the contrast between Hummel and the clairvoyant Student.) In both cases he relates his experiences to the Old Man, who is thereby reminded of his crimes against these two people. However, when the Milkmaid appears for the second time, she is seen not only by the Student but also by Hummel. At her last appearance, during the ghost supper, she is seen only by the Old Man. (The Student is on this occasion in another room.) These variations illustrate a change within Hummel, whose evil is gradually revealed both to himself and to us. Hummel's reactions make this clear. After the Milkmaid's first appearance, he asks the Student to whom he, the Student, has been talking. When the Student astonished says "Didn't you see?", Hummel does not reply. After a pause he changes the topic of conversation. Already here Hummel feels that he is in the grip of supernatural powers. He is beginning to suffer from pangs of conscience. When he later learns that the Student has been talking to the Milkmaid, he "*shudders.*" When she appears for the second time, he "*collapses with horror.*" The third time, she is "*unseen by everyone but* THE OLD MAN, *who shudders.*" Gradually Hummel's sense of guilt awakens.

It is evident that the visions have been incorporated into the play as a theatrically effective means of dramatizing inner processes. There is also a point to the fact that the Strindbergian ghosts, unlike their Shakespearean counterparts, do not differ conspicuously from the living characters who are, as we have seen, the true ghosts of the play.[65]

This paradox applies also to the beginning of the play as compared to the final vision of Böcklin's monumental *Toten-Insel*, the logical outgrowth of the death screen of Acts II-III. Böcklin made, in fact, five versions of this painting, slightly different from each other.[66] Strindberg does not indicate, in his stage directions, which of these versions he had in mind.[67] And although the biographical evidence provides no definitive answer, it points in the direction of the first 1880 version.[68] This version shows an isle with high, crater-like rocks, surrounding a group of tall cypresses. In the rock to the right are openings similar to those of sepulchral chambers. On the shore below, centre, there is a staircase of white marble. Here the recently dead are received. "*A black boat with a black rower, carrying a white coffin with a white figure standing next to it*" (SV 63:329) – the stage directions for the drama fragment *Toten-Insel* – approaches the staircase across the still water.

In *The Ghost Sonata's* final picture of *Toten-Insel* we find a spiritual counterpart of the solid façade at the beginning of the play. The marble staircase of the house – the entrance to Life – corresponds to the marble steps of the isle, the entrance to Death, that is, to the afterlife; the laurel bushes framing the house entrance to the cypresses of the isle;[69] the windows of the house to its sepulchral openings. The white marble statue inside the house, "*surrounded by palms*," corresponds to the erect white figure in the boat, surrounded by the cypresses of the isle. The Dark Lady, "*standing immobile on the stairs*" has a counterpart in the black rower in the boat, whereas the dead Milkmaid, "*in summer clothes*," resembles the recently dead white figure in the boat. Even the fresh water of the street drinking-fountain, in which she mirrors herself, can be linked with the still water around the isle in which the white figure is reflected.

The final tableau may also be seen in the light of Swedenborg's concept of the afterlife. This appears both from the drama fragment entitled *Toten-Insel*,[70] and from the little piece called "Higher forms of existence; *Die Toten-Insel*" appearing in *A Blue Book III*. The first station where man arrived after death, we here read,

> consisted of isles, swimming in something which could be air or water. [-] On every isle there was a castle, where guardians, helpers and teachers dwelled. Good people who had come out of the ordeal reasonably well were now living here. They had mostly suffered in life, had been dragged down by sins and crimes but had then come to feel such a loathing for evil that they had turned in the direction of good. Liberated from the base

human body and from what is evil and untrue, they were all beautiful and pure. They were half transparent, so that they could not conceal anything or lie. [-]

This was the station of rest, or the summer vacation after the first death; and the days seemed as short to them as a feast. (*SS* 48:1034-36)

It is to this paradisaic existence that the Milkmaid belongs, as her "*summer clothes*" indicate. And it is to this existence the Young Lady journeys in the final tableau. The house of earthly existence has collapsed to give way to its spiritual counterpart, the Isle of the Dead, "a home without dust," the station of rest.

The connection between the beginning and the end is also underlined by the sound effects.[71] When the curtain rises for Act I, we hear the ringing of "*the bells of several churches [which] are audible in the distance.*" While the Milkmaid washes her hands and looks into the water of the street drinking-fountain, "*a steamship bell can be heard, and now and then the silence is broken by the bass notes of an organ in a nearby church.*" By these acoustic means, Strindberg from the very beginning creates a strange and solemn mood.

The sound effects return at the end. When the Young Lady feels death approaching, she "*rings the bell*" and the servant enters. As she is dying behind the black folding-screen, the Student prays for her:

Poor little child, child of this world of illusion, guilt, suffering, and death, this world of endless change, disappointment and pain! May the Lord of Heaven have mercy on you on your journey...

We then see how "*the room disappears*" and how "*Böcklin's* Toten-Insel *becomes the backdrop.*" The Student's prayer clearly relates to the voyage depicted in Böcklin's painting. To the visual impression, Strindberg adds an acoustic one: "*soft, quiet, pleasantly sad music can be heard from the isle.*" Here, just as in the beginning, a voyage is combined with celestial music, but this time in an explicitly metaphysical fashion.

In *A Blue Book I* the teacher describes a vampiric character called Cinnober after E.T.A. Hoffmann: "You saw a cradle child without hair and teeth, but with beard and glasses, this arose pity and compassion..." (*SV* 65:129) Cinnober wears glasses to hide his true intentions. The glasses function as a mask. Similarly, the Old Man, provided with wig, beard and glasses, from his wheelchair appeals to the Student's compassion, only to reveal himself later as a vampire. With his glasses Hummel masks his true self not only to others but also, and especially, to himself. Not even when he looks at himself in the mirror, does he see himself. He does so only to check that the wig hides what it is supposed to hide.

The Fiancée devotes herself to another form of blindness. Instead of falsifying her self, she escapes it: "The gossip mirror's the only mirror she uses, because in that she doesn't see herself, only the outside world and in two directions, but the world can see her, she hasn't thought of that."

The Mummy who lives in the closet "both to escape seeing and being seen" represents another variety: the person who hides to the world and to herself because she cannot stand either and who therefore leads a semblance of life.

Hummel's glasses indicate that his eyesight is poor. The Fiancée, it says in the notes, is "half-blind." And the Mummy, who normally dwells in darkness, must have problems with her eyesight in daylight.

In *A Blue Book I* it says: "The material eye can mirror images; the inner eye can apprehend them. There are thus two ways of seeing, an outer and an inner one." (*SV* 65:198) Hummel seems to be provided only with the former kind. But his poor eyesight is not constant. It improves as he becomes more aware of the evil deeds he has done. Seeing yourself becomes identical to apprehending yourself. But, as it says in *The Burned Site*, "when you have seen yourself, you die." (*SV* 58:151)

With respect to the flaws of other people, Hummel is very sharp-sighted. Both his presentation of the inhabitants of the house and his unmasking of the guests at the ghost supper demonstrate that. Like most of us, he sees the mote in his brother's eye but not the beam in his own. His eyesight is distorted.

Even the Student seems blinded in the beginning by the sun that is reflected in the windows of the admired house.[72] At the end, when the hyacinth room is filled with "*white light,*" he sees the sun directly, as in a vision. His eyesight, too, improves in the course of the play. Yet from the beginning it is better than that of the other characters. He can see "what others cannot see": the little child he tried to save, the Milkmaid, the Dead Man and, possibly, *Toten-Insel*. But his second sight can also be regarded as a childlike ability to see others as essentially good. When the Young Lady first appears, the Student exclaims: "never did I see such a woman of woman born." And Hummel indicates that it is not the Young Lady's outward beauty the Student refers to: "You can see it! – Not everyone sees her beauty..."

In *A Blue Book I* the teacher describes two different attitudes to one's fellow-men. By adopting a "childish, unconscious condition," one can experience them as good or at least as harmless.

This is a kind of somnambulism. But I can sometimes wake up; then I see the company naked, their unclean underwear through the clothes, their decrepitudes, unwashed feet, but worst of all, I heard the thoughts behind their words, I saw their mimicry which did not fit the words, I caught a sidelong glance [-]. Then it is horrible to live! – I had a

friend who at a party became clairvoyant. He sat down in the middle of his table, revealed all he had seen during the evening; undressed his friends; and was, as a conse-
quence, brought to the asylum as being insane. There are many kinds of insanity, we
must admit! (*SV* 65:69)

This description agrees with that of the Student concerning his father. After a
life as a somnambulist, he is seized by clairvoyance. When he sees life as it is,
he is sent to the madhouse. When he turns sane, he is declared crazy. What
else can you expect in this world of illusions, peopled by madmen who kill
their saviour and let the robber loose? The episode about the father not only
motivates the Student's eruption at the end genetically; it also mysteriously
connects the father's eruptive veracity with Hummel's in Act II.[73]

However, unlike the eruptions of these two, the Student's is followed by an
endeavour to see a meaning in the misery of life. We may, in fact, in his case
speak of a highly compressed development, not unlike Hamlet's. Hamlet,
Strindberg claims,

> lives like an unreflecting sleepwalker, dependent, working by means of other people's
> thoughts and ideas which he learned as a child and imagines are his own. Then he
> awakens, his eyes open, he sees through the deception and the illusions, rages about
> having been fooled, and has to revise his whole philosophy.
>
> [-] in Ophelia's presence he analyzes love, which in its very nature is unreflected syn-
> thesis that cannot be analyzed. He wants to know what one is not permitted to know;
> and because of arrogantly wanting to know God's secrets which have a right to remain
> secrets, Hamlet is punished by the kind of madness called skepticism, which leads to ab-
> solute uncertainty, and out of which the individual can be saved only by faith: childish
> faith which through the sacrifice called obedience one gets as a sort of Christmas-gift
> wisdom, the absolute certainty that surpasses understanding.[74]

We find the three stages distinguished here also in the Student who initially
entertains the idea that life is a paradise; who later arrives at the idea that it is
an inferno; and who finally embraces the faith, amounting to a synthesis, that
although life is an inferno, there is a paradise beyond death.

By showing us the Student's visions, Strindberg allows us to share his point
of view. His subjectivism becomes ours. This is especially important at the end
of the play. Just before the Young Lady dies, "*the harp's strings begin to rustle*" and "*the room is filled with a white light.*" Swedenborg's idea that a sense
of light arises when a film is removed from the eyes of the dying person is relevant here.[75] Not until we die are our eyes opened. But the exoteric meaning is
that the Sun of Grace is shining on the dying woman. Then follows the vision
of *Toten-Insel* which, if shown unaccompanied by any character, objectifies
the Student's faith in a brighter afterlife.

According to popular belief, a vampire is a ghost who at night sucks blood out of the living. The blood gives the vampire vitality, whereas the victim fades away. Strindberg makes metaphoric use of this idea in a number of works around the turn of the century, not least in *The Ghost Sonata*.

The Old Man and the Cook are the two obvious vampires. The connection between the two is made explicit when the Young Lady declares that the Cook belongs to "the Hummel family of vampires" and when Bengtsson reveals that Hummel has once been "a vampire" in his kitchen, siding with the Cook and "sucking all the goodness out of the house."

Hummel's vampiric mentality is visually demonstrated early in Act I when he takes the Student's hand:

> STUDENT. But let go of my hand, you're taking all my strength away, you're freezing me, what do you want?

When Hummel later refuses to spare the Colonel, he significantly gives the following motivation: "I can't let go once I have my teeth in someone." This line points forward to the Cook who *"grins, showing her teeth."* Just as Hummel has earlier sucked the goodness out of Bengtsson's house, so the Cook now sucks it out of the Colonel's. "There's the one who's devouring me...and all of us," the Young Lady complains. But the Cook retorts: "You suck the strength out of us, and we out of you." As this speech indicates, the vampirism is linked to the class struggle, not least to the parasitic existence of the upper classes.

It is obvious that the vampirism in the play is more mental and social than physical and that it is a widespread phenomenon. A passage in *A Blue Book I* is in this respect clarifying:

> There are vampires [-] who through feigned services bind thankful people; or who demand too much interest, provision, book-keeping charges, etc. for modest charities. [-] I have met many such stranglers. They are always provided with filing cabinets where the promissory notes of gratitude are kept, although they should be returned. (*SV* 65:196)

This is a portrait of Hummel who, by pretending to be the victim of merchant Arkenholz, binds his son, the Student, to himself through a debt of gratitude. While in this quote economic terms are used metaphorically, in *The Ghost Sonata* it is often left suggestively open whether statements should be understood literally or figuratively. Take the case of the Consul. We have earlier assumed that he was economically indebted to the usurer Hummel. But nothing prevents us from seeing the notes of hand Hummel is said to have strangled the Consul with as notes of gratitude.[76]

We normally regard the sucking of the vampire merely as an act of cruelty and aggressiveness. But we must not forget that the increased vitality resulting from the sucking according to popular belief means that the transference to hell is postponed. The blood-sucking is, in other words, linked to self-preservation. Both the Cook's and the Old Man's vampirism should be seen in this light. When Hummel, for example, at the age of 80, feels the chill of death approaching and counters it by 'sucking' warmth out of the Student's hand, we sense that his vampirism expresses his need to stay alive.

Significantly, even the Student becomes a vampire towards the end of the play:

> STUDENT. Do you know what I think about you now?

> YOUNG LADY. Don't tell me or I'll die!

> STUDENT. I must, or I shall die!...

Like the Old Man, the Student cannot "let go" once he has got his teeth into someone. The passage reveals that the vampirism can also stand for the brutal disclosure of other people's most private shortcomings.

With regard to flowers, Strindberg limits himself to one kind – the hyacinth – connected with one space, the hyacinth room, and one character, the Young Lady.

Already in Act I we see her busying herself with the hyacinths in the window of her room. "She is talking to the flowers," Hummel says, and he adds:

> Isn't she like the blue hyacinth herself?...Now she gives them a drink, only pure water, and they transform the water into colours and fragrance...

The comparison adds a narcissistic touch to Adèle's concern for the flowers. In Act II she is sitting reading in the hyacinth room, while Hummel states that she is "withering" in an air breathing crimes and betrayal. In Act III we see "*hyacinths in various colours everywhere.*" The act opens with a song of praise to the hyacinth-cum-woman:

> YOUNG LADY. Sing now for my flowers!

> STUDENT. Is this the flower of your soul?

> YOUNG LADY. The one and only! Do you love the hyacinth?

> STUDENT. I love that above all others, its virginal form which straight and slender rises from the bulb, rests upon the water and sinks its pure white roots into the colourless liquid; I love its colours: the innocent, pure snow-white, the honey-sweet yellow, the youthful pink, the mature red, but above all the blue – the dewy-blue, the deep-eyed, the faithful...

Do we not here, in the description of the white hyacinth have a counterpart of the white marble statue, surrounded by green vegetation, in the round room? When the Student nevertheless claims to prefer the blue hyacinth, it testifies to his romantic mind, his search for the original kind: *die blaue Blume*. His love for the flowers expresses obliquely his love for their owner, the Young Lady.

The hyacinth, the Student points out, has its own "story" (Sw. *saga*, meaning 'fairy-tale'). According to the myth, Hyakinthos was a handsome prince, loved by Apollo who accidentally killed him. This corresponds to the Student's unintentional killing of the Young Lady.[77] Apollo used Hyakinthos' blood to help the hyacinth grow. Similarly, the Student's intercession for the Young Lady may be seen as a penitentiary attempt to restore her to life, albeit in a *post mortem* existence.

But the hyacinths have also another, even more esoteric meaning. In *A Blue Book III* Strindberg writes:

> There are people, who spend their whole life sleepwalking, and if you wake them up they get angry, turn around and go to sleep again. They live like plants and sleep like plants. (*SS* 48:834)

> The hyacinth is beautiful to look at, its scent is delightful to inhale, it feels perhaps something like pain or joy; but without sensibility, self-consciousness and free will no mental life can arise, and to be soulless is almost to be dead, for us human beings at least. (*SS* 48:847)

The description fits the Young Lady. When we first see her, she "*walks slowly, without looking at anyone*" – like a sleepwalker. In the first two acts she is mute and devotes herself to her plants rather than to her fellow-men. She leads, it seems, a vegetating existence. Just as the Mummy has locked herself up in the closet, the Young Lady seems to shut herself up in the hyacinth room. Surrounded by the scent of the hyacinths, she seeks to keep other odours, "the impurity of life," at a distance.[78] The Student disturbs her 'sleep' when he expresses doubts about her purity. And it kills her.

Before that happens she arouses not only the Student's admiration but also his desire. The fragrance of the hyacinths, he says, "assails me with poisonous arrows that make my heart sad and my head hot." Eros with his bow is here linked with the strong scent of the hyacinths, functioning as an aphrodisiac.

The polarization between heaven and earth characterizing this whole act culminates when the Student states that "the most beautiful flowers [-] are the most poisonous." What he means is hardly that the most beautiful women affect men's sexuality the most. More likely, he is commenting on the nature of all women, on womanhood. In his *Hamlet* essay, Strindberg writes:

In good and evil, with her roots in the manure and her flower in the light, the most beautiful grafted to the most ugly, the masterpiece of creation but utterly spoiled, hating when she loves, and loving when she hates, that is how Shakespeare depicts woman, the sphinx, whose riddle cannot be solved, because it is unsolvable or does not exist![79]

A portrait of the Young Lady and the Cook in combination! In the opening of Act III the Student is still admiring the flower. Later, after the Cook's entrance, he discovers the roots.[80] He sees the the connection between what is beautiful and what is ugly, between good and evil, spirit and matter. Separated they cannot exist. Together they form the complete plant, woman, creation. This is why the Young Lady cannot dismiss the Cook. With this interpretation, the expression "sick at the source of life" points to the roots, the Cook.[81] The Student's bitter remark that "the most beautiful flowers [-] are the most poisonous" is visually supported by this interpretation: the Cook, animal-like and as fat as the Young Lady is thin, carries the poison, "the colouring bottle with the scorpion letters" as an attribute in her hand.[82]

The characters of *The Ghost Sonata* are a sickly lot. Amalia is mummified. The Colonel wears a corset. The Young Lady is "sick at the source of life." The Cook is abnormally fat. Hummel tells the Student: "You see I'm a cripple; some say it's my own fault; others blame my parents; I myself tend to believe that it is life itself with all its snares..." Is his invalidity a result of syphilis, self-inflicted or inherited? Hummel's statement *can* be regarded in this way.[83]

Hummel's son is homosexual and his daughter is sickly. If we accept the idea that the Old Man suffers from syphilis, it seems natural to ascribe the same illness to his daughter.[84] This would throw light on the following passage:

YOUNG LADY. [-] I can never be yours.

STUDENT. Why not?

YOUNG LADY. That you mustn't ask.

It would also explain the Student's conclusion: "Why didn't you want to be my bride? Because you're sick at the source of life..." In line with this, the beautiful, aphrodisiac hyacinths which poison the Student may be seen as a warning of the Young Lady's venereal disease.

The expression "sick at the source of life" may, however, also be combined with a few words belonging to the preliminary notes for the play: "the Daughter with Cancer" (*SV* 58:132). Our conclusion would then be that the Young Lady suffers from cancer of the uterus, an interpretation which is supported by the fact that the Cook, representing the Young Lady's base self, carries a soya bottle "with scorpion letters on it." The associative chain is fairly obvious in Swedish, where *skorpion* relates to *kräfta* meaning both 'crayfish' and 'cancer.'

But beyond these individual meanings, and more relevant than these, is the signified that unites the Young Lady with the rest of the characters. Like them, she is not only marked by Original Sin;[85] conceived in sin, she is also the individual product of a fall. It is in this context interesting to note that Strindberg places a 'well' – the street drinking-fountain – on the stage in Act I and behind this a paradisaic vision: "*a white marble statue of a young woman* [the Young Lady's mother], *surrounded by palms, brightly lit by sunlight.*" This is clearly a picture of Eve in the garden of Eden before the Fall.[86]

When the Student tells the Milkmaid that he has witnessed the collapse of a house and that he has "bandaged up injured people and kept watch over the sick," the word "sick" seems surprising in connection with the accident that has just occurred. When he utters this word, he is standing next to the Milkmaid who has just 'purified' herself in the street drinking-fountain, in front of the marble statue, a picture of woman before and after the Fall. The Milkmaid's washing prepares for the Young Lady's attempt to keep the impurity of life at a distance, to find a cure for the sickness at the source of life: Original Sin.

Hummel's manner of bringing the Student and the Young Lady together is devious. Since he is banned from the house and since the Young Lady is not officially his daughter, it must be done indirectly. A poster on the advertisement column informs us that *The Valkyrie* is to be given as a matinée at the Opera. Since Hummel knows not only that the Colonel and the Young Lady are going to attend the performance but also where they are going to sit, he asks the Student to get himself a ticket for a seat next to theirs. In this way he can become acquainted with them and receive an invitation to the supper offered by the Colonel the same evening. The Student, who is "musical, sings, writes poetry," finds the proposal attractive – especially since he is in love both with the Young Lady and the house in which she lives. All this does not, however, explain why Strindberg has chosen to name the opera he will attend no less than six times in Act I.

What function has Wagner's musical drama *The Valkyrie* (1870), the second part of the sequel *The Ring of the Nibelungs*, in the chamber play?[87] In *A Blue Book I* Strindberg calls Wagner "the musical representative of evil" and he speaks contemptuously of his "cavalry music (trumpets and kettle-drums)" (*SV* 65:230). This is, however, music that a character like Hummel would appreciate, especially since he is not unlike the god of the opera, Wotan, and since his daughter, the Young Lady, is not unlike Wotan's daughter Brünnhilde. Hummel claims to know "everyone, their fathers and forefathers." But no one knows him properly. We do not even learn his real name; compare Wotan who on earth appears under a false name. Hummel is "very rich." "He wants to rule...All day long he rides about in his waggon like the god Thor." And he "plays havoc with people's fates, kills his enemies, and never forgives."

In Old Norse mythology the valkyries are handmaidens who ride across the battlefield before the battle takes place and select which heroes are destined to be killed. The boldest of the warriors are chosen and will have a blissful afterlife in Valhalla. The title of the opera refers to Brünnhilde. It is in this context interesting to see that when *The Ghost Sonata* opens, the Young Lady is "out riding"; that she wears, literally translated, an *"amazone dress"*; and that she later accompanies the Student's recital of an old Icelandic poem on a harp, a bardic and celestial instrument. Leifer has observed the most essential connection between the two women:

> Just as Wotan's daughter Brünnhilde in her slumber awaits her liberator, so 'Thor's' daughter, the Young Lady, awaits *her* hero, but [-] instead of liberating his love, he ends by 'murdering' her.[88]

It could be objected that the Student's 'murder' of the Young Lady means that she is in a sense liberated – from the pain of living. "The liberator is coming," the Student prays, adding: "Welcome, you pale and gentle one!"

Hummel's interest in *The Valkyrie* ties in with his egoistic, reckless, 'pagan' mentality, so different from the Student's Samaritan altruism and belief in the mild Buddha. Similarly the loud music of the opera is a far cry from the intimate 'music' – *"soft, tranquil, and pleasantly melancholy"* – with which Strindberg's sonata closes.

Two: Target texts

Strindberg's plays in translation are texts not only for actors, directors and spectators, texts to be transformed into visual and aural reality in the theatre. When published, they are also texts for readers. A reader of the translated plays is only once removed from the Strindbergian text. For the spectator and listener, on the other hand, the director functions as a go-between. Few non-Scandinavian directors – and, we may add, actors, drama scholars and theatre critics – have any knowledge of Swedish. They are therefore totally dependent on translations.

In this situation there is a risk that Strindberg's text is criticized for what are actually shortcomings – unavoidable or not – in the translations. Faithfulness towards the source text must be a primary demand. But not least because play translations are usually undertaken with a production in mind, it is equally important that the lines are idiomatic and easily spoken. The text must also be easy to grasp, since in the theatre we have little time to ponder. It is obvious that these three criteria to a certain extent compete with one another and that the balance between them must be settled from case to case. The problems involved will be examined here with regard to how *Spöksonaten* has been translated into one language: English, British or American.[1]

Spöksonaten has, to my knowledge, so far been published in fifteen different English translations, all of them listed and chronologically numbered in the bibliography. In the following, references to these translations are made by means of the numbers mentioned there.

The first question a translator should ask himself is: Which edition of the source text shall I use? In the case of *Spöksonaten*, SS 45 has, we may assume, been used until 1991,[2] SV 58 after this date.[3]

Another question relevant especially with regard to plays is: How has the translation come about? Is it based on a production? This is obviously the case in (6, 12, 13). In many cases information is lacking on this point.

Already the play title provides us with two alternatives: while (1) has chosen to call the piece *The Spook Sonata*, all the others have preferred *The Ghost Sonata*. In (9) there is a certain vacillation in the sense that "spook supper" appears twice in the text – while the expression "ghost supper" is used the third time. An interesting comment on the alternatives is given in (3):

> I have called this [-] *The Ghost Sonata*, in spite of the tempting alternative *Spook* [-] because I believe "ghost" is a truer translation of the author's "spök" than "spook." The latter word has, in English, a facetious flavour – one inevitably thinks of "spooky" –

which the Swedish word has not and, fantastic, in part even grotesque though the play is, it is very far from being facetious.

A similar view, this time biographically motivated, appears in (5):

> Strindberg did not want his play called *The Spook Sonata*. To his German translator he insisted that the play be "called *The Ghost Sonata* after Beethoven's *Ghost Sonata* in D Minor and his *Ghost Trio*. Hence not *Spook Sonata*."

Although the situation is hardly as simple as the commentator – by translating Strindberg's "Gespenstersonaten" and "Spuk" into English – claims, one can agree with the view that the author's information to Schering supports the alternative "ghost."

As we have earlier noted, the drama contains a number of inconsistencies. It is also obvious that certain lines call for particular movements/gestures not indicated in the acting directions. The principal question then is: should a translator retain these inconsistencies/lacunae or should he amend them? The question is touched upon in the "Translator's foreword" with which (6) opens:

> I have [-] added casts of characters [-] and have inserted additional stage directions wherever urgently needed – details that Strindberg, in his feverish and impassioned absorption in the fundamental labor of the play itself, often neglected or left to the discretion of the publisher and the stage director.

This principle is more or less adhered to by all the translators. Most of them omit the Caretaker from the list of characters, while the Cook, the Maid and the Beggars are included. Practical concerns here motivate the amendments.

The translators rarely omit anything of Strindberg's text. Examples are the omission in (6) of the initial stage direction *"det är en klar söndagsmorgon"* (it is a bright Sunday morning) and in (7) of the line "Väl, så är det skrivet!" (Well, so it is written!).

The same moderation is not shown with regard to additions. Although the three parts of the play have not been given any designations by the playwright, most translators prefer to call them 'scenes,' presumably because of their brevity.

Quite disturbing are the additional acting directions containing evaluations. In the original we find the following:

> GUBBEN *i tamburen [-] smyger sig fram och lyssnar.*

> The OLD MAN *appears in the hall [-] steals forward, and eavesdrops.*

Gubben *har försökt resa sig och taga ordet, men har fallit ner i stolen och krympt ihop, krymper allt mer och mer under följande.*

The Old Man *has tried to get up and speak, but has collapsed in his chair and shriveled up, shrinks more and more during what follows.*

(5) adds *"like a spider"* in the first example,[4] and *"like a dying insect"* in the second. Openly siding against the Old Man, the translator takes over the role of the director.

The play's list of dramatis personae is quite unconventional. Consider the following:

The Colonel.

The Mummy The Colonel's Wife.

His Daughter, is the Old Man's Daughter.

We are here explicitly told that the Young Lady is not the daughter of the man who is taken to be her father. The discrepancy between seeming and being indicated in the initial presentation of the Young Lady, whose very name, Adèle, raises the question whether she *is* noble or merely *seems* so, is found also in the presentation of "The Posh Man, called Baron Skanskorg. Engaged to the Caretaker's Daughter." The implication is here that Skanskorg is *not* a baron – just as the Colonel is not a proper colonel. From the information given earlier in the list of dramatis personae, we know that the Dark Lady is *not* the Caretaker's daughter. The relationship between Skanskorg and her, in other words, is based on mutual ignorance of the true identity of the other person. Again we are confronted with a case of discrepancy between seeming and being, in one case conscious, in the other unconscious. Strindberg makes us, in other words, already in his list of dramatis personae, take part in what is to be the major theme of his play. It is therefore unfortunate when the presentation of Skanskorg is rendered by (11) as "Baron Skanskorg, *engaged to the Lady in Black.*" The point the playwright wants to make is blurred.

The rendering "The Lady in Black" for Strindberg's "Den Mörka Damen," appearing also in (2, 3), may seem preferable to the literal "The Dark Lady" (5, 9, 15) since it clarifies that the woman in question is neither dark-skinned nor necessarily dark-haired but, as the reader may eventually conclude from the Old Man's remarks, dressed in mourning. But a literal translation, which retains Strindberg's vagueness, has arguably the advantage that it more strongly suggests that she represents death.

Strindberg's stage directions sometimes seem capricious with regard to the order of presentation. This is, for example, the case in the directions opening the play. Here (1) and (3) have chosen to change the sequence. In this way, the stage directions are easier to grasp but the associative Strindbergian order of presentation has a thematic-symbolic value which is lost.

Theatres have their national conventions. The entrance of the house is placed by Strindberg to the left. (6) instead places it to the right; we deal in this case with a consistent principle, accounted for in the "Translator's Foreword":

> For the purpose of conforming to the American stage custom, I have reversed the author's directions – Right and Left – to their opposites. Thus they are given here from the viewpoint of the actor on the stage.

This remark calls attention to the fact that playwrights and translators rarely indicate whether their stage directions are from the viewpoint of the actor or of the spectator.

Although Strindberg never explicitly says so, it is obvious that the play is set in Sweden. (In an additional stage direction (5) unnecessarily locates it in Stockholm.) When the references to Swedish habits are quite local, a translator is faced with the question: maintain or change?

In the opening of the play, the Student assumes that the Milkmaid believes that he has been drinking "punsch" the preceding night. We here deal with a national drink, relished not least by Swedish students around the turn of the century. (8, 9) translate the word with "punch" – which leads the thoughts of an English-speaking audience to a much weaker drink. Aware of this, (12) speaks of "arrak" and others (1, 3, 6) more generally of "liquor." (2, 4, 5) avoid a noun. (7) proposes a drink, whiskey, which is as natural to American students today as it was rare to Swedish students around the turn of the century.

A typical example of old Swedish mourning ritual is found in the fact that the windows to the left are *"covered with white sheets."*[5] Three approaches can be distinguished here: (a) the source text is literally translated, (b) idem, but complemented with a note explaining this national custom, (c) the explanation is included in the running text:

(a) *hung with white sheets* (2)

(b) *hung with white sheets* *
   * Sign of mourning. (3)
*draped with white sheets [in Sweden the
indication that someone has died].* (11)

(c) *hung with white mourning sheets* (7)

Of these solutions, only (b) seems recommendable. (a) means that the English-speaking reader is not put in a position to understand what to his Swedish counterpart is a matter of course. In a play where ghosts haunt the stage and where the characters speak like parrots, it may be difficult for a foreign reader to know what is realistic and what is not. If no explanation is given concerning the white sheets, there is a risk that these are considered one of the bizarre ingredients of the play. As for (c) it is, of course, incorrect not to point out that we deal with an explanative addition by the translator.

To what extent should a translator explain references to national customs and habits? Some (1, 7, 9, 11) provide very few explanations, others (5, 8, 14, 15) a great many. It is usually difficult to distinguish any firm selective principle. Much of the provided biographical information seems unnecessary for an understanding of the text – whereas words/expressions such as *"reflexions-spegel"* (gossip mirror), "Sursum corda," "Cor in aethere" are often left unexplained. In the last two cases the translator could, of course, argue that these Latin expressions are as incomprehensible to the average Swede as to the average Englishman or American. But this is a poor argument.[6] Occasionally the explanation is incorrect – as when *"reflexionsspegel"* is said to be "set at an angle inside [should be: outside] the window, so as to show what is going on in the street" (3). Or when (1) and (5) erroneously claim that "The Song of the Sun" is taken from the Old-Icelandic *Edda*, a misunderstanding which may have contributed to the choice of metre in (5). Beate von Holsteinkrona is referred to as a "stiftsfröken." Few Swedes would know that by this is meant "an unmarried noblewoman who belongs to an order providing her with an income designed to cover the basic necessities of food, shelter, clothing, and keeping up appearances" (8). The word is difficult to translate. The closest equivalent seems to be "secular canoness" (1, 2, 8). Misled by the first part of the compound – "stift" meaning 'diocese' – (3) and (7) turn the old lady into "a pillar of the Church," while (6) makes her "active in her church." Here this representative of old Swedish aristocracy has been enrolled in American sectarianism.

A similar vagueness concerning the place of action is found in another context in (7). "Your father robbed me of seventeen thousand crowns," it says with a reference to Sweden. But a little later it is pointed out that the Consul "cheated the state out of another fifty thousand pounds" (Sw. "50,000 kronor") which, irrespective of the incorrect rendering of the amount, makes the reader believe that we either deal with a British consul or that the action is set in Britain.

At the end of the play the Student remarks: "Befriaren kommer!" While either the more everyday "The liberator is coming! (13) or the more solemn "The Deliverer cometh!" (10) may here be chosen – the Student refers to death – "The Saviour is coming." (12) seems misplaced in its suggestion of Christian redemption.

A time reference, not without interest, is lost when the original's *"en modern husfasad"* – as we have seen an indirect critique of contemporary life – in (9) is rendered as *"a fashionable house,"* where the thematically meaningful *"fasad"* (*façade*) has also been left out. It can be argued that *"modern"* is not very informative unless we know in which period the play is set. A comment by the translator, provided by (15), is called for here.

In the initial stage directions, Strindberg three times mentions the words *"fasad"* and *"synes,"* which denotes 'is seen' and connotes 'appears,' 'seems.' Both words allude to the fact that the House of Life is a mirage. It is therefore regrettable that this idea does not fare well in the translations. While the connotation of *"synes"* seems impossible to retain in English, the translators either neglect the *"façade"* altogether or mention it only once.

Strindberg's Caretaker's Wife sweeps *"farstun"* (the hallway). In some translations she sweeps *"the doorstep"* (3), *"the stairs and the sidewalk in front of the house"* (5), *"the front step"* (4, 9). On the balcony rail we see a blue spread and *"två vita sängkuddar"* (two white pillows). In (5) they are just *"pillowcases."* The Milkmaid wears *"bruna skor"* (brown shoes). In (6) they are *"black."* The Mummy *"stryker"* (strokes) the Old Man on his back. In (8) she *"strikes"* (misprint?) his back. In these examples we deal with carelessness rather than lack of knowledge.

Very occasionally, the translators misunderstand the meaning of the source text. When the Student asks "Var finns heder och tro? I sagorna och på barnföreställningarna!" (Where are honour and faith? In fairy tales and performances for children!), he nihilistically implies that all positive qualities are merely fictitious, illusory. "Barnföreställningarna" is somewhat freely but essentially correctly rendered with "children's plays" by (8), while (1) and (3), confusing the preposition "på" with the preposition 'i,' wrongly translate the word with "childish fancies" and "children's fancies." Closer to the meaning of the source text are the alternatives "children's games" (5) and "games that children play" (9).

Class circulation plays an important part in the play. When Johansson declares that he has once been "bokhandlare" (a bookdealer) we get a measure of his social decline. When (2) translates this phrase with "used to be in a bookshop," this perspective disappears.

The Cook's "Nu går jag, men stannar ändå, så länge jag vill!" (Now I'll go, but I'll stay just the same, as long as I want!) is in (5) translated as follows: "I'm leaving now, but that doesn't mean I haven't stayed as long as I wanted to." In other words: Strindberg's Cook remains while the Cook of the translator leaves. Strindberg's idea that the Young Lady cannot free herself from the vampire in the kitchen until she dies is lost.

Bengtsson's remark that Hummel "höll på att få oss i fängelse, när vi kallade kokerskan tjuv" (nearly got us into prison, when we called the cook a thief) is by (9) exaggerated into: "he had us put in prison." What is grotesque with Strindberg becomes completely incredible in the translation.

Sometimes a translator ascribes a role to one character which actually belongs to another. When Strindberg writes "som han [Hummel] måste bort klockan tre, så gjordes middan färdig klockan två" (since he [Hummel] had to leave at three, dinner was ready at two), we must imagine that it was the Cook, courted by Hummel, who prepared the dinner. When (7) says that "he prepared dinner at two," as though Hummel would cook either for himself or for the whole family, he turns the vampire into its opposite. When the Young Lady's reference to the "colouring bottle with scorpion letters on it" is put in the mouth of the Cook (1, 2), the reason is either carelessness or yet another example of translators usurping the job of the director.

Sometimes the vagueness of the original is determined by a wish to maintain suspense through mystification. For example:

GUBBEN. [-] Där kommer fröken...

STUDENTEN. Överstens dotter?

GUBBEN. Ja! Dotter!

In (8) this is rendered quite literally as:

HUMMEL. [-] There comes the young lady...

STUDENT. The colonel's daughter?

HUMMEL. Yes! Daughter!

The Old Man does not explicitly state that the Young Lady is the Colonel's daughter, well aware that she is his own daughter. But almost all the translators here make themselves guilty of what in German is called *Vorausübersetzen*, i.e. translating with regard to information presented later in the play, rendering the last speech with an unequivocal "Yes! *His* daughter!" (10) or something to this effect. The Old Man is more honest in the original than in the translations.

The polysemy of a word may cause confusion. When the Student towards the end remarks that he and the Young Lady "diktade, sjöng och spelade," the last three words meaning "sang and played" seem to steer the translators in a literary direction with regard to the first word, which is rendered tritely as "composed things" (14) and more satisfactorily as "made poetry" (11) or "wrote poetry" (15). But next to this formal, literary meaning, "dikta" has the related and more general meaning of 'indulge in fancies.' Since the Student has just referred to the discrepancy between the crudeness of life and his embellishing "imagination," this meaning seems here to be the more relevant one.

Early in the play we find the following puzzling passage:

GUBBEN. Är ni sportman?[7]

STUDENTEN. Ja, det var min olycka...

GUBBEN. Så skall den vändas i lycka!

OLD MAN. Are you a sportsman?

STUDENT. Yes, that's my misfortune...

OLD MAN. We'll make it your fortune!

The Old Man's question has to do with his desire to get the Student attached to the Young Lady, who enjoys horse-riding. She is, in other words, a sportswoman. If the Student happens to be a sportsman, the chances of pairing them off would seem favourable. But beyond this literal meaning, the word "sport(s)man" has a figurative one, both in Swedish and in English: an honest, chivalrous person. This suits the Student who has just demonstrated these qualities when distinguishing himself as a "brave rescuer" of human lives.

But how are we to understand the Student's peculiar answer? How can it be a "misfortune" to be a sportsman, literally or figuratively?[8] I have earlier ascribed this to a sense of discrepancy on the part of the Student between his own sensitive Sunday child mentality and what may be considered normal human behaviour.[9] The problem with this interpretation is that it does not rhyme with the Student's attitude in the beginning of the play, where he still believes in the goodness of humanity.

A more plausible explanation, perhaps, is that when the Student talks about his "olycka" (misfortune), he has the "olyckshändelse" (disaster) of the previous night in mind. More specifically, he is thinking of the child who mysteriously disappeared as though he did not manage to save it from the collapse of the house. He has in this case failed as a "brave rescuer," as a sportsman. This child metaphorically represents the Young Lady the Student wants to save from the evil of this world. But the house collapses and the Student is left empty-handed when the Young Lady is brought to the Isle of the Dead. He has again failed as a "brave rescuer," as a sportsman. This is why, being a Sunday

child provided with second sight, he can say: "Yes, that's my misfortune...".
He is talking about his predetermined lot in life rather than about a particular
event. To be intelligible, the Student's answer must be seen in the context of
the whole play, a task for the rereader rather than for the spectator.

If this interpretation is correct, the conclusion must be that it is essential to
render the word "sport(s)man" literally, and many translators do so. (12)
tries a variation:

> OLD MAN. You like a good adventure, don't you?
>
> STUDENT. Yes, that's my misfortune...

But (3), who has obviously found the Student's answer incomprehensible,
translates "sportsman" with "gambler," thereby providing the Student's answer with a logical motivation. "Gambler" returns in several of the following
translations. By exchanging the "sport(s)man" of the original for a word with
the opposite connotations – duplicity, frivolity, greed, recklessness – the translators provide a characterization of the Student that is in total conflict with
that of the source text.

Another cryptic example we find at the end, where we are told not that the
Young Lady is dying but that she "*synes döende*," that is, "*seems to be dying*"
(8).[10] What Strindberg is suggesting here is that we, the living, are deluded.
Like the characters in the play, we mistake seeming for being. Actually, the
death of the Young Lady is no death at all, only a transformation, a rebirth to
the true life. This appears also from the acting direction referring to the Young
Lady's 'dying': "*Det höres ett kvidande bakom skärmen.*" (*A wailing is heard
behind the [death] screen.*), i.e. a sound suggesting both birth and death; as it
says in *A Dream Play*: "Why do you awaken to life [-] with a cry of [-] pain?"
Our tendency constantly to mistake the mask for the face, appearances for reality, the playwright seems to say, applies also to our view of life and death.
Strindberg's idea is obscured in renderings like "*it is seen that she is dying*" (3)
and "*She is obviously dying.*" (5).

A good example of how Strindberg's habit of thinking in metaphoric terms
may puzzle translators,[11] is the following:

> OLD MAN. Wealthy perhaps?
>
> STUDENT. Not at all. Quite the contrary! I'm extremely poor!
>
> OLD MAN. One moment --- I think I've heard that voice before --- I had a friend when I
> was young, who couldn't say window [Sw. fönster] but always said winder [Sw.
> funster] – I've only met one person with that pronunciation and that was him; and now
> you – are you related to Mr Arkenholz, the merchant, by any chance?

Since the Student has never said "funster," most of the translators, assuming that Strindberg has been careless, amend:

> HUMMEL. Wealthy, I suppose?
>
> STUDENT. Not at all – on the contrary – poor as a durmouse!
>
> HUMMEL. Look here...It seems to me as if I recognised your voice. When I was young, I had a friend who always said "dur" instead of door. (1)

The same 'improvement' is used by (2) and (4), whereas (3) prefers a vague paraphrase: "When I was young I had a friend who pronounced certain words just as you do." Not until (5) do we get a better solution: "I had a friend who couldn't pronounce window, he always said winder." That this is a premeditated choice appears from the introduction, where the translator comments on the passage:

> If this were a realistic play, there would be no explanation, just as there would be no explanation for the appearance of the Milkmaid as an apparition visible at first only to the Student. On the other hand, if the apparition can be accounted for as a symbol, so can the window. For Hummel is described later as a thief who enters through windows to steal human souls, and here we see him as he first steals into the Student's life by means of a "window."[12]

One would perhaps expect later translators to be influenced by this interpretation, and the concomitant solution, and this is the case in (7), but in (5, 8-9) we come across different attempts at emendation.

Sprinchorn is certainly right in seeing an intended symbolic significance in the window rather than a sign of carelessness on Strindberg's part. But his argumentation is somewhat misleading. Hummel does not claim that the Student has uttered the word 'funster'; he merely says that the Student's pronunciation reminds him of the way in which someone used to pronounce the word "fönster," which is something else. Since the Student has just uttered the word "beröm" (praise), presumably pronouncing it 'berum,' Hummel's remark seems quite appropriate. Yet it is strange in another way. Hummel's implication that the pronunciation of the vowel ('u' instead of 'ö') is unique, or at least very rare, is absurd since this was, and still is, standard Stockholm pronunciation.[13] It is in this way that Hummel "steals into the Student's life."

It should be clear from the foregoing that "fönster-funster," when enunciated on the stage, present a problem even to many source text recipients. The passage in which the two words are found, apart from being exceedingly mystifying, presupposes a knowledge about regional pronunciation that cannot be taken for granted.

Turning back to the translations we can distinguish different strategies. As we have seen, (3) empties the passage of its significance by paraphrasing it. (1, 5) try to find equivalents for Strindberg's implied variation "fönster-funster" with their "door-dur" and "window-winder"; but since neither "dur" nor "winder" are widespread regional pronunciations, the manipulative nature of Hummel's claim is lost. By rationally 'emending' the source text, (9) demystifies it. He makes the Student stammer and suggests that the way in which he stammers is inherited from his father. Something of the irony of the source text is nevertheless retained, since stammering in this case, like regional pronunciation, is not an individual mannerism.

Occasionally Strindberg's clause sequence is puzzling, as when the Old Man tells the Student:

> And if I were to tell you that she [the Mummy] left him [the Colonel], that he beat her, that she came back and married him again [-], then you'd think I was crazy. (15)

Whereas almost all the translators retain Strindberg's clause sequence, (9) reverses it into the more logical "that he struck her, that she left him."[14] But what the source text implies is, rather, that she returns *although* he has mistreated her, either because she has deserted her lover, Hummel, or, more likely, because she has been deserted by him. Rather than assume carelessness on Strindberg's part, we may see the clause sequence as an example of elliptic style. Put differently: although her behaviour may seem absurd, there may well be a reason for it. The world sees only the façade, not what is behind it.

Sometimes translators are forced to resign themselves to the fact that some subtleties of the source text will be lost. The two vocative forms in Swedish (du, ni) create possibilities which cannot be rendered in English translation. The change of vocative form is subtly utilized in Act III. Here the Student and the Young Lady address one another with a formal "ni" – they have just met – until, after a crescendo-like antiphony, they find one another in an ecstatic, informal "du." But the short moment of communion is soon gone. The misery of life makes itself felt and separates them again. The renewed distance is indicated by a return to the formal "ni." Not until the end, when the Young Lady is 'dying,' does the Student revert to the intimate form of address: "Sov du sköna, osälla, oskyldiga, utan skuld till dina lidanden..." (Sleep, you beautiful, unhappy, innocent creature who bears no blame for your suffering). Neither the gentleness of the "du" nor the coolness of the "ni" can be communicated by the "you" that replaces both.

Ambiguities and puns are often untranslatable. "Är han klok?" (Is he sane/wise?) the Student asks, referring to Hummel, and Johansson answers: "Ja, vad är *det*?" (Well, what's *that*?). Most translators have rendered "klok" with "in his right mind" etc., but (3) and (7) prefer "wise." Both alternatives are legitimate. The point is that Strindberg's Student phrases his question in such a way that wisdom and madness conjoin – compare his remark about his father: "he was sane but he was crazy." This meaningful ambiguity inevitably disappears in the translations.

The Student is again ambiguous when he declares that "prestaven hade älskat den avlidnes son" (the mace bearer had loved the dead man's son). "Älska" can here be understood either in a spiritual or in an erotic sense. The Young Lady's reaction – she *"fixerar, för att utleta meningen"* (*stares at him trying to understand what he means*) – reveals that she hesitates between these two meanings. In this way Strindberg pinpoints the word "älska" (love). What does it actually mean? The Student's phrasing becomes uninteresting and the Young Lady's reaction incomprehensible if the ambiguity is not preserved. How do the translators solve this?

(1) and (2) translate "hade älskat" with "had been rather too friendly." The ambiguity is replaced by a euphemistic phrase. As a result the Student seems slightly prudish and the reaction of the Young Lady is difficult to account for. (3) and (6-7, 9) use the expression "had been in love with" which is so straightforward that the Young Lady's difficulty to grasp the meaning seems unconvincing. Far too direct is the alternative "had been the lover of" (5). As so often, a literal translation – "had loved" (8, 15) – proves to be the best solution.

Surprising words, expressions, compounds are often due to an attempt on the part of the playwright to give his play an extra dimension. When the Old Man states that the Posh Man hopes to become rich and that he is getting divorced from his wife who offers him "ett stenhus" (a stone house) to get rid of him, we may be surprised at the classification "stone." But at the turn of the century, when wooden houses were still the rule in Sweden, a stone house had social prestige. More important, however, is that stone elsewhere in the play connotes materialism. The house we see on the stage is a prestigious stone house. The Posh Man's expectations are apparently identical with those of the Student and Johansson who both dream of entering this house. Ultimately we are dealing with the illusory hope of man that happiness can be gained from worldly stability and success.

This being the case, it makes a difference whether "stenhus" is rendered as "apartment-house" (1), "big house" (2), "stone mansion" (3), "mansion" (4), "town house" (5), "great mansion" (7), "stone house" (8), "manor house" (14), or "a big house, all in stone" (15). Again the most literal translations, unidiomatic as they may be, are thematically the most adequate.

The names of the dramatis personae often form a problem to a translator. A name like Skanskorg, meaning literally 'entrenchment-basket,' may imply the Posh Man's attempt to secure a social position. But it would definitely not be recommendable to translate the name into English. There is no reason, however, for reducing the original's "kallad baron Skanskorg" (called Baron S.) to "Baron Skanskorg" (3, 5-6). For Strindberg's phrasing is an indication that Skanskorg is not what he seems to be.

Nor is there any reason for changing the speaker-labels and substitute "HUMMEL" (1, 6, 8) for Strindberg's "GUBBEN" (THE OLD MAN). The appelative here corresponds to most of the other speaker-labels in the play and underlines the significant generation motif.

Extremely important in Strindbergian drama are the correspondences in the text. As we have seen, the sound effects in the beginning and at the end correspond. The organ music from a nearby church in the opening has a counterpart in the miraculous sighing of the harp strings towards the end, and the chiming of distant church bells in the opening is echoed in the "*soft, quiet, pleasantly sad music*" from the distant Isle of the Dead at the end. It is therefore unfortunate when the ringing of the bells in (3) is said to come not only from distant but also from nearby churches; when in (5) we hear "*the deep notes of the organs in the nearby churches*"; and when in (6) the final sound effect is sentimentally rendered as "*the soft strains of ecstatic music, mournfully ending on a note of peace.*"

A special problem is presented by the literary, notably biblical allusions which appear in several places in the play.[15] The opening conversation between the Student and the Milkmaid offers an example. As we have noted, it relates both to the story of the good Samaritan and to Jesus' conversation with the Samaritan woman at Jacob's well. When the Student declares that he has "bandaged up injured people and kept watch over the sick all night," we are reminded of the Samaritan who, having compassion on the man who had been mistreated by robbers, "went to him, and bound up his wounds, [-] and took care of him" (Luke 10:33-34). While (15) emphasizes the biblical allusion by using the expression "binding up wounds," the others prefer more common expressions such as "dressing wounds" or "bandaging wounds."

A biblical allusion which has usually been preserved in the translations is found at the end of Act I, where Hummel admonishes the crowd: "Clap your hands, citizens. It's Sunday, of course, but the ass in the pit and the ear in the field absolve us..." In Luke 14:5, as (8) points out, we read: "Which of you shall have an ass or an ox fallen into a pit, and will not straightway pull him out on the sabbath day?" Most translators use the phrase "ass in the pit," but (8) prefers "well" – surprisingly enough, since he is aware of the biblical reference. (7) and (9), on the other hand, seem to be ignorant of it. The former translates "the ass at the draw well," the latter "the ass at the well." The lack of biblical knowledge has here resulted in 'emendations.' The translators have assumed that Strindberg has carelessly written "i brunnen" instead of the in-

tended "vid brunnen," that he has been referring to the ass as a working ani-
mal – even on the Sabbath day.

It is, of course, essential that the recipient is aware of the fact that the
words following upon the 'killing' of Hummel – the Mummy's "Det är
fullbordat!" (It is finished) – are identical with Christ's last words on the cross
(John 19:30). The allusion can be interpreted in different ways. It may be seen
as an indication that Hummel at this moment is 'crucified'; as a reminder that
even he has something in common with Christ; or, on the contrary, as a reference to the contrast between the two. Whichever way we see it, it adds a dimension to Hummel's death.

Several translators faithfully stick to the corresponding biblical phrase and
translate "It is finished!". (9) is close to the Bible stylistically but diverging
from the Authorized Version with his "It is accomplished!". In the trivial "It is
over!" (5), "Now it is done!" (6) and "It is done!" (8), one looks in vain for
Strindberg's biblical reference.

A more cryptic biblical allusion is found at the end of the play where the
Student prays:

> Du vise, milde Buddha, som sitter där och väntar att en himmel skall växa upp ur
> jorden, förläna oss tålamod i prövningen, renhet i viljan, att hoppet icke må komma på
> skam!

> You wise, gentle Buddha, sitting there waiting for a heaven to grow out of the earth,
> grant us patience in our trials, purity of will, that the hope be not put to shame.

In Rom. 5:3-5 we read: "tribulation worketh patience; and patience experience; and experience, hope: and hope maketh not ashamed." It is this faith, in
the sense of suffering, that the Student at the end of the play tries to embrace.
When Strindberg uses the definite form "hoppet" (the hope), it is because it
agrees with the form in the Swedish Bible. The form adequately represents
both Buddha's hope and the hope of mankind.

With regard to the phrase "att hoppet icke må komma på skam," the translators are faced with the problem of how to retain both the biblical allusion
and the double reference of "hoppet." A literal quotation from the Authorized Version would have emphasized the biblical nature of the phrase too
much. But several translators have given the phrase an archaic touch by using
such words as "thy" and "come to nought." The exception is (15) who comes
close to King James with his "may not maketh ashamed." Several translators
combine the hope with Buddha: "thy hope(s)" (1, 5) "your hope(s)" (4, 6,
13). (2) combines it with humanity: "our hope." And (3, 8, 15) maintain the
vagueness of the original: "this hope," "hope."

The special problems related to the translation of biblical allusions can schematically be described as follows:

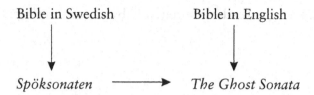

Bible in Swedish   Bible in English

Spöksonaten   ⟶   *The Ghost Sonata*

As appears from this diagram, the translator has a double loyalty. The more faithful he is to the source text, the less faithful he will probably be to the English Bible and vice versa. The difficulty consists in finding a favourable balance, so that the biblical allusions are indicated but not emphasized.

So far I have concentrated on the *meaning* of the original text and to what extent and in what way it has been preserved in the target texts. In the following I shall pay attention to problems related to *form*. To what degree has the style of the play been retained in the translations?

The language of *Spöksonaten* in many ways differs from that of present-day Swedish. Here a translator is faced with the question: Shall I settle for the kind of English spoken around 1907 or shall I choose present-day English? Here we find great divergences between the oldest translation (1916) and the latest one (1999). Even the source text is in this respect problematic. When staging Strindberg's plays in Sweden, the language is usually slightly modernized. Irrespective of whether a production is based on the source text or a target text, modernization is the director's and not the translator's task. It is another matter that it is difficult to reproduce a linguistic environment many decades later. In this respect old translations, which are temporally close to the source text, have a certain advantage over later ones.

In modern prose drama, the dialogue is almost always characterized by simple vocabulary and syntax, similar to what we find in everyday spoken language. *Spöksonaten* is no exception. What distinguishes Strindberg's dialogue from that of many other dramatists is that it provides a maximum of information and suggestion with a minimum of words. A comparison with the target texts reveals that though the natural tone is in most cases retained, the translators tend to use more words and provide less information than the author. As for the power of suggestion, this normally has a reverse relation to the number of words: the more laconic a speech is, the more suggestive it is. Consider for example this short passage, the meaning of which I have discussed earlier:

STUDENTEN. Är han klok?

JOHANSSON. Ja, vad är *det*?

This short exchange of speeches is rendered differently by all the translators. Here are four of them:

Is he in his right mind?
Who can tell? (1)

Is he a wise man?
Depends what that is. (3)

Is he compos mentis – you know, 'all there'?
I'm sure I don't know, sir... (4)

Is he quite right in his head?
Well – just what does that mean, exactly? (6)

As we have noted earlier, the ambiguity of the Student's question cannot be transferred. The translators are forced to make a choice. As a result, the suggestive element disappears. But apart from this, most of them have not been able to retain the laconic, yet natural phrasing of the original.

One of the hardest tasks for a translator is finding the right register, the right stylistic level. In *Spöksonaten* the style varies considerably, and a translator must be sensitive to subtle nuances. Take, for example, the 'monologue' opening the play. Strindberg's Student here makes use both of a number of everyday words and of words given a more careful, even solemn form. The reason for the two styles is that Strindberg has a double purpose. On the one hand he is anxious to demonstrate at once that we deal with realistic characters in a contemporary setting. (That the Milkmaid is a vision we do not realize immediately.) The Student must therefore speak like a Swedish student around the turn of the century. On the other hand we must soon sense that he also, and primarily, represents goodness and innocence. To clarify this, Strindberg has him not only perform actions in the spirit of Jesus and the good Samaritan but also describe these actions in words recalling the biblical paragons. This is how (8) translates a part of his 'monologue':

Give me a drink of water, girl, I deserve it! [-] Well! Then I'll have to tell you – I bandaged up injured people and kept watch over the sick all night;

Here the elevated tone of the original has largely been preserved. It is disturbed when (12) has the Student address the Milkmaid with "darling" – and even more so in (5):

Come on, let me have a drink of water. After last night, I think I've earned it. [-] I guess I have to tell you the whole story. I've spent the whole night bandaging wounds and taking care of the injured people.

Presumably (5) has found it strange that the Student suddenly begins to express himself quite solemnly. He has therefore settled for a homogeneous portrait of the young man by keeping the everyday jargon throughout. As a result, the biblical allusions cueing the recipient to the symbolic significance of the situation are virtually absent in his version. A comparison between the number of words used in Strindberg's 'monologue' compared to the renderings in (8) and (5) results in the figures: 48-52-70.

If the loftiness has here been set aside in (5), examples of the opposite – raising the stylistic level – can also be found. This is the way the Student describes his father in the final monologue:

> Men en dag höll han en stor bjudning – det var om aftonen; han var trött av dagens arbete, och av ansträngningen att dels tiga, dels prata skit med gästerna...

In (15) this passage is rendered quite literally as:

> One day though, he gave a big party – it was in the evening and he was tired, what with working all day and the strain of keeping quiet on the one hand and talking shit with his guests on the other...

The Young Lady reacts strongly to the Student's use of the word "skit" (shit): She "fasar" (shudders). By choosing an equivalent of Strindberg's coarse word, (15) can account for the Young Lady's violent reaction to this verbal intrusion upon her pure hyacinth world. Other translators, opting for more naturally idiomatic versions – "rot" (1, 2), "rubbish" (3), "nonsense" (5, 6-8), "filth" (10) – fail to motivate her reaction and make her overly prudish. In all respects misleading is "spiteful gossip"(9).

Even when translations come very close to one another, suggestive differences, providing different incentives to the actor, may be discerned. A good example is found in the final words of the play, concluding the Student's intercession for the Young Lady. In *Spöksonaten* they read:

> Du stackars lilla barn, barn av denna villornas, skuldens, lidandets och dödens värld; den eviga växlingens, missräkningarnes och smärtans värld! Himmelens Herre vare dig nådig på färden...

This is how four of the translators render this passage:

You poor little child! Child of this world of illusion and guilt and suffering and death – this world of eternal change and disappointment and never-ending pain! May the Lord of Heaven have mercy on you as you journey forth... (5)

Poor little child, child of this world of illusions, guilt, suffering, and death, the world of everlasting change, disappointments, and pain! May the Lord of Heaven be merciful to you on your journey... (8)

Unhappy child, born into this world of delusion, guilt, suffering and death, this world that is forever changing, for ever erring, for ever in pain! The Lord of Heaven be merciful to you on your journey. (9)

Poor little child, child of this world of illusion, guilt, suffering and death; this world of endless change, disappointment and pain. May the Lord of Heaven have mercy on you on your journey... (15)

Of these versions, (8) and (15) come closest to the original, in (8) somewhat at the expense of natural American English, as in the plurals "illusions" and "disappointments." The maintenance in three of the renderings of *points suspensifs* after the final word is praiseworthy. The sign corresponds to what is being said in the final sentence: that we are dealing with a journey, with something unfinished.

In (8) and (15) the asyndetic parataxis of the original is retained in the phrase "illusion(s), guilt, suffering," while in (5) it is replaced by parataxis through conjunction ("illusion and guilt and suffering"), which gives the line a certain naïvety. (9) in several respects differs from the others. "Unhappy child" sounds somewhat high-flown next to the more intimate "you poor little child," but the expression "born into this world" to a certain extent compensates for this.

Of special interest is the final sentence. Strindberg here has a line consisting of three dactyls and two trochees: "Hi'mmelens He'rre va're dig nå'dig på fä'rden..." The three dactyls give a harmonious movement to the line suggesting the idea of a voyage to an isle which, although it is called the Isle of the Dead, is in fact, as we have seen, the Isle of the Living. In (5) and, notably, in (15) we find a metric approximation to Strindberg's very poetical closing line which forms a bridge to the concluding soft music from the isle.

In a play where so much is written between the words, lines, and speeches, and where the dialogue is so musical, even the punctuation is of significance.[16] The different signs for silence, for example – *points suspensifs*, one or more dashes, asterisks, the words *"Paus"* (*Pause*) and *"Tystnad"* (*Silence*) – function as indications of the tempo. Of the translators, only (10), (13) and (15) comment on the problems involved here; in the words of the latter:

Precisely what these diacritical marks signify is not always apparent, but with the musical inspiration of his last works in mind, Strindberg appears to have been working towards a notational system that would convey to actor and director the spoken values of the line in question. It would be relatively easy to smooth out the text by omitting these marks and where necessary to substitute more conventional punctuation, but – with the occasional necessary exception – I have, wherever possible, elected to retain them in the belief that they indicate how Strindberg saw (or heard) the movement of the speaker's mind. [-]

I have, however, elected not to reproduce every detail of the punctuation in one respect, namely Strindberg's liberal use of the exclamation mark, which is often attached to the mildest or most straightforward of utterances.[17]

The phrasing indicates that the translator has tried to find a balance between adherence to and deviation from Strindberg's often surprising punctuation. This is certainly a sensible approach. Even the inconsistency of excepting the exclamation marks from the ruling principle of retaining Strindberg's punctuation seems reasonable. Many of the exclamation marks seem less a result of contextual concern than of Strindberg's passionate temper at the time of writing.

As could be expected, the translators have taken great liberties with the punctuation. The asterisks are generally omitted – understandably, since they normally do not indicate silence but entrances and exits. But when the translators replace the very frequent *points suspensifs* at the end of a line with a full stop, an open line is replaced by a closed one.

One example of the translators' handling of the punctuation may stand for many. In Act II we find the following passage:

GUBBEN *tar upp ett papper*. Om ni läser detta utdrag ur Vapenboken, skall ni se att den ätt, vars namn ni bär, har varit utdöd i hundra år!

ÖVERSTEN *läser*. Jag har visserligen hört sådana rykten, men jag bär namnet efter min far...-*Läser*.- Det är rätt; ni har rätt...jag är icke adelsman! – Icke ens det! – Då tar jag bort min signetring. – Det är sant, den tillhör er---Var så god!

In (15) this passage is translated as follows:

OLD MAN *taking out a piece of paper*. Read what the College of Arms has to say here and you'll see that the family whose name you bear has been extinct for a hundred years.

COLONEL *reads*. I've heard rumours to that effect, yes, but I inherited the name from my father. *Reads*. It's true; you're right...I'm not a nobleman! – Not even that! – Then I'll take off my signet ring. – It's true, it belongs to you---Here you are!

Compare this version, where Strindberg's punctuation is on the whole retained, to the translation in (3):

> OLD MAN, *producing a document.* If you read this extract from *The Armorial Gazette*,
> you will see that the family whose name you are using has been extinct for a hundred
> years.
>
> COLONEL. I have heard rumors to this effect, but I inherited the name from my father.
> *Reads.* It is true. You are right. I am not a nobleman. Then I must take off my signet
> ring. It is true, it belongs to you. *Gives it to him.* There you are.

In the Colonel's speech – which concerns us here – an acting direction (the first
"*läser*") is omitted. Instead another, rather superfluous direction – "*Gives it
to him.*" – is inserted. The suggestive line "Icke ens det!" (Not even that!) is
left out. Semicolon is replaced by comma, *points suspensifs*, and exclamation
marks by full stops. Five kinds of punctuation in the original are reduced to
two in the translation.

Let us examine the Strindbergian speech. Here the Colonel begins by reading the extract. He starts to defend himself, we may imagine, while still glancing through the beginning of the extract. *Points suspensifs* indicate that the
speech is not completed – presumably, as the second "*Läser*" (*Reads*) indicates, because the Colonel has now come to the heart of the matter which
takes all his attention. Then follows the confession. It is as though the Colonel
must bring home to himself that he has been wrong. Semicolon may at this
point represent a substantial pause. Then another pause (...) preceding the
conclusion, hard to accept for him and apparently spoken in an agitated tone
of voice (exclamation mark). Then a new pause. The Colonel is thinking. Another conclusion, mystifying to the recipient: "Icke ens det!" (Not even that!)
Later we understand that the Colonel here refers to the fact that he is not even
the father of the Young Lady, etc. Pause again (dash): the Colonel is thinking
about what he now must do. Then he takes a decision resulting in an action:
"Då tar jag bort min signetring." (Then I'll take off my signet ring.) New
pause (dash), suggesting that the Colonel has initially planned to put the ring
in his pocket; suddenly he recalls that the ring is now actually Hummel's: "Det
är sant, den tillhör er..." (It's true, it belongs to you...). *Points suspensifs* in *SS*
45 and triple dashes in *SV* 58 here indicate the unwillingness with which the
Colonel hands the ring over, until he finally parts with it with a correct "Var
så god!" (There you are!).

Strindberg's punctuation marks function as acting directions. They help to
record the Colonel's inner changes. When this 'score' is replaced by a more as-
cetic one, as in (3), it becomes more difficult for the reader, and for the actor
who is to play this part, to imagine what happens inside the Colonel.

We all know how a theatre performance can be spoilt by a tempo lacking in nuances because of wrong timing and absence of pauses. It is often during the silence between speeches or within one and the same speech that we intensely experience what goes on between and within the characters. The punctuation helps to indicate this subtext. Few translators seem to realize this.

My examination of how *Spöksonaten* has been rendered in English has led to a rather disapppointing result. In all fairness it must be said that this picture is somewhat one-sided. When discussing problems related to translation, it is natural to concentrate on striking discrepancies between the source text and the target texts, discrepancies which indicate insurmountable difficulties or unsatisfactory solutions. It goes without saying that the fifteen translations also comprise many imaginative solutions, some of which have been indicated here.

Translators naturally often influence each other. Many renderings can be explained this way. There is nothing surprising in the fact that a translator studies earlier translations of the same text. What *is* surprising, at least in this case, is that this seems to have been done to a very limited extent. Thus an earlier translator has sometimes offered a better solution than a later one. The desire to diverge from earlier target texts in order to create a translator's profile for oneself may lead to dubious results. A new translation does not inevitably mean a better translation – as the publishers' blurbs would have us believe.

Critics rarely comment at any length on how plays in target languages have been translated. Nor do they pay more than passing attention to this subject when reviewing stage or screen performances.[18] The reason is, of course, that they feel incompetent to do so, when they lack a knowledge of the source language which is usually the case when they are confronted with a minor language like Swedish. Those who translate from such languages find themselves in a position different from those translating from major ones like English, French or German. Unlike the latter, those who translate from minor languages can take great liberties with the text and get away with it. In this sense Strindberg is much more vulnerable than Wilde, Maeterlinck or Schnitzler.

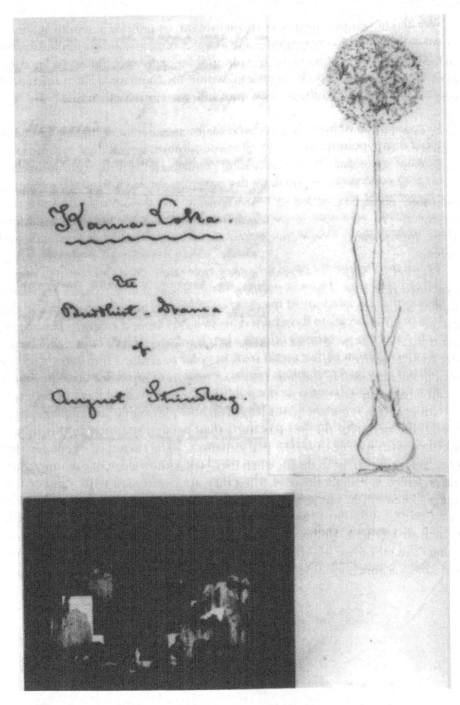

1   Title page of Strindberg's fair copy of *The Ghost Sonata*, including a cutting of Böcklin's *Toten-Insel* (first version) and a drawing of the Ascalon shallot (*Allium ascalonicum*). The text reads: "*Kama-Loka*. A Buddhist-Drama by August Strindberg." Courtesy Strindbergsmuseet.

2 A page of the original manuscript of *The Ghost Sonata*, in Strindberg's neat handwriting, showing how the Cook has been added in the margin.
Courtesy Kungl. Biblioteket.

3 Front cover of the first edition of *The Ghost Sonata*. The title is in red letters. The book actually did not appear until early 1908.

4　The stage of Strindberg's and Falck's Intimate Theatre in Stockholm (1907-10), seen from the auditorium. On either side of the stage replicas by Carl Kylberg of paintings by Arnold Böcklin, to the left the Isle of the Living, to the right the Isle of the Dead. Courtesy Strindbergsmuseet.

INTIMATEATERN

Spöksonaten.

Fantasistycke i 3 akter af
AUGUST STRINDBERG

Personer:

Direktör Hummel, gubben	Hr Ljungqvist.
Studenten Askenholz	Hr Wahlgren.
Mjölkflickan (vision)	Fröken Geijer.
Den döde, konsul	Hr Norrman.
Den mörka damen, den dödes dotter med portvakterskan	Fru Björling.
Öfversten	Hr Falck.
Mumien, öfverstens hustru	Fröken Åhman.
Hans dotter (är gubbens dotter)	Fröken Flygare.
Den förnäme, kallad baron Skanskorg, trolofvad med portvakterskans dotter	Hr Gustafson.
Johanson, tjänare hos Hummel	Hr Johann:son.
Bengtson, betjänt hos öfversten	Hr Kjellgren.
Fästmön, Hummels f. d. fästmö	Fröken Forsström.
Kokerskan	Frkn Alexandersson
Portvakterskan	

5　Program for the first production of *The Ghost Sonata* which opened at the Intimate Theatre on 21 January 1908. In the original program, the name of the theatre above and the stylized flower below are red. Note the subtitle: "Fantasy piece in 3 acts." Courtesy Kungl. Biblioteket.

6 Paul Wegener as the Old Man and Gertrud Eysoldt as the Mummy in Max Reinhardt's pioneering 1916 production at the Kammerspiele in Berlin. Drawing: Gerda Ploug-Sarp.

7 Act I in Olof Molander's famous 1942 production at Dramaten in Stockholm showing the so-called Red House where Strindberg lived when writing the play. Photo: Almberg & Preinitz. Courtesy Drottningholms teatermuseum.

8 Act II in Olof Molander's 1942 production showing the round room arranged for the ghost supper.
Photo: Almberg & Preinitz. Courtesy Drottningholms teatermuseum.

9 The Old Man (Lars Hanson) and the Mummy (Märta Ekström) by the marble statue, her youthful self, in Act II of Olof Molander's 1942 production.
Photo: Almberg & Preinitz. Courtesy Drottningholms teatermuseum.

10   Act III in Olof Molander's 1962 production at Dramaten in Stockholm,
showing the hyacinth room with the Buddha figure and the Ascalon shallot. The
Student (Allan Edwall) left, the Young Lady (Christina Schollin) by the harp, in
the background the Mummy and the Colonel.
Photo: Beata Bergström. Courtesy Drottningholms teatermuseum.

11   Act I in Ingmar Bergman's 1941 production at Medborgarhuset in Stockholm. Fr. l. to r. the Old Man (Erland Colliander), The Colonel, the Student (Peter Lindgren), the Dark Lady, the Milkmaid, the Young Lady (Karin Lannby).
Courtesy Drottningholms teatermuseum.

12   The ghost supper in Bergman's 1941 production. Fr. l. to r. the Fiancée, the
Mummy (Dagny Lind), the Old Man (Erland Colliander), Bengtsson, the Colonel,
the Posh Man, the Dark Lady. Courtesy Drottningholms teatermuseum.

13   The Student (Folke Sundquist) and the Milkmaid (Harriet Andersson), both in summer clothing, by the street drinking-fountain in Ingmar Bergman's 1954 production at Malmö City Theatre.
Photo: Skånereportage, Malmö. Courtesy Dramatiska Teater.

14   The Old Man (Benkt-Åke Benktsson) and the Mummy (Naima Wifstrand)
by the marble statue in Bergman's 1954 production. Note the physical contrast
underlining the difference between vampire and victim.
Photo: Skånereportage, Malmö. Courtesy Drottningholms teatermuseum.

15   The Student (Folke Sundquist) and the Young Lady (Gaby Stenberg) in pietà grouping at the end of Bergman's 1954 production.
Photo: Skånereportage, Malmö. Courtesy Drottningholms teatermuseum.

16   Act I in Ingmar Bergman's 1973 production at Dramaten in Stockholm
showing out-of-focus projections of two identical façades and part of a church.
Downstage the grandfather clock left and the marble statue right indicate the interior of the imaginary house in the auditorium. Cf. the ground plan p. 189.
Photo: Beata Bergström. Courtesy Drottningholms teatermuseum.

17   The Milkmaid (Kari Sylwan), in authentic costume, and the Student
(Mathias Henrikson) by the street drinking-fountain in Bergman's 1973 produc-
tion. Cf. the Milkmaid's costume in figs. 11 and 13.
Photo: Beata Bergström. Courtesy Drottningholms teatermuseum.

18   The Old Man (Toivo Pawlo) and the Student (Mathias Henrikson) looking at
the house-in-the-auditorium in Act I of Bergman's 1973 production. Cf. the use
of a skull-cap in figs. 11, 12 and 14.
Photo: Beata Bergström. Courtesy Drottningholms teatermuseum.

19   The Young Lady (Gertrud Fridh) by the brightly lit, semi-nude marble statue in Act I of Bergman's 1973 production. Note the identity of hair fashion.
Photo: Beata Bergström. Courtesy Drottningholms teatermuseum.

20   The Milkmaid (Kari Sylwan) drowning in the memory of the guilty Old Man
(Toivo Pawlo) at the end of Act I in Bergman's 1973 production.
Photo: Beata Bergström. Courtesy Drottningholms teatermuseum.

21 Act II in Bergman's 1973 production showing out-of-focus projections of the overloaded walls of the round room and five sturdy black-and-red chairs arranged for the ghost supper. In the background the hyacinth room with a harp and two slender white chairs. Cf. figs. 8 and 12.
Photo: Beata Bergström. Courtesy Drottningholms teatermuseum.

22   The Mummy (Gertrud Fridh), her hands raised in a 'parrot gesture,' by the marble statue, partly sunlit, in Act II of Bergman's 1973 production. Cf. fig. 19. Photo: Beata Bergström. Courtesy Drottningholms teatermuseum.

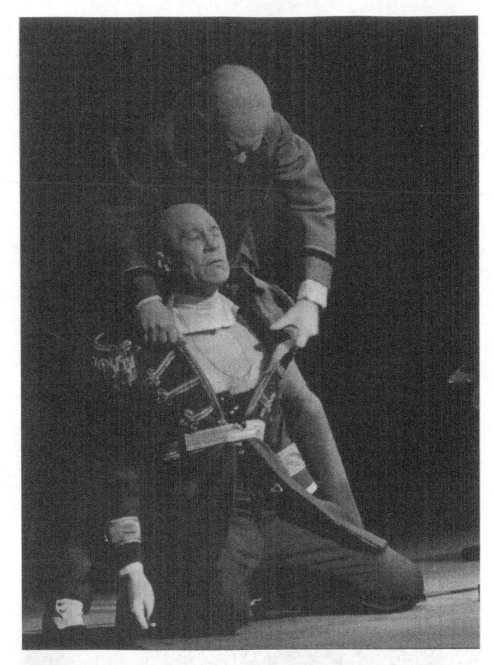

23 The Old Man (Toivo Pawlo) unmasking the Colonel (Anders Ek) in Act II of
Bergman's 1973 production.
Photo: Beata Bergström. Courtesy Drottningholms teatermuseum.

24   Bengtsson unmasking the Old Man at the ghost supper towards the end of
Act II in Bergman's 1973 production. Fr. l. to r. the Colonel (Anders Ek), the
Mummy (Gertrud Fridh), the Old Man (Toivo Pawlo), Bengtsson (Oscar Ljung),
the Fiancée (Dora Söderberg) and the Posh Man (Frank Sundström). Cf. fig. 12.
Photo: Beata Bergström. Courtesy Drottningholms teatermuseum.

25   Act III in Bergman's 1973 production showing out-of-focus projections of
the walls of the hyacinth room. To the left the black death screen. The slender
white chairs contrast with the sturdy black-and-red ones in the round room upstage. Cf. fig. 10.
Photo: Beata Bergström. Courtesy Drottningholms teatermuseum.

26 The vampiric Cook (Hjördis Petterson) by the shaded marble statue in
Bergman's 1973 production.
Photo: Beata Bergström. Courtesy Drottningholms teatermuseum.

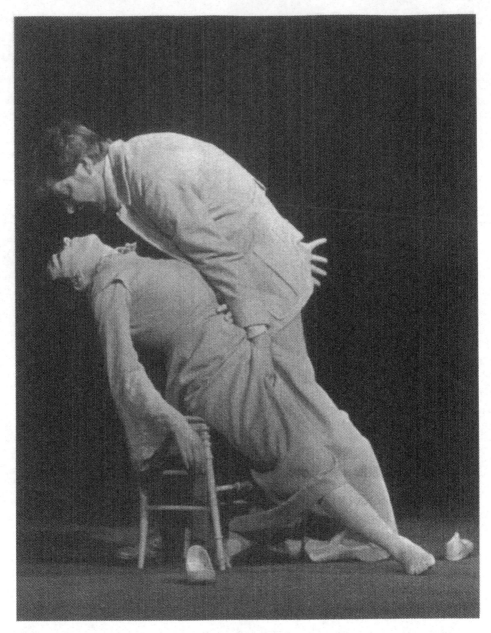

27 The Student (Mathias Henrikson) 'raping' the Young Lady (Gertrud Fridh) towards the end of Bergman's 1973 production.
Photo: Beata Bergström. Courtesy Drottningholms teatermuseum.

28   The Young Lady (Gertrud Fridh), curled up, in her petticoat after the blue
hyacinth dress has fallen off her. In the foreground the disillusioned Student
(Mathias Henrikson). From Bergman's 1973 production.
Photo: Beata Bergström. Courtesy Drottningholms teatermuseum.

29   The ending in Bergman's 1973 production, showing a human trinity: the dead Young Lady (stand-in Karin Thulin), the Mummy (Gertrud Fridh) and the Colonel (Anders Ek).
Photo: Beata Bergström. Courtesy Drottningholms teatermuseum.

30   The Milkmaid (Virpi Pahkinen) drowning in the memory of the guilty Old
Man (Jan Malmsjö), surrounded by the Beggars, in Bergman's 2000 production at
Dramaten in Stockholm. Cf. fig. 20. Photo: Bengt Wanselius.

31   The anguished Mummy (Gunnel Lindblom) and the sly, bald Old Man (Jan
Malmsjö) in Act II of Bergman's 2000 production. Cf. figs. 9 and 14.
Photo: Bengt Wanselius.

32   The Student (Jonas Malmsjö) attacking the Young Lady (Elin Klinga) towards the end of Bergman's 2000 production. Cf. fig. 27.
Photo: Bengt Wanselius.

33   The Old Man (Allan Edwall) and the Student (Stefan Ekman), with a Swedish student's cap, by the advertisement column showing the poster of *The Valkyrie* in Johan Bergenstråhle's 1972 TV production. Photo: Lars Wiklund.

Three: Stage productions

The world premiere of *The Ghost Sonata*, at Strindberg's own Intimate Theatre, took place on a stage that was only 6 meters wide and 4 meters deep for an audience counting at most 161 persons. The play was subtitled "fantasy piece," after E.T.A. Hoffmann, possibly in an attempt to counteract criticism.[1] Nevertheless both the play and the performance were severely criticized and only twelve performances were given.[2] One critic remarked:

> The play which when read is undoubtedly suggestive, seems completely unactable even for the most artistic actors, while at the same time, with regard to direction, it demands such extensive resources that the tiny stage of the Intimate Theatre in no way can yield.[3]

Though the actors were both talented and committed, they were also young and inexperienced, a problem in *The Ghost Sonata*, where most of the characters are quite advanced in years.[4]

The critics were mystified by what they called Strindberg's peculiarities. Writer-critic Bo Bergman, however, was sensitive to the uniqueness of the piece when writing:

> In the vision the chamber play wants to present on the stage the invisible becomes visible. The only law governing the play is the author's imagination. It is a dream that is to be recreated in flesh and blood, a very delicate matter theatrically. One has to retain the visionary element without losing touch with realities.[5]

Act I made little impression, partly because of "a misleading scenery."[6] But the ghost supper "provided mood and illusion."[7] The guests were characterized as "a monstrous collection of human caricatures and wooden puppets"[8] or as "mannikins" making the real "ghosts," the Milkmaid and the Dead Man, "far more real and almost more human"[9] – a reversal quite in line with the theme of the play. The references to household problems in Act III were experienced as parodic.

At the end a couple of doors opened to show "a landscape with fir trees"[10] rather than Böcklin's *Toten-Insel* (a copy of which, of course, could be seen next to the stage).

The acting, especially the diction, was highly stylized. In "an attempt at a Maeterlinckian mood," the words, one critic observed, "are laboriously breathed out as though part of anguished visions by actors who have painted themselves chalk-white to look starved."[11]

While the actor playing the Old Man was not sufficiently demonic,[12] the actress playing the Mummy was in some sequences "highly suggestive."[13] Helge

Wahlgren's Student, "a deathly pale young snob with stiff movements,"[14] met with harsh criticism. Several critics found him affected, decadent, monotonous. Although it is quite possible to argue that the Student's position as the outsider and 'narrator' of the play should be indicated in his acting style, Wahlgren's approach was obviously not the way to do it. Even Strindberg reacted to it. In a letter to the actor, dated 2 February 1908, he remarks:

> [-] in *The Ghost Sonata* you did not play my part: the dashing student, the new, sceptical young man, who "doesn't go on about eternal love." Therefore I could do nothing to change it. You weren't affected, but something else, which I can't find the words for. But I said to the Director: this has a gravity and profundity for the future. [-]
>
> I don't really know what I can teach you. But I urge you next time in *The Ghost Sonata*: speak to the girl, it is with thoughts and words that he enters her soul.
>
> And stress the poisonous effect of the flowers, which drives him mad like his father, and motivates his eruption.
>
> In the final scene try gently to recall her to life, or at least take her hand and see if she is dead!
>
> To go down on your knees before death, not to the Madonna, would make the tableau more beautiful.[15]

Strindberg's comment is typical of his attitude to the actors of the Intimate Theatre. Significantly, his criticism of the rather realistic production took the form of self-criticism:

> *The Ghost Sonata* soon appeared to be impossible to stage the way it was written. But Falck loves difficulties; did not conquer them, however, for they were insurmountable. But the piece belonged to our stage, and it should be done again but with a simplified scenery. (*SV* 64:236).

What he had in mind appears from a letter to Falck, dated 8 February 1909:

> If *The Ghost Sonata* could be transformed, with a drapery, we could play for invited people [-]! [-] The Mummy, for example, is sitting in the opening of the drapery in the background representing the closet. This would lift the piece to its true level, which is not the material one; and now I see hyacinths on the barrier, see *Toten-Insel* (which you must paint large and grand) when the drapery at the back is drawn apart! If you wish, I'll transpose it for drapery and barrier.[16]

Strindberg's pleading for simple scenery – "A table and two chairs! The ideal"[17] – has a trivial reason. Because of the narrow space around the stage of the Intimate Theatre, the head of the fire brigade allowed only one scenery at a time on the stage; the rest had to be kept far away from it. Changing the scenery was therefore very cumbersome and one was forced to look for simplifying solutions.[18] But simplification also seemed attractive to the late Strindberg and his concern with dematerialization, not least because it meant trusting the audience's power to complement, in their imagination, what was missing in the scenery.

Strindberg's plans for a simplified production were never realized. In December 1910 his and Falck's Intimate Theatre ceased to exist. And a year and a half later Strindberg died. Twenty-three years were to pass before another Swedish director dared to tackle the play.

In the meantime *The Ghost Sonata* had received international attention in Germany, where Strindberg was one of the most frequently performed dramatists during and immediately after World War I.[19] The war had been devastating for Germany. Strindberg's combined unmasking of and pity for humanity in his post-Inferno dramas was therefore better understood there than in Sweden that had escaped the war. Moreover, while naturalism and symbolism were still prevalent on Swedish stages, the advanced German theatre climate was more receptive to Strindberg's pre-expressionist dramas.

Although he was not the first to produce *The Ghost Sonata* in Germany, Max Reinhardt was the first to demonstrate the significance of the play. Along with Stanislavski, Reinhardt was at this time Europe's leading director. Assisted by some of the period's outstanding actors, he managed not only to create ensemble playing of the highest order. He also knew how to utilize the technical possibilities in the theatre: lighting, sound effects, etc. Instead of having the scenery represent an outward reality, he let it visualize an inner one. Undoubtedly Strindberg's post-Inferno dramas were an inspiration in this respect.

Reinhardt's active interest in Strindberg can be traced back to 1902, four years before he created his Kammerspiele in Berlin. In the first decades of the new century he produced no less than seventeen Strindberg plays in different theatres. The most important of these productions are those of *The Ghost Sonata* in 1916 and *A Dream Play* in 1921. Both went on tour to Denmark and Sweden.

In his prompt book for *The Ghost Sonata*, based on Schering's 1908 translation, Reinhardt pays much attention both to the visual and the aural aspects of the play.[20] Although the directorial intentions mentioned in the prompt book on the whole seem to have been effectuated, we cannot be certain that this has always been the case.[21] In the following I shall discuss Reinhardt's intentions as presented in the prompt book in the major part of this section; by way of conclusion, I shall comment on the critical reception.

In Act I, Reinhardt writes, the house is "immense [-], showing all the details, [-] and with all the outward magnificence of modern city houses, over-

loaded, ghostly in its massive, stony luxury." When the curtain rises, the
house can barely be seen because of the subdued grey light employed, telling
the audience that what they witness is something dreamlike, perhaps the unreality of the world. However, two figures are brightly lit: the marble statue
and, by means of a lamp hidden in the fountain, the Milkmaid – suggesting a
connection between the two: youth, purity. Soon a third figure is even more
obviously connected with the bright light:

> When the Student enters, it gradually grows lighter on the stage; it is a clear, bright,
> mysterious light (from in front without support from the normal stage lighting).

The change of light enables the spectators to see everything "through the eyes
of this Sunday child in [-] super-clear sharpness." Identification is established
between the Student, the dreamer, and the audience. Along with him, we experience the world around him as something unreal. Time and again, the Student is to let his hand move across his forehead and temples, a gesture
indicating how he experiences the surroundings and events as dreamlike.

The Old Man first looks "small, old, shrivelled, lifeless, momentarily in-
sensitive like a dead person," then seems immense when he stretches to his full
length. In conformity with his shrinking and growing, his tone of voice varies
considerably. Some lines are spoken as if he is soliloquizing, others
commandingly, some blandishingly, others with the initial consonants
"squeaking like an old clock preparing to strike."

The vampire gesture in Act I is done as follows: the Old Man looks at the
Student "with a lifeless glance," then clasps his hand, "raises himself slowly
towards him, grows noticeably fuller." In the following scenes, he seems
"livelier, more powerful, bigger." Reinhardt here kinesically expresses the
folkloristic idea, which Strindberg used psychologically, that vampirism, the
sucking of someone else's blood, has to do with survival, transference of life
blood, rejuvenation.

How can one make it clear to an audience that the Milkmaid is a vision?
Reinhardt suggests that she should move "soaringly, as though she does not
move her feet." Similarly, the Dead Man should come soaring down the stairs
in his winding-sheet, "with pale-green face [-] and closed eyes, the bony hands
across his breast, open mouth."

Johansson's decline and present thralldom is visualized in his appearance:
"a grey, hollow man [-] with frayed, soiled clothes, dark spots in hair and
beard," "exceedingly tired, even bent."

At the end of the act, Strindberg's Beggars, in obedience to Hummel's order
to hail the Student, *"bare their heads, but without cheering."* Reinhardt's Beggars wave their caps and clap their hands without a sound being heard – in
true dream fashion.

After the Old Man has been wheeled out, "the figures remain standing, immobile." When the Student too exits, "the light slowly disappears with him." Reinhardt then adds a polyphonic, pantomimic sequence:

> In the darkness (as in the beginning of the act), different figures can be seen gesticulating. The Dark Lady and the Posh Man continue their struggle soundlessly. The Milkmaid remains immobile. The Caretaker's Wife polishes the brass. The Beggars, forming a group, first shout a soundless hurrah, then [-] put their heads together. The Young Lady in the window busies herself with the flowers, caressing them. The Colonel stands in front of the statue. The Maid on the first floor lowers the flag back to half-mast. The Old Woman in the window looks into the gossip mirror, and the Dead Man steals past the Beggars – back into the house, after having looked upwards at the flag. Sound of organ notes and church bells. Darkness. When the ship's bell sounds, it turns completely dark. Curtain.

The act, in other words, ends, much as it began, with a number of characters, left in the darkness, performing different actions – a picture of erring, helpless humanity.

Act II shows a room in exaggerated tassel style with velvet door-hangings, palms, family portraits, dark-violet furniture, and on the walls "poisonous, mould-green wallpaper with a mushroom ornament" – recalling the Student's words about the rotteness of the house. Upstage left the hyacinth room is seen, in mild colours and white fluttering bobbinet curtains contrasting with the poisonous atmosphere of the foreground.

While Strindberg gives a laconic description of how the Old Man enters the house – he is simply suddenly there – Reinhardt's Hummel

> swings soundlessly on his crutches (with rubber supports) into the room. He now seems immense, massive, diabolically swelled-up and sucked full of evil purposes. He swings himself soundlessly behind the two [servants], eavesdrops.

As Kvam notes, the fantastic manner in which Reinhardt here has the Old Man steal into the house verifies Johansson's earlier description of him as someone who "creeps in through windows" and "plays havoc with people's fates."[22]

Unlike Strindberg, Reinhardt pays great attention to the Mummy's appearance. She wears

> a wrinkled green silk dress, turned yellow, with yellow garniture, lively, understanding lustreless eyes, a thin neck in white ruche, sparse white-light-grey hair with a quite thin plait. The face grey, colourless, completely wrinkled. The hands idem. She speaks with a light, clear voice, repeats the initial words of every clause, rolls the 'r' parrot fashion. When she articulates the words, she does it with a long, hoarse, light-creaking tone.

As in Act I, light is linked with Arkenholz: "When the Student enters, again unnoticeably light in room. When he goes upstage, again darker."

The guests at the ghost supper are carefully individualized. "The Fiancée, with a constant thin smile on her lips, old-fashionedly dressed, appears in the door, looks around, curtsies and slowly and carefully trips into the room." After her the Posh Man, "with a long, elegant frock coat, gloves (black), black neckerchief with a big pearl, high black hair and moustache," walks "with accentuated elastic steps." When seated, he regards "with a pince-nez those present, then talks to the Fiancée, who keeps smiling. The Posh Man also constantly has an ironic smile on his lips which [-] is there only to hide "the lurking uncertainty of waiting."

The ghost supper is a major kinesic challenge. How forestall stasis? After the clause "especially in those cases where paternity needs to be proved," there is a significant pause, during which the Old Man drums his fingers against the table. "The drumming increases and becomes a roll which suddenly stops." The sentence ending with "when the villain is exposed" is directed to the Colonel in a rather quiet tone. During the following two pauses, the stereotype smile of the guests disappears. The Old Man enjoys his manifestation of power,

> sucks himself full, drinks the anguish of the others, seems to widen, expand. The others are sitting in a shrunk-up position keeping their breath in the painful stillness before the storm.

Hummel speaks the following lines in a rational tone and the words "Now I grant you leave to go" in a calm, friendly way, while he looks at the guests in turn.

His "Time's up! Time's up!" is synchronized with the ticking of the clock, very audible in the silence called for by Strindberg. When it is heard preparing to strike, the Old Man

> rises, stands there immense and broad, strikes powerfully with the crutch on the table and shouts with powerful voice: "I, too, can strike! Do you hear?" All sit still, depressed, sunk in themselves. The Posh Man has lost all his superiority, the Colonel his stiff dignity, the Fiancée her smile. They seem quite small. Only the Mummy trembles from inward excitement.

During the Mummy's verdict on Hummel,

> the Old Man, whose face has noticeably darkened, starts brokenly, clings during the following to the table, seems to waver, grows gradually smaller. Sinks and shrinks slowly in himself.

When the Mummy then rings the bell for Bengtsson, the sound "is roaringly echoed by the distant church bells whose sound enters from without" – while a bright light spills out from the hyacinth room, connecting the young couple there with the visionary Milkmaid.

As the Old Man disappears into the closet, the other characters gradually go back to their old roles. When Bengtsson has put up the death screen, "the harp prelude begins," while

> the Mummy stands in deep sorrow, moved and bent in front of the screen. The others sit immobile staring in front of them. In the foreground, it turns dark and shady. In the background by the young people, it is still clear evening light. The curtain slowly falls to the harp notes of the postlude.

Act III shows "a small room with high walls." Aspiring, vertical lines and high burning candles around the Buddha statuette turn the room into a kind of oriental temple.[23] Spread out in the room are hyacinths in mild, pink colours. Hyacinths are also inscribed in the *art nouveau* wallpaper. The dominant colours are grey and violet. At curtain rise, Reinhardt writes, "evening is nearing. Violet colours in the sky. In the room an indefinite, bright light, as if coming from flowers."[24]

One of the problematic characters visually is the Cook. How can one avoid making her a comical character? Not without risk, Reinhardt accentuates her grotesqueness. "Immensely fat, exaggeratedly huge," she

> forces herself through the door-hangings, puts her arms on her hips, looks distrustfully into the room. She has a red, fat face, thick eyebrows, fatty black hair, a red, checkered dress with a monochrome apron, red fatty hands.

To enlarge both her giant figure and her unreality, the director lets her appear in a small wallpaper door which she closes with a bang when she exits. When she appears again, she "brutally pushes the door open, so that everything rattles and wavers." Before leaving the second time, she turns

> contemptuously her behind to [the Student], exits, goes on scolding outside, again closes the door with a bang, apparently crashes the [Soya] bottle and other objects outside. One hears objects being thrown and broken, rattling and scolding.

Reinhardt calls his Cook "challengingly revolutionary." In her exaggerated voluminousness, dressed in red and lit from behind by a red lamp, she can be seen both as "a punishing representative of the lower classes" and as a nightmarish incarnation of the guilt feelings of the suppressing upper classes.[25]

In Act III the world becomes more and more unreal to the Student. Reinhardt indicates this by means of body language: "He looks around, shakes his head, touches his forehead and temples, wonders whether it is all a dream." He now experiences the room – the world – as claustrophobic. "He can no longer breathe, violently pushes the window open, breathes deeply. The wind blows into the room." In this directional addition, Reinhardt provides the Student with a psychological reason why he wants the window open.

When the Student towards the end "murders" the Young Lady "with words," as Strindberg's notes have it, Reinhardt's Adèle starts, "picks up flowers (hyacinths), hides her face in them" and then stands "trembling, bent under his beating, sighing softly," then "is mute, stands immobile leaning on the chair, as if annihilated."

Strindberg's harp miraculously begins to play by itself. Reinhardt's is somewhat less miraculous:

> The wind increases in the room, can be heard. The curtains flutter. The wind plays some notes in the strings of the harp, from which the soft accompaniment of the song develops.

Suddenly we realize why the window had to be opened. The harp notes 'dissolve' not into soft music from *Toten-Insel* – Reinhardt omits Böcklin's isle – but into a sound collage consisting of

> distant church bells as in the opening of the piece, the distant organ and finally something like a soft funeral march develops: organ, harp, dull kettle-drums. The Student now speaks the concluding words in an exalted, beautiful voice, while the room is swept in darkness and nothing is seen but the restful, star-spangled firmament.

Rather than voyaging to a blessed Isle of the Dead, Reinhardt's Young Lady is journeying into the Great Unknown. The Student's – and the playwright's – hope for a better life hereafter is replaced by an agnostic question mark.

Reinhardt's *Ghost Sonata* was enthusiastically received by the critics, both in Germany and in Sweden. Sigfried Jacobson found the production essentially musical in conception. The nature and form of *The Ghost Sonata*, he claimed, could be attributed as much to the musical orchestration of the piece as to the text.[26]

In Sweden, Anna Branting remarked that "everything is shadows, everything is illusion, everything passes away as though it has never existed." The Caretaker's Wife was as immaterial as the visionary Milkmaid. She concluded that the director saw the play as a variation on the theme of "life is a dream."[27]

Bo Bergman found that the ghost supper visualized

> a strange nightmarish game of puppets, who had severed themselves from life and led a shadow life governed by some secret curse. It was as if something behind and above the

humans had held the strings of these dolls with their automatic and stylized movements.[28]

There were also more specific observations. The Old Man "sat in a wheelchair
half-way hidden by the cast-shadow from an advertising column."[29] His bare
arms, which contrasted with the Colonel's quasi-elegant, pulled-down cuffs,
strikingly testified to his greediness.[30] In the doorway stood "a woman in dark
clothes, immobile and with her arms crossed, silhouetted against a greenish
light [-] like a painting by Munch from the 90s."[31] The Young Lady was, not
surprisingly, dressed "in a hyacinth-blue dress," the Fiancée, more surprisingly, "in a rococo costume" and the Colonel, apparently even in Act I, in uniform.[32] The Student appeared bareheaded. In Germany this might be natural
but for the guest performance in Sweden, Branting remarked, he should have
worn a white student's cap. "For us the white cap has become the symbol of
youth and dreams of the future. Strindberg has not made a note of this, for it is
self-evident."[33] One critic found it strange that the Dead Man "threw a
shadow on the wall of the staircase," since dead people according to popular
belief "lose their shadow."[34] In Act III, the Young Lady's dress had the same
colour as the wallpaper – "to indicate the languishing, half immaterial nature
of the young woman."[35]

With one or two exceptions, even those critics who had mixed feelings
about the text lauded Reinhardt's production. Sven Söderman gave a representative summary of its characteristics. Remarking that the director had
found "the most sensitive dramatic expressions" for what is essential in the
text, he praised the director's

> implicit moods, the vaguely fleeting symbols, the unexplained emotional shades and vi-
> sions, as well as an ingenious combination of music (or musical sounds), changing light
> effects and expressive psychological decorations, in which not an object is found which
> has no meaning. Through a combination of natural conversation and supernatural at-
> mosphere, he gives the audience the impression that he carries out the play's original
> conception.[36]

And this despite a far from optimal translation!

The Swedes were slow in staging *The Ghost Sonata*, as they had been with
Miss Julie and *A Dream Play*. Not until 1942 was the play professionally
staged in a production that was soon considered a landmark in Swedish theatre history. Responsible for this production at Dramaten was Olof Molander,
who had earlier been head of this theatre and who was generally considered
the leading Strindberg director in Sweden at the time.

Not surprisingly Molander, who eventually converted to Catholicism, took a particular interest in Strindberg's post-Inferno dramas, especially *A Dream Play* which he staged no less than seven times and *The Ghost Sonata* which he directed five times. In either case his first productions were the most remarkable.

Although he was impressed, as a young man, by Reinhardt's Strindberg productions, he soon took a critical attitude to the Austrian's presentation of the so-called dream plays, convinced as he was that Reinhardt was not really in rapport with Strindberg. "Perhaps because of poor translations," he later remarked, "Reinhardt did not understand Strindberg's religious view of crime and punishment, he didn't understand his view of life."[37] By the latter he meant that the late Strindberg experienced life as something fairly unreal, more *Schein* than *Sein*. Nonetheless, like Martin Lamm in his biographically oriented studies of Strindberg's work, he had come to the conclusion that the plays are full of elements taken from real life though filtered through the playwright's subjective and creative mind.

Consequently, the aim of a production must be to recreate the delicate balance which the Poet in *A Dream Play* indicates when he says: "Not reality, but more than reality...not dreams, but waking dreams..." As Nils Beyer put it in his review of Molander's first *Ghost Sonata*:

> The action must resemble a dream. Whatever seems grotesque in the play then receives meaning, for in the world of the dream all proportions are changed and the tiniest things become important. Yet, as long as the dream lasts it is experienced as reality. The dreamer does not realize that he is dreaming. Therefore the dream, when presented on the stage, must seem both unreal and real.[38]

Unlike Reinhardt's nightmarish version with its terrifying effects, Molander's was subdued, closer to what Strindberg meant with his suggestive term "half-reality." The dreamlike impression stemmed from the self-evidence with which the grotesqueness was acted out. This was obvious already when Molander, unlike Reinhardt but in agreement with the text, opened his performance in bright sunlight.

The house façade was an almost exact copy of the so-called Red House at Karlaplan 10, where Strindberg lived when the play was written.[39] Even the number of the house was made visible. "At first it looks simply like a colour photograph," Herbert Grevenius wrote, "but there is a slight overexposure that quickly emerges with dreamlike clarity in the colours and contours."[40] The red-brick façade was greeted by the audience with "a curious mixture of happy recognition and a lurking sense of agitation."[41] For those living in just such stately turn-of-the-century apartment houses in the vicinity of Karlaplan, the stage picture became a kind of mirror.[42] Not until the second act would the satiric thrust of this device be fully evident to them.

Molander set the play in a period that more or less agreed with Strindberg's. Apart from the costumes, the clatter of horse-hoove's in Act I served as a general time indicator. The Dark Lady, one critic found,[43] was dressed according to the 1890s. The Colonel's apartment, another remarked,[44] was filled with "furniture of the 1870s," while a third ascribed it to "bourgeois magnificence of the 1880s."[45]

To Georg Svensson, the Dark Lady was "a discrete indication that the clarity with which we see everything on the stage is not that of reality but of the dream."[46] Lit by a sickly green light, she had heavily painted lips. Since a glaring red petticoat was visible in a slit in the front of her black dress,[47] the blackness connoted sin as much as mourning.

In Act II, the statue and the tiled stove had "precisely that kind of unnatural relief, that kind of super-reality that objects acquire in a dream."[48] That the furniture had covers "looking like ghosts" contributed to the dreamlike impression. The considerably smaller hyacinth room of Act III with its apex mid-upstage was obviously designed to suggest first intimacy, then claustrophobia as the Student found himself cornered there. On either side were terraces of potted hyacinths. To the right was the tiled stove with the Buddha statuette on top; in front of it the harp and a stool; behind it, the opening to the round room; to the left an alcove with a bed and in front of it a small desk with a stool. With the last pieces of furniture, added by the director, Molander presumably wished to indicate how the Young Lady spends both her days and her nights in the room, that she is 'imprisoned' in it. But at least to one critic, the room had "a fatal connotation of boudoir."[49]

Though Molander abstained both from the white, 'Swedenborgian' light towards the end and from *Toten-Insel*, he retained the metaphysical mood of Strindberg's ending, when the walls of the room glided apart allowing the audience to look into a grey haze in which the Student – Man – disappeared. To many this undoubtedly meant not only substituting the Student for the Young Lady but also replacing Strindberg's Isle of the Blessed with an image of the Great Unknown – much as Reinhardt had done. To others, who let their knowledge of the text influence their experience of the performance, it could be seen as "a glimpse of another life, where mankind is released from the nightmares of earthly existence."[50] Even the way in which the critics optically perceived the "hymn-like ending" differed. Whereas one spoke of a "heavy and impenetrable darkness,"[51] another talked of a "pale dawn."[52]

Similarly, the Old Man was seen by one critic as the incarnation of evil, a "big spider" with the mouth of a reptile, insidious and resentful,[53] whereas according to another, Lars Hanson who played Hummel did this "as friendly as it could possibly be done. There was not only cunning but also benevolence in this expressive old man's face."[54] And while the same critic found Hummel's end touching when he, "half lame and crushed" dragged himself into the closet, another stated that "it was just a crawling beast who crept in to the waiting rope."[55]

The Old Man's mask was impressive:

> the face, withered from inside, where the lurking and roving glance, when needed, hides behind the curtains of the eyelids, and the mouth which cuts like scissors or turns into a smile, full of false bonhomie. It is with this smile and with the voice which is ingratiating and authoritative at the same time that he entangles the Student [-] in order to suck his youth and poison his faith like a vampire.[56]

An ingenious device were "the all-too-long crutches" which made him fly "with soundless kangaroo leaps among the furniture in the Colonel's uncozy salon."[57]

Beijer had reservations about Strindberg's Student and, implicitly, against Molander's. Seeing the Student as an innocent victim, he found him unrepresentative of mankind. Moreover, the 'motto' – "This is what you, human beings, are like" – he found "uncanny" in its accusing misanthropy.[58] What Beijer did not see is that the Student towards the end becomes another Hummel and consequently yet another sinful human being and that the play's 'motto' is rather the Mummy's "We are poor human beings."

The Mummy, with her "corpse-brown face," her "hair like a cock's crest," her "garnished white dress with the red rose," and her "strutting bird's walk" in her "cheap-gaudy tournure dress" was a masterly "combination of ghost-like coquetry and stale senility."[59]

The Young Lady appeared in a light blue dress, the Colonel in "an appearance typical of the period with a parting at the back of the head and a black turned-up moustache,"[60] the Dead Man barefoot in a winding-sheet looking "like a nightgown."[61] The Cook "appeared only as a giant shadow on the wall" but her mocking laughter reverberated through the apartment "like an echo of life's own meaningless brutality."[62]

Molander's productions in Gothenburg, Copenhagen and Oslo differed little from the Dramaten performance. In Gothenburg, Ebbe Linde complained,[63] "The Song of the Sun" was omitted in Act II; as a result the deep meaning of having it repeated at the end of the play was lost. After the production in Copenhagen, the critic of *Sydsvenska Dagbladet* wondered if the dream aspect should not be more pronounced.[64] In the Oslo ending, the Student moved "towards a shining ball of light – as though he knew where light is to be found."[65] Ebbe Linde found the tempo, intended to augment the ghost-like mood, too slow:

Monotonously hard speeches with a lot of pretentious silence in between. [-] This made earlier a strong impression in Sweden, but it has aged more swiftly than the play, and I wonder if the time is not ripe for [-] quicker changes and more nuances in the dialogue.[66]

For his fifth production, Molander returned to Dramaten. The Dead Man now appeared not in a winding-sheet but "in the tails of a diplomat." He was "a little green in the face but for the rest quite alive."[67] As a result, his appearance was hardly shocking and a shock, Linde argued, is needed at this point to transfer the action into the supernatural. Similarly, the shadow of the Cook was normalized; as a result, "it was hard to understand what the shadow was supposed to represent."[68]

The most obvious deviation occurred at the end, where the Student lifted his arms so that he formed a cross as he walked through the room opening up to *Toten-Insel*. The projected painting was not shown full-scale, only in detail, vaguely and in black-and-white. According to Linde it worked. "Far from seeming banal, it is a beneficial period indication; at the same time it is engaging and has universal significance." Though this ending came somewhat closer to Strindberg's than Molander's earlier solutions, it still differed in having the Student leave for the Isle of the Dead, *nota bene* with a cruciform gesture, rather than have him remain in this world. It could, perhaps, be argued that this gesture, more natural in the Swedish context than a prayer to Buddha, counterbalanced the 'buddhism' and made the ending more syncretistic. But it seems more likely that most spectators found this explicitly Christian gesture disturbing and saw it as undermining the syncretism of the ending.

Ingmar Bergman's interest in *The Ghost Sonata* can be traced back to 1930:

> When I was twelve, I read *The Ghost Sonata* for the first time. I had bought it in a second-hand bookshop and planned to stage it in my puppet theatre. The title seemed especially attractive to me.
>
> I would not say that the play made a great impression on me at that time. What I liked best was the closet inhabited by a mummy, the dead man on the stairs and the Young Lady's dislike of food.
>
> Not surprisingly, these strongly infantile moments of horror appealed to my imagination, linked as they were to rather recent childhood experiences.
>
> Later, I have found quite a few examples of infantile horror in *The Ghost Sonata*: the giant cook, the secret ticking of the clocks [sic], the discomfort vis-à-vis cripples, the gruesome imitation of the parrot... Even the ghost supper itself with its semi-ritual monstrosity between very old grown-ups could mirror a child's frightened and fascinated imagination.[69]

When Bergman staged his first production of *The Ghost Sonata* in 1941, he had been a director for three years of a group of amateurs affiliated with Mäster Olofsgården, a Christian settlement house in Stockholm. And he had already directed six Strindberg plays, five of them belonging to the post-Inferno period.[70] The group played to small children in a small theatre, seating 99 people. But "one day we began to play to grown-ups, beginning with *The Ghost Sonata*, which had not been produced [in Sweden] since the days of the Old Intimate Theatre."[71] Given the "infantile" elements of the play, the choice must have seemed rather natural for a group used to playing for children. Bergman later remembered

> how the frail cast was carried away as though on a huge wave by the immensity of the drama. We experienced theatre as magic: to be thrown outside our own limitations, to be supported rather than crushed in our insufficiency.[72]

There were seven performances.[73] The pictures of this production in the Malmö theatre program, the Markers note,[74] bear a certain resemblance to the pictures of the old Intimate Theatre productions.

Some of the photos show the actor playing Hummel with beard, glasses and, as a directorial addition, a big skull-cap. This Jewish-looking headgear was to return in Bergman's next productions of the play as an icon in defense of Hummel. It is hard to believe that it served the same purpose in 1941, when Bergman by his own admittance "was on Hitler's side."[75] Whatever the director's intentions may have been, worn by the villain of the play, it is more likely that it appealed to anti-semitic feelings among the audience – one reason, perhaps, why Bergman was later to qualify his first attempt at *The Ghost Sonata* as "a confused production."[76]

The deficiencies of his own staging of the play were clear to him already a year later, when Bergman witnessed Molander's pioneering production at Dramaten. "What I experienced that night in the theatre," he declared a decade later, "seemed to me absolute and unattainable – and it seems so still."[77]

In his second production at the City Theatre in Malmö, he "consciously built on Molander's production."[78] He narrowed the proscenium opening of the huge Malmö stage from 22 to 14 meters, raised the stage 40 centimeters and extended it 6 meters into the auditorium – thereby improving the acoustics – and reduced the seating capacity from 1,700 to 1,100. Behind the proscenium masking on either side of the stage, movable light towers were erected. These could provide sidelighting so that the faces of the actors were 'sculptured' in relation to the scenery.[79]

The ordinary curtain, one critic observed, was replaced by a neutral one, smooth and rat-grey like the human consciousness just before sleep comes. When it opened up, you sat in pitch-darkness and watched white clouds drift by on a transparent scrim (which remained during the whole evening, serving as a barely visible gauze between the stage reality and the auditorium). After that the exterior of the first act released itself from the darkness [-].[80]

From the very beginning, Bergman in this way not only informed the audience that they were to witness a dream play. He visually put them in a 'hypnotic' situation to help facilitate identification with the dreamer of the play, the Student. Identification was also secured by having the Student dress and behave "like a young chap of today." One critic even saw him as "Bergman's alter ego."[81] In quite another sense Bergman was implicitly linked with Hummel. When the Old Man described the people in the house and they looked out of their windows like puppets, Hummel was "sitting at the edge of the stage like a dispassionate director."[82] On the whole, another critic remarked, the voluminous Hummel "had nuances and was human. His evil was superficial."[83]

Wahlund felt that Bergman had retained Molander's Östermalm environment in his first act, whereas Ivar Harrie was of the opinion that he had done away with "the Stockholmean couleur locale."[84] A detail not mentioned by the critic supports the former view: on the advertisement column a concert at "Skansen" – the famous open-air museum in Stockholm – is advertised.

The Dead Man's entrance was a piece of grand guignol, first a pointing hand in the door, then the face of the Consul with a cramped, gaping mouth. More bewildering was the Milkmaid's entrance at the end of Act I. Apparently in imitation of her drowning, she came in falling down, then rolled over a couple of times before stretching her arms out towards the Old Man.

Each act had its own distinct scenery, increasingly stylized. Contrasting with the heavy draperies of the round room was the white hyacinth room.

At the end the Student was seen in a tender position next to the dead Young Lady. "They remained in this position for quite a long time. Slowly the sight faded away and the clouds on the gauze curtain started moving."[85] This final 'tableau vivant' could arguably be seen as an inverted pietà, in which the Student "was transformed into a 'Madonna' [-] able to express compassion for all mankind."[86]

During the rehearsals Bergman told critic and filmmaker Vilgot Sjöman:

[-] as much as I love the first two acts, as much do I detest the last one; but it is my damned duty as a director to shape it with exactly the same objectivity [-].[87]

There is an indication here that Bergman intuitively felt that he had not managed to integrate the third act properly. This was to be one of the major chal-
lenges in his next production of the play.

Bergman's third *Ghost Sonata* opened at Dramaten on 13 January 1973. The
original plan was that the play should be produced in the paint room of the
theatre, a locality which had been used for stage purposes before. Since
Molander had earlier produced this play on the big stage of Dramaten, it
would have been a relief for Bergman to make use of a completely different
stage. But this plan had to be abandoned for security reasons. Although Bergman found the paint room interesting "as a challenge," he did not feel that the
choice of stage was of great importance to him, and readily agreed to produce
the play on the large stage of the theatre, with an auditorium seating 794 people.

  Another important change concerned the cast. The original idea was that
the Young Lady and the Mummy should be played by two actresses, following both the text and tradition.

> As soon as Ingmar got the idea that they should be done by one actress, Gertrud Fridh
> came into the picture. We knew already in the spring [of 1972] who would play the
> leading parts. But the complete cast was not worked out until a couple of weeks before
> the rehearsals started, at the end of October.[88]

A comparison between the structure of Strindberg's drama text (Appendix 1)
and that of Bergman's production (Appendix 2) reveals that the latter contained almost twice as many configurations as the former: 94 against 49. Of
these, no less than 59 belonged to Act I, 26 to Act II and merely 9 to Act III.
While Strindberg opens the play with three people on the stage, Bergman limited himself to one: the Old Man. Very quickly he then had five characters enter. Not until conf. 8 did the Student appear. Bergman opened, you might say,
with a piece of silent film: people entered from various directions; but no one
said anything; only the chiming of church bells was heard.

  Even more striking was the discrepancy between text and production at the
end of the act. Here Strindberg's three configurations (20-22) correspond to
eleven (49-59) with Bergman. Instead of having all the people appear on the
stage when the Old Man is wheeled in by the Beggars, Bergman had them enter, one after the other, until the Milkmaid, in the culminating conf. 53, appeared – only to let them disappear successively after this event. The rather
symmetrical pattern had a dynamic, wavelike quality.

  During the greater part of Act I, the Old Man and the Student were positioned at or close to the centre of the stage. It indicated their central roles and

provided the Old Man with good possibilities to turn the Student's attention in different directions.

According to the text, the Caretaker's Wife appears twice on the stage. She then sweeps the entrance, polishes the brass of the banisters and waters the laurels. Bergman had her enter no less than six times. Her fifth entrance coincided with that of the Young Lady. In the text the latter *"says a couple of words to the* CARETAKER's WIFE.*"* Bergman had the two whisper with one another about the recently occurred death of the Consul. When the Young Lady left the Caretaker's Wife, her mother, she curtsied humbly to her – as if to disguise their relationship.

More than Strindberg, Bergman made the Caretaker's Wife, poorly dressed, a representative of the hard-working proletariat vividly contrasting with the idleness of the upper classes. As such she formed a telling background for the Cook's and Bengtsson's class-determined revolt in Act III.

Strindberg has the Dark Lady stand immobile on the stairs in the beginning; she then keeps walking on the pavement; when the Posh Man starts talking to her, the two move over to the advertising column where they inaudibly continue their conversation. Bergman instead had the Dark Lady walk restlessly to and fro, impatiently waiting for her lover. Would he come? Three times she sought consolation from her mother. When the Posh Man finally appeared, he pretended not to see the Dark Lady. She then followed him. The triangle mother-daughter-lover became a little play within the play.

Moreover, since the tragedy of the Dark Lady was visualized more or less simultaneously with the dawning love between the Student and the Young Lady, the audience witnessed two aspects, or stages, in the relationship between man and woman. Bergman indicated the connection by having the Student at the fountain wipe his eyes with a handkerchief (conf. 16) right after the Dark Lady had done the same at the same place. In conf. 14 the Dark Lady hurried out crying, because she doubted that the Posh Man would marry her. In conf. 32 the Student was crying, realizing that the Young Lady would never be his. In conf. 43 the Dark Lady and the Posh Man formed one loving couple on the stage, the Student and the Young Lady another.

The Colonel, too, was by Bergman integrated in the action to quite another extent than is the case in the text. With Strindberg we see him appear behind one of the windows of the round room, in civilian clothes, to read the thermometer, a property measuring the temperature of human relations, here serving also as an excuse to get the Colonel to the window. He soon walks away from the window and remains, for seven pages, in front of the marble statue. He then approaches the Young Lady who is seen behind the window of the hyacinth room and shows her the newspaper. Seven pages later we learn that when the Student is celebrated, the Colonel *"stares out of his window."*

Bergman retained and developed the Colonel's attention to the statue and to the Young Lady. But he abstained even from an imaginary thermometer, since the Colonel's concern with such an object would have been hard for an audience to grasp. The Colonel was also allowed to take part in the celebration of the Student, be it in a reserved manner.

The Colonel's first entrance had no counterpart in the text. Dressed in a silk dressing-gown, he demonstrated his erotic interest in the marble statue. When he appeared next he was dressed in a frock coat – corresponding to Strindberg's "*civilian clothes.*" In addition, he was provided with a riding-whip to indicate that he is an officer and 'father' of the Young Lady who soon appeared in riding costume and with a riding-whip. The Colonel's interest in his outward appearance was demonstrated through his intense polishing of his nails. He used his handkerchief to dust the marble statue after he had reverently bowed to it – a comical illustration of his worship of the Mummy as she once was. He then circumstantially took out the painful letter from Hummel which Johansson had just delivered and read it "for the tenth time" (Bergman). In the brief newspaper passage (conf. 34) the tender love between 'father' and 'daughter,' especially his for her, was demonstrated – in anticipation of his reaction to her death at the end.

Strindberg's Colonel is on stage for a very long time with a minimum of occupations, a situation that cries for directorial supplementation. Bergman solved the problem by shortening the Colonel's stage presence and by providing him with various occupations. Thus the Colonel's pantomimic acting indicated his aristocratic manners and façade mentality as well as his attitude to the Mummy and the Young Lady. The unwelcome letter (conf. 20) was linked to Johansson's report (conf. 38-39) and returned in conf. 70. The Colonel's attention to the marble statue visualized a third aspect of the man-woman relationship.

Bergman's second act contained 9 configurations more than the text. To the added ones belonged those which showed Johansson, framing the act, alone in the round room. When he first entered it (conf. 60), he was seen putting on his social persona. When he left it (conf. 84), it was with a gesture of self-willed lack of respect indicating that he was now "*free from the slavery.*"

Two other added configurations, 73 and 77, had to do with the ghost supper. In the former the servants arranged the chairs. In the latter they entered with tea. By letting the servants be in the room with teapot and tray when the Old Man rejected the Colonel's suggestion that the tea be brought in, Bergman sacrificed realistic illusion for a comic effect but he also demonstrated the Old Man's humiliation of the Colonel and the latter's bewildered state of mind. This was further underlined when the Colonel, after Hummel had had his say, sent the servants out by pointing with his riding-whip, a parodic gesture illustrating his cramped attempt to retain his military dignity.

Very striking, and lacking a counterpart in the text, was the Mummy's entrance in conf. 67. She entered from 3, disappeared as soon as she saw the Old Man but returned again, now via the closet. The double entrance indicated that the Mummy's closet existence was a bit of a fake, a mask behind which she hid from the world. Making people believe that she spent her life in the closet – cf. the Colonel's expectation to find her there in conf. 77 – she played the role of a penitent. When suddenly caught out of this role, she was eager to repair her mistake and return to her role-playing. Bergman's device was at once comic and psychologically illustrative.

In Act III the number of configurations in text and production agreed more or less. This does not mean that they looked alike. Two of the configurations in the production (92-93) were determined by a circumstance Strindberg need not worry about: the female double role necessitating a change of costume.

While Strindberg's Colonel and Mummy remain silently seated in the round room throughout this act, Bergman had first the Colonel, then the Mummy enter the hyacinth room. The reason for this will be clarified later.

Bergman's decision to do *The Ghost Sonata* on an almost empty stage while utilizing projections to indicate the locality agrees both with Strindberg's ideas in 1908, quoted by the director during rehearsals, and with Bergman's own tendency, not least as a filmmaker, to focus on the characters, notably on their faces. As he told me:

> [-] we have very few properties [-], nothing that can distract from the faces. What is important, is what happens to the bodies. No furniture must conceal the action, nothing must stand in the way anywhere. It is a choreographic pattern that should be able to move freely in relation to the space and the scenery.[89]

The absence of properties enabled Bergman to appeal to the spectator's imagination, thereby involving him in the action. The Milkmaid washed herself with imaginary water, the Old Man read an imaginary poster on an imaginary advertising column, the Young Lady closed an imaginary window and busied herself with imaginary hyacinths. This non-realistic device naturally helped to increase the feeling of witnessing or being part of a dream world.

In Act I a beautiful white *art nouveau* building – in agreement with Strindberg's demand, in 1907, for a *"modern façade"* – was projected on the screens and part of a church on the cyclorama.[90]

However, when the Old Man and the Student watched the house, they did not look at the projected house upstage. They looked in the opposite direction, into the auditorium. Bergman in other words chose, quite paradoxically, to place the modern house not only upstage, as Strindberg has it, but also in the auditorium. A major reason for this was that with this arrangement the characters would no longer turn away from the audience. To Bergman this was of paramount importance. As he constantly stressed during rehearsals, what the characters witness is less important than their reaction to it.

In *The Ghost Sonata*, where the house represents Life and its inhabitants stand for humanity, the spatial reversal was meaningful also in the sense that it linked the audience with the characters on the stage. Appearing on either side of the proscenium frame, the inhabitants of the house came to function as mediators between the audience inside the House of Life and the characters out in the street.

As the Old Man and the Student watched the imaginary house in the auditorium, the spectators watched the house they were describing on the screens. The similarity between the shape of the stage, enclosed by concave screens, and the horseshoe shape of the auditorium, turned the whole locale into a *theatrum mundi* and actors and spectators alike into members of humanity. The fact that exactly the same building was projected, out of focus, on the two screens further served to affect the audience directly, to bewilder them, make them doubt their own eyes and make them feel that they were part of a dream.

By including a church, that is, a building visualizing a belief in an afterlife, behind the House of Life, Bergman also compensated, as it were, for the omission of The Isle of the Dead at the end, while relativizing Strindberg's idea.

In Act II Strindberg designs a tripartite space. Bergman omitted the least functional of these spaces: the green room. With a bisected stage, he could find a counterpart of the bisection stage-auditorium. More importantly, he could effectively visualize the spatial reversal from Act II to Act III, the movement from the world of the old to the world of the young, thereby emphasizing the generation theme.

From the very beginning, Bergman had the idea that the play represents a dream by Strindberg himself. In his 1963 TV production of *A Dream Play* he nourished the same idea. There it was indicated by having the performance begin and end with a close-up of the author.[91] In his 1970 stage production of the same play, he repeated this idea by turning the Poet, at his desk, into the author's alter ego. In *The Ghost Sonata*, it is the Student who has a similar function but since he is directly involved in the action, Bergman here more discretely limited himself to a projection of the face of the aged Strindberg on the curtain between Acts II and III.

What I have earlier called the Student's Dantean journey in reverse was necessarily obscured when the house was placed in the auditorium. Instead, the generation motif was emphasized in the scenery of the last two acts, where the old, experienced, sin-burdened characters occupy the round room and the young, innocent, hopeful ones, the hyacinth room; in the two rooms two phases of life and two contrasting views of it are exposed. The contrast appeared with Bergman not least in the interior decoration. In the round room, an out-of-focus projection showed a typical turn-of-the-century wealthy, overloaded, dark bourgeois interior; five sturdy black-and-red chairs completed the impression of sombreness. In the much loftier hyacinth room, on the other hand, two slender white chairs and a white-and-gold harp dominated the picture; only gradually did the spectators become aware of a contrasting property: the black death screen.

Three times (once in each act) the projected exterior or interior scenery was momentarily replaced by a projected high stone wall. Whenever this occurred, there was a sound reminiscent of thunder. The wall projections appeared in moments of intense anguish on the part of the Old Man (Act I), the guests at the ghost supper (Act II), and the Student and the Young Lady (Act III). By these audiovisual effects the director wished to communicate a sense of claustrophobia, a feeling of being imprisoned in "this madhouse, this prison, this charnel-house the earth," as the Student puts it, and the concomitant longing for "the liberator," death.

The wall could also be seen as the quay near which the Milkmaid was drowned. Or, in Act II, as the wall in the house stripped of its wallpaper and its boastful collection of paintings, an unmasking corresponding to the one Hummel performs vis-à-vis the guests. In Act III, finally, the wall was clearly a visualization of the Student's reference to the world as a "prison." Bergman:

> The Student and the Young Lady are now in that same prison in which the others have lived all their life, those who have deformed them. They are locked up together in a kind of hell and it is not until she dies that there is suddenly air and light.[92]

The dreamy note struck in the opening was not only maintained but augmented in the course of the performance. Twice, for a minute or so, the curtain dropped to allow for necessary changes of scenery and costume. But even during these short intervals the audience was kept in a dreamlike mood through a strange 'snowfall' – rising and falling dots of light projected on the curtain – creating a sense of dizziness. As earlier noted, the second time the snowfall appeared, the face of the aged Strindberg could be vaguely divined in it, allowing the audience to share the playwright's dreamlike experience of life – although this experience of course was Strindbergmanian.

Apart from the diffuseness of the projections and the non-realism of the bare wall and the snowfall, the dreamy impression was created by the variability of the scenery. Thus when the house-and-church in Act I returned, after having been replaced by the bare wall, they had become larger, as though they were now closer to the spectator. In Act II, the bare wall was replaced by blackness when the Mummy launched her counter-attack, a suitable 'death screen' for the Old Man. When the real death screen was put up as a sign that he had hanged himself, the projection of the overloaded interior returned.

A similar pattern was adhered to in Act III. The interior projection faded out in favour of the bare wall, which in turn gave way to a neutral background, light and airy, when the Young Lady died, an indication that the room, visualizing her life, had disappeared and that death had come to her as a liberator.

The projections thus served three important purposes. They indicated mental changes within the characters. They strengthened the impression that life is a dream by catching some of the dream's fleeting quality. Most importantly: they had the spectators share the feelings of some of the characters; in this sense they helped to break down the barrier between stage and auditorium and emphasize the *theatrum mundi* aspect.

With regard to stage light, we may distinguish between functional, realistic, symbolic, and atmospheric lighting. Functional light was provided in conf. 21 when the Student started to tell the story about the house that collapsed the preceding day; at this point, the light on the stage was dimmed, while the Student was strongly lit. As a result, attention was focused on him and the story he had to tell. The light here helped to emphasize a thematically important passage in the play. In conf. 53, similarly, the light was primarily functional when especially the Old Man, the Student and the Milkmaid, the latter coming out of the trap in the floor, were lit. Since she *"is seen only by the Student and the Old Man,"* it was logical to unite the three.

Seemingly more realistic was the *"strong white sunlight"* in conf. 27, directed towards that part of the stage to which the Student was wheeling the Old Man in response to his request to be wheeled *"into the sun."* However, the sunlight here had above all a symbolic significance. Sensing that he is soon to die, the old sinner, hoping for divine Grace, was drawn to the warm sunlight. In conf. 85 the Student's face was bathed in light as he recited from "The Song of the Sun." The past tense of the poem – "I saw the sun", etc. – contributed to the impression that the light was supernatural and that you were witnessing the recreation of a vision. Viewed thus, the lighting helped to express a state of mind, a belief in a just god.

The sunlight in conf. 27 was momentary. In a realistic performance the front part of the stage would have been lit much longer – in line with Strindberg's indication that the marble statue is *"brightly lit by sunlight."* Bergman's dynamic light direction, allowing characters, properties and stage areas to be lit momentarily, was much more effective in keeping the spectator constantly alert. Viewed from another perspective, it meant a removal from a realistic presentation of the play in favour of what is mystifying, dreamlike.

Atmospheric light was frequently adopted. The functional light in conf. 21 is also an example of atmospheric light, since the dimming of the characters around the Student, all of them immobile, contributed to create a dreamy mood. By isolating the Student in this way, Bergman increased the impression that his narration at this point seemed less a piece of dialogue, addressed to the Old Man, than a soliloquy, a thinking aloud, underlined by his central and frontal position on the stage.

Especially in Act III, atmospheric light was important. Here there was a change from warm to cold and back to warm light, corresponding to the three "notes" the director sensed in this act: tenderness-bitterness-tenderness. The hyacinths mentioned in the text were merely indicated in the Young Lady's hyacinth-blue dress and in the lighting: mixed blue and white light. As she was kneeling on the floor, stretching out her hands, the bluish-white light coloured her dress to indicate that she surrounded herself with "a barrier of colour and warmth and fragrance."[93] By contrast, an uncharitable cold light accompanied the Student's cruel unmasking of the Young Lady, which directly led to her death.

When Bergman, in addition to the faint, mild light at the end of the play, used a strong, beamed light from above to accompany the Colonel's and the Mummy's intercession for the Young Lady, the purpose was hardly to demonstrate how Divine Grace was bestowed on the recently dead woman. It was rather to make the audience share their compassion for her, their hope that in the afterlife she would "be greeted by a sun that does not burn" and that "the Lord of Heaven" would be merciful to her. That the Student did not share their confidence, was indicated both by his isolated position, his skeptical way of reciting "The Song of the Sun" and his absence during the Mummy's final speech.

As we have seen, Strindberg opens his play with various sounds, including the ringing of bells from several churches in the distance. Bergman limited himself to one sound: the tolling of the bells of a nearby, visible church (conf. 1-9).[94] Strindberg does not indicate how long the ringing is to continue. Bergman had it tone away when the Milkmaid left the stage. It was heard again when the Dead Man appeared (conf. 35-37) and, again, in connection with Hummel's reliving of the Milkmaid's drowning (conf. 52-59). In short, the tolling was heard whenever the ghosts appeared. Creating a funereal mood, it could be linked with the Consul's recent death, replacing, as it were, Strindberg's white sheets. More importantly, it could be associated with the Old Man's sense that he is "going to die soon" and the acute pangs of conscience on account of past misdeeds caused by this awareness.[95]

Act I culminated with the Old Man's horror when he was faced with the memory of the drowning Milkmaid (conf. 52-54), Act II with his collapse when she appeared again (conf. 81-82), Act III with the Young Lady's death after the Student had attacked her. Each of these unmaskings was acoustically accentuated by dull 'thunder claps,' created by mixing loose strings of a grand piano. The 'thunder' during the intermissions was, similarly, created through the acoustic vibrations of loose strings, mixed with occasional notes, high and low in the first intermission and only high in the second one. These unrealistic sound effects served to transmit the anguish felt by the characters as they were unmasked.

A sound effect clearly intended by Strindberg is the ticking of the grandfather clock in Act II; this is implied when it says that the Mummy *"stops"* the clock. Before this happens, the Old Man has compared the clock's ticking with the sound of the death-watch beetle, a sound which according to popular belief forebodes death. Ironically, he does not realize that the foreboding relates to himself. Aware that a prolonged sound effect counteracts its own purpose, Bergman limited the ticking to strategic moments. When the act opened, it had a realistic, preparatory function. It simply served to inform the audience that there was a clock in the room. When this impression had been established, the ticking could die away and continue only in the imagination of the audience – until the Old Man's unmasking of the guests called for it again (conf. 78). Whereas Strindberg's clock merely warns, Bergman's clock struck twice. At the opening of the act, it struck five, a little later (conf. 71) it struck six, indicating an early ghost supper, unrelated to the ghost hour (midnight). The indication of a one hour time lapse was yet another dreamy detail in the production.

The most spectacular sound effect in the text has to do with the harp, which plays different 'music' at the end of Acts II and III. In the former act, the Young Lady accompanies the Student's recital of "The Song of the Sun," in the latter the harp is at first "deaf and dumb" – corresponding to the Student's despair – whereas later, when he expresses a faith in a benevolent god, its *"strings begin to rustle."* This harmonious rustle then 'dissolves' into the faint music heard from the Isle of the Dead.

In the production the same harp notes (see conf. 84) were heard in both acts, the only difference being that the series of notes was repeated once in Act III. The composer, Daniel Bell, gave the following comment:

> The harp music has the form of a vault, a bow. It gains its special character from the fact that it comprises exactly half a [twelve-tone] series, with a particular tension between short and long intervals – the declining ones are half a note longer than their climbing counterparts. The music also has the form of a prolonged diminuendo and rallentando. The last note, which is the dissonance E/F, is played somewhat more loudly and was artificially prolonged in a studio.[96]

Considering Bergman's rearrangement of the ending, it was logical to have the harp music accompany not the Student's skeptical recital but the Mummy's conciliatory intercession. When the tonal series nevertheless ended with a dissonance, it clashed, in Act II, with the Student's belief that goodness is rewarded, in Act III with the Mummy's hope for a blessed afterlife for her daughter.[97]

Bergman's costumes were meticulously designed, sometimes with regard to factual circumstances but more often with an eye to their symbolic significance. In addition, there was an overall colour pattern. Act I was dominated by greyish tints – according to Bergman himself a heritage from Molander's *Ghost Sonata* productions. In Act II, the characters appeared in costumes which were realistic in cut but so glaring that they looked like dresses for a fancy-dress ball; here "the world of illusions" was at its strongest. In the final act, by contrast, the costumes were pale. The masquerade was over, and the characters seemed to incarnate the Mummy's contrite recognition that "we are poor human beings."

Bergman's Colonel first wore a long, black silk dressing-gown, announcing his aristocratic pretensions. In Act II, he had dressed up for the ghost supper in uniform. Although he claimed to have been "an acting colonel in the American voluntary service," his gold-braided, scarlet uniform did not seem to fit this claim.[98] Instead the glaring colour served to bring out the fact that the Colonel was disguising himself behind a socially impressive persona. In addition, the red colour linked him with his wife, the Mummy, and his servant, Bengtsson.

In Act III, however, his red uniform was replaced by an old, worn, grey velvet dressing-gown, strongly contrasting both with his pompous uniform and his elegant silk gown; the boots had been replaced by slippers; the wig and the monocle were gone; so was the iron corset, and as a result he had lost his artificial erectness. The stiff gait had been replaced by a tired man's bent shuffling along. At the end he had arrived at a resigned acceptance of suffering and compassion for all human beings reminiscent of a Buddhist outlook.

The explicit references to Buddha in the play text were all omitted in the production, partly because these ingredients would be alien to a Western audience, partly because Bergman's version did not allow for any divine superstructure. Instead the Colonel in the final act was turned into a 'Buddhist monk' with shorn head, simple gown, mild voice and radiant face. Sitting next to the death screen in a humble, harmonious position, he incarnated the attitude to life which the Student in the text prays to Buddha for: "patience in the trials, purity of will."

The Mummy's costume underwent a similar change. Her ghostly parrot-dress, intensely red below in Act II, became almost colourless in the final act.

Sapped of her life blood, she was now proclaimed a living corpse in her long grey-yellow-white dress.

Corresponding to the Mummy's dress in Act II was the Young Lady's petticoat in Act III: dirty, blood-stained around the womb, a visual confirmation of the Student's suspicion that the most beautiful flowers – the smeary petticoat was disguised by an ethereal hyacinth-blue dress – are the most poisonous and that the Young Lady is "sick at the source of life."

A fundamental idea behind the production was "the fact that the Young Lady is slowly turning into another Mummy."[99] To convey this idea to the audience the director had the same actress play the roles of mother and daughter, assisted by a mute stand-in when necessary. The idea that the Mummy has once been what the Young Lady is now and, conversely, that the Young Lady is an embryonic Mummy was indicated in various ways. By position: the Young Lady in Act I and the Mummy in Act II were placed in the same position next to the marble statue representing the Mummy as young; moreover, the Young Lady's coiffure was strikingly similar to that of the marble woman. By gesture: the Young Lady would flutter her hands in a manner reminiscent of the Mummy's parrot gestures. By costume: as we have seen, the Mummy's dirty and tattered dress turning red from the womb downwards resembled the dirty and bloodstained petticoat in which the Young Lady was finally revealed. By movement: notably in conf. 88.

In Bergman's production it was made clear that the catalogue of unpleasant chores mentioned in Act III should not be understood literally but figuratively, as so many examples of the obligatory "drudgery of keeping the impurity of life at bay." In addition, the passage became the most telling instance of the thematic connection between the Young Lady and the Mummy, of how the former is destined to turn into the latter. In the Young Lady's speech, the development from childhood (thumb in mouth) to old age (mummification), the gradual 'dying' to which we are all condemned in the course of life, was demonstrated by tone of voice and body language.

Just as the outward similarity between the Mummy and the Young Lady, between mother and daughter, suggested the frightening destiny of human development, so did the outward resemblance between the Old Man and the Student. Like Strindberg's Old Man, Bergman's was provided with a beard (plus a moustache) and glasses. So was his Student. In this way the idea was conveyed that the Student incarnates an earlier stage in the Old Man's life and that, conversely, the Student is destined eventually to turn into another Old Man – an idea that Strindberg hints at, not least through his age-oriented speaker-labels. Taken together, the male and the female couples thus presented a picture of the inevitable fate inherent in the process of ageing.

When he provided the Old Man with a skull-cap and a diamond ring, indicative of his Jewish origin, Bergman took a risk. Turning the most dislikeable character into a Jew would inevitably be seen as a racist statement by some spectators. Actually, the reason was quite the opposite. The Old Man was meant to appear as a pariah revenging himself on the society which oppresses him. His usurping mentality, his desire to unmask people of higher station could in this way be, if not socially wholly justified, at least accounted for. There is, however, no real support in the text for the idea that Hummel has been socially oppressed; besides, the emphasis on this aspect reduces his mythic status.

The correspondence between the Colonel's and Bengtsson's outward appearance in Act II was retained in Act III, where Bengtsson was seen in big, baggy, grey-yellow-white linen clothes and slippers. But his closest counterpart in terms of costume, was the voluminous Cook. Their clothes, Bergman explained, were meant to give the impression that they belonged to a lunatic asylum. These costumes served, in other words, to make the spectators identify themselves with the Student's view of the world.

In his choice of costumes, Bergman followed his basic conception that we gradually move into a deep dream. In Act I the costumes were still realistic. In Act II this was still true of those of the Student, the Young Lady and the servants, while those of the participants at the ghost supper were phantasmagoric. In Act III, only the Student retained a realistic costume. He was, in fact, the only character who did not change his costume, an indication both of his lack of a social persona – his childlike straightforwardness – and of his exceptional position as 'narrator,' Strindbergmanian alter ego and Everyman.

In the section on structure, I touched on what Bergman calls "the choreographic pattern": the positions, movements and gestures of the characters. Like most dramatists, Strindberg provides very little information about these matters in his acting directions. He leaves it to directors and actors to recreate what Bergman calls "the spiritual blocking" – positions, movements and gestures which express mental conditions.

Bergman opened with the Old Man alone on the stage. Then the Milkmaid entered. Although the Old Man could not see her, he sensed her. This was indicated by having him look around anxiously and tucking his blanket around him as if he suddenly felt cold. By isolating the two on the stage and by having the Old Man's (re)action coincide with the entrance of the Milkmaid, Bergman indicated that she was a product of his pangs of conscience rather than a character of flesh and blood. When the Student began to talk to her, the Old Man startled (conf. 8). His violent reaction in conf. 53 was in this way properly prepared.

The Student's ambivalent relationship to the Old Man was indicated by having him alternately approach and move away from Hummel, who constantly tried to keep him close to himself. Even the Old Man's comments on the inhabitants of the house could be seen as a device to prevent the Student from leaving him. In conf. 10, his remarks on the portrait in the newspaper were a clear example of this. Instead of letting the Student remain close to Hummel during the following conversation, Bergman had him move away from the Old Man as though he wanted to free himself from him. Hummel tried to counteract this by asking the Student questions which forced him to stop short and answer. The tug-of-war soon appeared to be uneven. In conf. 12 the Student took over Johansson's occupation. With Strindberg the relevant passage reads:

> OLD MAN. First of all, push my chair so I can read the playbills. I want to see what they're putting on tonight...
>
> STUDENT *pushes the wheelchair*. Don't you have a man with you?
>
> OLD MAN. Yes, but he's running an errand...will soon be back...

Here the Student immediately obeys; only from his question may we conclude that he does so unwillingly.

Bergman strengthened the contrast between the two and indicated the Student's ambivalence more clearly. In answer to the Old Man's order, the Student approached him, as if he was inclined to obey him spontaneously – only to stop short and put his question which seemed like a protest, since he had not yet complied with the Old Man's command. Not until Hummel made it clear that he was rather helpless and commandingly snapped his fingers, did the Student begin to push the wheelchair. Bergman, in other words, explicated and expanded the power struggle implicitly contained in the Strindbergian situation. In the following configuration he let the Old Man himself roll his wheelchair, thereby indicating that his helplessness was exaggerated, a trick to bind the Student to himself.

Whereas Strindberg clearly demonstrates the Student's attraction to the Young Lady early in the play, her attitude to him is more enigmatic. When she first enters, she "*walks slowly*," like a sleepwalker, "*without looking at anyone*," but when she sees the portrait of the Student in the newspaper, "she is not indifferent." When she loses her bracelet through the window, the Student picks it up and hands it to her. She "*thanks him stiffly*." She later motivates her loss by saying that her "hand has grown so thin." Can we trust her?

Bergman's Young Lady and Student were attracted to one other. As soon as she appeared (conf. 30), the Student approached her. Instead of having the Old Man draw the Student's attention to the Young Lady (the text), Bergman had him observe her even before Hummel had discovered her. As a result, the Student's interest in the Young Lady seemed a question of love at first sight, wholly independent of the Old Man's attempt to act as a procurer. Bergman's Student had, in fact, eyes for nothing but the Young Lady. When the Old Man noticed the Fiancée (conf. 35) and believed he was informing an interested listener, the Student was engrossed with admiring the Young Lady. For a moment there were, again, two 'loving couples' on the stage, to the left one representing extinguished love, to the right another representing dawning love.

Bergman's Young Lady quickly glanced at the Student as she walked past him (conf. 30), thereby indicating her interest in him even before she read about his heroic deed in the newspaper. While caring for the hyacinths, she now and then regarded him. In the bracelet passage (conf. 46), the director disregarded her prescribed stiffness and instead had their hands touch. Towards the end of the act (conf. 58), they found themselves alone together on the stage; for a second they established eye contact. The short configuration helped to indicate that the relationship between them was to develop later in the play. As a result of these changes, the Young Lady's claim that she had lost her bracelet unvoluntarily would not convince the spectators, who would rather see this act as her cunning way of establishing contact with the Student.

In his recreation of the celebration of the Student at the end of Act I, Bergman deviated noticeably from Strindberg's acting directions which read:

> The BEGGARS *bare their heads, but without cheering. The* YOUNG LADY *at the window waves her handkerchief. The* COLONEL *stares out through his window. The* OLD LADY *stands up at her window. The* MAID *on the balcony hoists the flag to the top of the mast.*

We here have five different reactions: the solemn-subservience of the Beggars, the enthusiasm of the Young Lady, the unconcern of the Colonel, the curiosity of the Fiancée and the ceremonious action of the Maid. The impression is dispersed.

In Bergman's version (conf. 52) the celebration was uniformly stylized, forced upon the participants by the dictatorial Hummel. Everyone except the Colonel celebrated the Student by raising their right arm, a gesture unpleasantly familiar to most spectators, not least to Bergman.[100] As the arms were lowered, the 'ice' in the foreground – the grey carpet covering the trap – was split by the drowning Milkmaid's upstretched arms. At the same time the Old Man was seen, leaning forward in his wheelchair, reaching out as if to get hold of her. The choreographic pattern of the passage seemed highly ironic in its indication that the Old Man's high-handed behaviour had retributively called forth the Milkmaid, whose upstretched arms, indicating her drowning, in this context became a parodic celebratory gesture.

In Act II the Old Man appears uninvited in the Colonel's apartment. The text reads:

> OLD MAN [-] *To* BENGTSSON. Announce me to the Colonel!
>
> BENGTSSON. Yes, but we're expecting guests...
>
> OLD MAN. I know! But my visit is almost expected, if not longed for...
>
> BENGTSSON. Oh! What's the name? Mr Hummel![101]
>
> OLD MAN. Quite so!

This passage appears neither particularly interesting nor very dramatic. One wonders how Bengtsson can know the name immediately after he has asked for it. When we later learn that Hummel has earlier been a sponger in Bengtsson's kitchen for two years, we are even more amazed that he does not recognize the Old Man. Even if we assume that Bengtsson is merely feigning this lack of recognition – he certainly does not welcome Hummel's visit – Strindberg has clearly left something for the director to fill in. This could be done in different ways. The Old Man may, for instance, present Bengtsson with his card; Bengtsson then reads the name aloud from the card. Or the Old Man may whisper his name in the ear of the servant, who then repeats what he has heard. Either way we have motivated Bengtsson's sudden mention of the name. But that is all.

Bergman, realizing that the passage draws its strength from the fact that it concerns a meeting between two old acquaintances, chose a solution which makes the exchange psychologically tense (conf. 64). Bergman's Bengtsson was condescending as long as he did not recognize Hummel. Recognition came when the Old Man turned his face to him, and it was verified by Bengtsson's mentioning of Hummel's title and name. The company director now smiled triumphantly at the terrified servant who reverently bowed to him and hurried out. Recreated this way, the short passage illuminated the reversal of roles that characterizes the relationship Hummel-Bengtsson. Through an effective use of kinesics – a change of facial position – Bergman gave depth to a seemingly rather insignificant passage.

When the two meet again (conf. 81), Bengtsson takes his revenge by revealing Hummel's past crimes against himself and, above all, against the Milkmaid. With Strindberg, the appearance of the Milkmaid forebodes Bengtsson's unveiling: she appears and disappears shortly before the servant enters. With Bergman, she appeared somewhat earlier, when the Mummy spoke of the "black spot" in Hummel's life. Here, according to Bergman, the

Old Man is reminded of his crime against the Milkmaid; this is (psycho)logi-
cally when she should appear. Unlike Strindberg, Bergman also had her remain on the stage during Bengtsson's unmasking of Hummel. Bengtsson's
speech is in two parts, the first concerns his own fate, the second that of the
Milkmaid. Bergman had him demonstrate both his hatred and his powerless-
ness towards Hummel. When commenting on himself, he lifted his arm as if to
strike the Old Man but instead broke down. When commenting on the fate of
the Milkmaid, he changed his tone of voice and became a rational reporter in
a neutral position – as though her fate did not concern him. At the same time
the Milkmaid who so far had been immobile began to raise her arms like a
drowning person. As a result, the attention of the audience shifted from him
to her. The end of his speech became an epic comment on her movement. To
put it differently: when the Old Man heard Bengtsson reveal the black spot of
his, Hummel's, life, this black spot was visualized by the Milkmaid to the Old
Man and to the audience who, unlike the other characters, were allowed to
share his vision.

  The Old Man's long monologue in Act II, full of pauses, is hard to make
dramatically arresting. Strindberg only once informs us how the four 'accused' participants react to Hummel's 'verdict.' "*All look at each other in silence,*" it says when the Old Man has warned them about the impending
unmasking. The acting direction indicates that they are aware that they are all
in the same trap.

  By having the four look stiffly in front of them, Bergman (conf. 79) instead
stressed their isolation, their concern with their own fate. The main choreographic pattern showed them gradually drooping, burdened by their crimes
that were now revealed by the Old Man. Their contrition culminated when
Hummel, identifying himself with inexorable justice, violently struck his
crutch against the table. Both the Colonel and the Posh Man at this point reacted like naughty boys about to be caned. The Mummy, on the other hand,
whose smouldering feelings of revolt were now released, began her counter-
attack. As the constraint was eased, the bodies straightened up, the heads
raised. It was now the Old Man's turn to fall back powerlessly in his chair.

  Just as in the celebration at the end of Act I, Bergman here applied a slightly
stylized pattern to make Hummel's monologue at once consistent and dynamic. Insofar as they have all sinned, the four have something in common.
This explains why Bergman could choreographically treat them as a group.
But they have sinned in different ways. Bergman made this clear by having the
Old Man kinesically pronounce individual 'verdicts' on them and by having
them respond individually. In this way the monologue, which may easily become a static and prolix passage, was turned into an intense battle between
him and them.

The conception of life underlying Bergman's secularized production was almost the opposite of Strindberg's. In line with this, the end was rearranged. The projection of *Toten-Insel* was omitted and "The Song of the Sun," which the Student had recited in a romantic-idealistic way, to the accompaniment of occasional harp notes, at the end of Act II, was now recited tonelessly, without any accompanying music, the harp having turned "deaf and dumb" to him.

The final speeches of the play express faith in a better afterlife and compassion for the dead Young Lady. Strindberg, who has the Student deliver these speeches, stresses the former; Bergman, who gave them to the Colonel and the Mummy, the latter. In the performance, the divine aspect was constantly toned down in favour of human love and compassion.

In the text the Colonel and the Mummy seem to share a mummified matrimonial existence. In the production, they were turned into two people who despite their crimes – or because of them – were tied to one another in a feeling of mutual loyalty. When the Old Man during the ghost supper revealed that the Young Lady was *his* daughter, not the Colonel's, the Mummy grasped the Colonel's hand. A little later, when she testified to the misery of mankind, she stood behind the Colonel with a protecting gesture, while he in turn grasped her hand. A little later she forced Hummel to hand over the notes of hand and the will – to the Colonel.

In Strindberg's final act, the Colonel and the Mummy are seen in positions illustrating that they have drifted away from each other. They are sitting close to the death screen in the round parlour, "*inactive and silent*" – a pre-Beckettian couple waiting for death, "the liberator." In Bergman's version they took the same deadly positions for a long time. But in the end they were reunited.

"We have broken up and gone our ways infinitely many times, but we're drawn together again," the Mummy states in Act II, referring to her marriage to the Colonel. Bergman demonstrated how the two were "drawn together" first when the Old Man threatened them, then when the Young Lady was taken from them. Her death was not in vain.

By giving the Student's concluding prayer for the dead woman to both of them, the director was able to stress their unanimity. This was further indicated by the choreographic pattern in the final tableau, where the Mummy's hand rested tenderly on the Colonel's shoulder, while he in turn lovingly held the hand of the Young Lady. Both of them regarded their dead 'daughter' – a secular holy trinity harking back to Jof, Mia, and their little son Michael in THE SEVENTH SEAL, the loving trinity that is saved from the Black Death. Bergman's positive evaluation of the Colonel's and the Mummy's relationship was one of the striking innovative traits in the production.

In the closing moments the harp that was earlier "deaf and dumb" to the Student begins to play. With Bergman, this happened when the Mummy prayed for her dead daughter. In addition, there was a combination of soft light, representing the love and compassion experienced at this moment by the Colonel and the Mummy, and strong light from above, indicating their hope – Bergman did not cut this religious reference – that "the Lord of Heaven" would show the Young Lady the same compassion as they did. Yet the separate harp notes, composed for the occasion, ended in dissonance, undermining the hope expressed in the Mummy's concluding prayer.

In four places Bergman cut the dialogue. The first concerned the Dead Man:

> OLD MAN. [-] But look now, up there on the balcony, the maid's hoisting the flag to half-mast for the Consul...and now she's turning the bedclothes...Do you see that blue quilt? – That was meant for two to sleep under, now it's for one...

The reason for this omission was undoubtedly that Bergman's projected house(s) did not allow for the Maid's activity.

In the beginning of Act III eight speeches dealing with the correspondence between macro- and microcosmos were omitted. The references to Buddha in this passage seemed out of place both with regard to the setting of the play and to the audience for which it was to be presented. The latter part of the passage was deleted because it does not concern the central hyacinth motif; a bit of a digression, it is rather undramatic in its combination of botanic examination and Swedenborgian doctrine of correspondences.

The third omission, concerning the Student's prayer to Buddha, followed logically from the second. Finally, the words "Sursum Corda" (lift up your hearts) – the introductory words to the Roman Catholic Mass – were deleted from the Student's final monologue as being unintelligible for the average Lutheran spectator, whereas the Latin expression "Cor in aethere" (a heart in the heavens), equally unintelligible but deemed to be of greater importance, was retained.

The dialogue of *The Ghost Sonata* necessarily bears the stamp of the linguistic environment in which it has arisen, Stockholm in the early years of the century. Director and actors are here faced with the question whether to keep this temporal couleur locale or fashion the dialogue in order to make it more accessible to a modern audience. Bergman's production in this respect signified a compromise between these two standpoints.[102]

How a speech is interpreted often has to do with how it is accentuated. Consider the following example:

> COLONEL. [-] Are *you* to run my house?

OLD MAN. Yes! Since I own everything you can see here: furniture, curtains, china, linen cupboard...etcetera.

Bergman's Old Man chose to accentuate the last word (conf. 71). As a result, the word seemed to refer to the 'object' he valued most highly in the house, the Young Lady who is seemingly the Colonel's daughter but who in fact is Hummel's.

A pause inserted in the right place can add an ironic touch to a speech. Compare Strindberg's "COLONEL. Miss Holsteinkrona, Mr Hummel..." with Bergman's "COLONEL [-]. Miss Holsteinkrona, Mr...Hummel." (conf. 75) The pause here indicates the Colonel's pretended difficulty of remembering the Old Man's name, a subtle way of humiliating him.

At one point Strindberg's Old Man asks: "What does her father say, I mean the Colonel? Your husband?" Compare this to Bergman's version:

OLD MAN [-]. What does her father say?

MUMMY *looks puzzled.*

OLD MAN *ironically, hissing.* The Colonel? Your husband?   (conf. 68)

The acting direction for the Mummy here corresponds to a pause on the part of the Old Man, a pause which serves to accentuate the ambiguity of the words "her father." The Mummy's puzzled expression underscores the absurdity of the fact that the real father in front of the mother 'denies' his fatherhood.

The meaning of a speech is, of course, highly determined by the way in which it is pronounced. As in most drama texts, there are very few paralinguistic indications in the acting directions of *The Ghost Sonata*. Consider the following passage:

OLD MAN. [-] I'll probably die soon, that I know, but before that I have a few things to do – take my hand and feel how cold I am.

How is this phrased, in which tone of voice? Matter-of-factly or pathetically? Does the Old Man turn to the Student in the first part of the speech or does he mumble the words to himself? Is his admonishment to the Student done commandingly or appealingly?

Bergman's version was as follows:

OLD MAN. [-] *Nonchalantly.* I'll die soon. That I know. *Ominously.* But before that, I have a few things to do. *Stubs the cigarette, appealingly.* Take my hand and feel how cold I am. (conf. 28)

We here get three different intonations. The first tells us that Hummel pretends not to worry about his impending death; the second indicates his desire to revenge himself; the last shows how he is seeking contact with the Student.

When the Old Man grabs the Student's hand, the latter reacts: "Let go of my hand, you're taking my strength away, you're freezing me, what do you want?" Thus according to the text. It would be rather natural to have the Student scream the line and that was also the way it was done during the early rehearsals. It soon proved more effective to have him say the line "*anguished, feebly*" (conf. 28). After all, the Student has just been 'blood-sucked' by Hummel and is now weakened, powerless.

The same intonation returned in Act III. The text has it:

STUDENT. Send her [the Cook] away!

YOUNG LADY. We can't.

The exclamation mark may seem to be a hint. But Bergman chose to have the Student's line phrased as a powerless whisper, and the Young Lady's as a lamentation. In this way they were paralingustically defined as victims of the Cook's vampirism. Their intonation became an illustration of the Young Lady's remark that the Cook had taken their strength away.

Most of the critics were enthusiastic and impressed by Bergman's third production of *The Ghost Sonata*. Negative statements were rare. The majority found the combination of the Young Lady and the Mummy interesting although, surprisingly enough, several admitted that they did not see its deeper significance. Only one or two seemed to realize that the doubling was intimately connected with Bergman's attempt to relate the third act to the first two, to make the play an organic unity.

The scenery was generally praised, and several commentators noted that Marik Vos' bare stage agreed well with the ageing Strindberg's demand for the simple staging of his plays.

Of the actors, Toivo Pawlo was highly commended, whereas Gertrud Fridh did not quite get the praise she deserved for her exceedingly difficult double role. Mathias Henrikson's Student was lauded by some reviewers, while others were not quite convinced of his role interpretation. Much the same was true of Anders Ek (the Colonel), a remarkable actor whose somewhat idiosyncratic style bothered certain reviewers.

Leif Zern, by many considered the outstanding Swedish theatre critic, devoted four columns to the production which he found intriguing, provocative and deeply personal.[103] But because he could share neither the Student's idealism nor his subsequent bitter disappointment he found it difficult to identify

with him. Åke Janzon tempered his praise by expressing certain doubts about
Bergman's version of the ending. Although he appreciated the director's new
approach, he was not certain that it would have received Strindberg's blessing.[104] Åke Perlström called the production "one of the most splendid that
Swedish theatre can bring forth,"[105] and Allan Fagerström considered it "the
perfect performance."[106]

When Bergman staged his first *Ghost Sonata*, in 1941, he was 23 – the same
age as the Student. When he staged his fourth version, in 2000, he was 81, the
age of the Old Man. If any play can be said to have been his companion
through life, it is this one. This does not mean, however, that he has shifted his
point of view and has become more conciliatorily towards the Old Man as
time has gone by. But surveying his own long life, he can now better see what
separates and what links the young man that he once was with the old man he
now is – a fundamental theme, as we have seen, already in his third production, visualized in the outward similarity between the Student and the Old
Man and, more obviously, in the double role of the Young Lady and the
Mummy.

In his new version these correspondences were not stressed. The two
women were played by different actresses and the two men did not look
very similar – although the actors playing these parts happen to be father and
son.

To underline that the whole play is a dream, or a nightmare, Bergman rein-
troduced the generic subtitle of the original production: "fantasy piece." He
also chose to have the play performed, not on a large stage as in 1954 and
1973 but on a small one, the paint room of Dramaten, seating about 150 people, that is, about the same number as Strindberg's Intimate Theatre. And this
time the performance took place on a stage, surrounded by black velvet curtains, with even fewer properties than before – the harp was gone – very much
in agreement with the late Strindberg's ideas for simplified stagings of his
plays.

While Bergman had earlier largely abstained from music, in his new version he made incidental use, not of the Beethoven sonata or trio, as indicated
by Strindberg, but by Béla Bartók's *Music for Strings, Percussion and Celesta*,
which helped to create a kind of unity of mood while at the same time the contrasting instruments could be linked to the divergent characters, ages and in-
clinations in the play. The Student's report concerning the collapse of the
house the preceding night, for example, was accompanied by a fragment from
Bartók's piece, giving a lyrical, dreamlike profile to his narration about his
vain attempt to save the child walking under the wall.

In his fourth production, Bergman harked back to the view he held in his
Malmö version, that the Student is the dreamer of the play. It was this time indicated not by means of a gauze between stage and auditorium but, more effectively, by having the Student, alone, appear on the stage from the entrance
found in the middle of and below the sloping auditorium. Crawling onto the
stage in his dirtied clothes, he was not only escaping one house to be confronted with another; he was also waking up from a nocturnal dream soon to
be revivified on the stage; and, born out of the 'womb' of the dark auditorium,
he was entering life as another Everyman.[107] He and the audience, to paraphrase his words in Act III, had given birth to something together.

As in 1973, a black-and-white photo of the same turn-of-the-century
apartment house was projected on the black velvet draperies framing the
claustrophobic, magic black box where the dream was to be enacted. Representing the House of Life, this stately 'fortress' behind which mankind, notably the well-to-do bourgeoisie, are hiding their frailties, visualized the Red
House where Strindberg lived when he wrote *The Ghost Sonata*[108] and which
Molander had recreated in his productions of the play. Pulled down in 1969,
this building was replaced by an apartment house where Bergman now lives.
Whereas Molander's spectators could still find the Red House in their city,
Bergman's had to locate it in their memory, as one of those buldings that had
to 'collapse' to give place to a younger, more modern one. Inscribed in the
grey stage floor in front of the house was a green rectangle, at once a stylized
reproduction of the square, Karlaplan, in front of the Red House and a symbolic indication of how the greyness of life surrounds our hope for something
better, as the old people surround the young in the play. The green returned in
Act II as background for the young couple in the hyacinth room, whereas the
red formed the backdrop for the old couple in the round room of Act III. The
lighting – green and red shades on the black draperies – was subdued; ironically, the only stark white light provided was that of death, at the end.

As in his 1973 production, Bergman placed the House of Life at once in the
auditorium and on the stage, thereby creating a *theatrum mundi* – and a dizzy
dream effect. Again the emblematic grandfather clock to the left and the marble statue to the right indicated that the spectators were inside the house entered by the Student-mediator in Act II. In Acts II and III the upstage room,
framed by so-called Wagner pulls, had the appearance of an inner stage – with
a theatrical quality characteristic of turn-of-the-century upper-class interiors.[109]

The street drinking-fountain to the right was this time placed below the
stage floor, underground. From it, radiating with a mysterious green light,
real water was scooped up by the Milkmaid. Similar to a wholesome well –
Bergman's THE VIRGIN SPRING came to mind – this fountain of life was obvi-

ously meant to correspond to "the source of life" – the womb, the Paradise before the Fall – mentioned in Act III. To the left of this 'well' was another hole in the ground, a sewer into which the Caretaker's Wife matter-of-factly emptied a bucket full of latrine – thereby anticipating the Student's discovery in Act III that the Young Lady is "sick at the source of life" and the spectators' discovery by the end of the performance that freshness and foulness, beauty and ugliness are subterraneously connected and exist side by side as inevitable parts of life.

The unmasking of the characters, especially of the Young Lady, was synchronized with the withering of the hyacinths, an idea that was in Bergman's mind already in 1973 but which was then abolished. While Strindberg calls for hyacinths of various colours, Bergman limited himself to the white – pure, innocent – kind. In Act I the Young Lady was seen watering and silently talking to the lovely hyacinths in her window. In Act II the hyacinths had already begun to wither. In Act III the beautiful giant white hyacinths projected on the side walls corresponded to the Student's enamoured illusions about the nature of the Young Lady as an ideal representative of (wo)mankind. Contrasting with these 'projected' hyacinths were the tiny, withered, real ones in front of the Young Lady, smelling so badly that she had to sprinkle herself with perfume around her neck, in her armpits and, significantly, around her behind to quench the odour.

The sick condition of humanity was visualized in ways that could lead the thoughts to Pär Lagerkvist's early expressionistic dramas with their crippled characters. The Dark Lady had an ugly red boil on her cheek which she desperately tried to hide behind her crape. The Posh Man constantly kept licking a red – syphilitic? – wound below his mouth with his tongue. The Fiancée had an ear that was stark red from the constant use of an ear trumpet and her laughter at the most inopportune moments indicated her lack of wits. The Mummy's entangled hair bore witness of her inner confusion. The Old Man's warped mouth and slow patter suggested that he had suffered a stroke, motivating his awareness that his days are counted. His bleeding, bandaged hands indicated either psoriasis – from which Strindberg suffered when writing the play – or stigmatization. Johansson wore a shoe that seemed considerably longer than the other one; an oily, ingratiating figure, he showed, like Hummel's son, homosexual leanings. The Colonel's iron corset was, again, revealed when the Old Man stripped his – this time blue, Swedish-looking – uniform open. The Young Lady showed self-inflicted scratches on her arm and, as in 1973, blood around her womb, once her shiny, light-blue Amazon 'armour' was removed. Stiffly moving around as if in trance – a sleepwalker in life – she showed at an early point "only the white" of her eyes "like a blind person."[110]

The thematic focus was this time on virginity or rather virginity lost, linking the street drinking-fountain, the marble statue (Eve after the Fall), the Milkmaid, killed by Hummel, and the Young Lady, 'killed' by the Student. In Act II a gobelin tapestry was projected on the side walls showing a lancer on horseback piercing a unicorn, the traditional symbol of virginity, with his lance – an obvious reference to the killings just mentioned. By showing the Milkmaid as undesirably pregnant (as is the Dark Lady and as was the Mummy); by having the Old Man contaminate the marble statue by placing a mark of blood on its stomach; and by having the Young Lady, in Act III, violently beat her stomach, Bergman further linked the key line of the play – the reference to the sickness at the source of life – to the origin of us all: the womb. At the end the connection between the Young Lady and the Milkmaid became explicit. As the Young Lady was dying, standing in her petticoat behind the death screen with its Japanese letters meaning "life, death, eternity,"[111] the Milkmaid, identically dressed, rolled onto the stage through the black curtain at the back and joined the Young Lady, now lying on the floor. As the Mummy approached them for the final intercession, her use of the singular made it clear that the two women now represented one and the same child (of man). The Young Lady was carried out by four lilac-dressed, top-hatted bearers with gauzy – anonymous – faces, whereas the Milkmaid, now alone on the stage and seen only by the Student, positioned in the auditorium, performed a final, oriental-looking, upward-striving dance, Bergman's non-verbal substitute for the Student's prayer to Buddha. The message was clear. The death of the Young Lady meant a separation of body and soul, the former doomed to annihilation, the latter, in the Student's hope – an important qualification – blessed with survival. No *Toten-Insel*, no angelic harp, no "Song of the Sun" at the end, not even a secular family reunion. And yet consolation, be it a subjective one in the final vision of the spiritualized Milkmaid, 'born' by the Student and the audience together. His hope, our hope.

As in 1973, the grey-black-white pattern dominated in the costumes of Act I. In Act II they were more realistic, less gaudy than in 1973. In Act III they adjusted, more or less, to what was seen then. As the outsider-narrator of the dream, the Student appeared throughout the performance in the same clothes: white shirt, light grey dress, light grey shoes. The Old Man wore in Act I dark glasses as an indication of his bad eyesight, black fur cap and black, fur-edged coat – both status symbols – and grey fingerless woollen gloves. On his wheelchair he kept his cane and a worn bag, containing the sweets with which he tried to catch his victims. "All the others walk around in thin clothes," one critic noted.

> He is sitting in his winter coat protecting himself against inner cold. Through his dark Beckett glasses he observes the world conspiringly.[112]

In Act II the Old Man appeared in a black top hat; when removed, it showed a bald head; Bergman in other words this time abstained both from skull-cap and wig. Hummel now wore dark-green clothes, including a waistcoat with a black-green, frog-like pattern. The Milkmaid wore a grey dress with a grey-and-white striped apron in Act I, later a long, white shroud-like petticoat. The Young Lady wore a light-grey riding habit in Act I, in Act III replaced by a light-blue dress, pearl-embroidered above, at once a star-studded heaven and a shiny armour covering her soiled grey petticoat. The Mummy's entangled grey hair around a head that twitched like that of a parrot dissolved into her grey dress turning red below – just as her voice subtly fluctuated between anguished humility and passionate condemnation. Bengtsson appeared like an anachronism in an 18th century red costume, with a huge black bow-tie, his patriotic medal proudly fastened to his breast.

Suggestive visual correspondences occurred when the Colonel's handling of his monocle was mimicked by the Dead Consul's handling of his. More importantly, when the Old Man vampirically gripped the Student's hand, the anguish of the latter was echoed in a silent, nightmarish cry à la Munch by the Dark Lady, who herself was being utilized by the Posh Man.

Comical touches centred on Johansson who, combining self-importance with ingratiation, walked around with a briefcase out of which he eventually produced, not documents or even books but a pocket-flask which he evidently regularly sipped. When he told the Student that the Old Man was reputed to have been in Hamburg, he laughed insinuatingly and waved his grey bowler hat like a cabaret artist; the implication was obviously that Hummel had been a customer of the famous red light quarter of that city, Reeperbahn.

As in 1973, Bergman indicated a tender relationship between the Mummy and the Colonel. He had the Mummy this time eavesdrop when the Colonel was stripped by the Old Man, thereby strengthening her motivation to pronounce judgement on Hummel later. But unlike the situation in 1973 the Mummy and the Colonel were not united at the end. They stood in frozen positions isolated from each other and from the dead in front of them – as though the director wanted to underline that whether alive or dead, we are ultimately alone.

The prelude to the ghost supper was this time more elaborate and the supper – where tea and biscuits were never even brought in – included, as in 1941, one more guest: the Dark Lady. Hiding her boil with one hand, she reached out the other to be kissed by the Colonel – in vain; the Mummy similarly turned away from her; and she was placed at the right end of the row of chairs, half turned-away from the others, collectively rejected.

The drowning of the Milkmaid was repeated pantomimically when she unexpectedly appeared, from the entrance below the auditorium, writhing in front of the Old Man who was standing in his wagon, surrounded by the Beggars, like a king surrounded by his courtiers. With his cane he tried to repress (the painful memory of) the Milkmaid. She then placed herself in the painful position of the Crucified[113] next to the grandfather clock, thereby anticipating Hummel's death.

When Bengtsson had revealed the Old Man's hitherto hidden crime, Hummel tried to escape from the death penalty that had been pronounced on him but he was prevented from doing so by the guests. Having run the gauntlet, he was carried by Johansson into the closet, where the Milkmaid put the rope around his neck. All Hummel's victims in this way took their revenge. Johansson picked up the Old Man's cane, waved it like a cabaret artist to indicate that he, now free from his slavery, had replaced his master.

In Act III the Cook, a small, grey, dirty, fat woman, more repulsive than terrifying, held the brown soya bottle with the Japanese "scorpion" letters in her hand. At her second appearance, she was accompanied, as in 1973, by Bengtsson, he too in grey proletarian clothing, brushing one of the Young Lady's riding-boots. The two were "an aged Jean and an old Kristin"[114] serving a descendant of Strindberg's Miss Julie. The plans that were abolished in 1973 to have their "You suck the strength out of us, and we out of you" reverberate were now put into effect. The line was unevenly echoed as if by an anonymous, mumbling proletariat.

Bergman's fourth and presumably last production of *The Ghost Sonata* was praised by most critics as a coherent, fluid and highly meaningful presentation of the play. "Everything is supremely restrained and sonorous," Henrik Sjögren summarized.[115] As usual the actors playing the Old Man (Jan Malmsjö) and the Mummy (Gunnel Lindblom), two thankful roles, were especially praised, while the actors incarnating the Student (Jonas Malmsjö) and the Young Lady (Elin Klinga), two less rewarding parts, received less attention. "A rare treat at Dramaten," was the headline of one review,[116] "Bergman's definitive *Ghost Sonata*" of another,[117] "Bergman touches the heart" of yet another.[118] Several critics pointed out the puppet-like nature of the characters,[119] leaving it open whether Hummel, Bergman, God or Fate should be seen as the master puppeteer. The bare stage caused Zern to think of an empty rehearsal room – Bergman's favourite 'stage' – whereas Margareta Sörenson reminded the reader that this was a stage production made by a filmmaker; to her the performance – the Student's nightmare – was "a horror film from the period of the silent film."[120]

Four: Adaptations

Reading a play and listening to a radio performance of that same play are activities which have something in common but also differ markedly; in Martin Esslin's words:

> [-] by having to provide the visual component, which is undeniably present in any true dramatic experience transmitted by radio, [the listener] is an active collaborator with the producer. In this respect he is in exactly the same position as the reader of a book who has to imagine the action in his mind's eye. The difference, however, is that the voices, music, and sounds of the radio play are of a far greater immediacy, have an infinitely more powerful emotional and sensuous impact in themselves, than the abstract symbols of print on the page.[1]

How the immediacy and emotional impact of radio drama compare with that of stage drama is another, hitherto empirically unexplored matter.

Radio drama is an intimate form of drama. Deprived of any visual correlative, the listener, like a blind person, will be very sensitive to aural nuance. The actor very close to the microphone may be compared to the actor close to the camera in a TV or film production. The listener receives in such a case an aural close-up corresponding to a soliloquy. The Old Man's talking to himself at the opening of Act I in Per Verner-Carlsson's production is a good example. Christopher Martin makes no use of this possibility; his dialogue is throughout – dialogue.

One of the great assets of radio drama is its ability to present inner processes. As in the case of many novels, we learn as much, or more, about what the characters are thinking and feeling as about what they are doing. Another asset is the ease with which a running commentary – a commentary not about what has happened but about what is happening – can be dealt with.[2] In this respect the Old Man's presentation to the Student of the people in the house is not unlike the running commentary of a radio reporter. When he admonishes the Student "Look at her [the Young Lady]! – Have you ever seen such a masterpiece?", it is easier for the listener than for the spectator to agree with him; tastes differ but in our imagination we can always create a masterpiece to our own taste. The total reliance on the aural code also favours ideological and poetical drama, both aspects relevant with regard to *The Ghost Sonata*.

Sound effects naturally play an important part in radio drama. These must be easy to decode by the listener; the director must avoid sounds which resemble one another too much and consequently are difficult to identify. A sound may well be undecipherable at one point and fully intelligible at another;

many sound effects "come to dramatic life *after* the listener has been *told* what they represent."[3] Next to ordinary, objective sounds, radio drama frequently employs subjective sounds, mirroring the way a character experiences a sound rather than the sound itself.

In the following I shall compare Verner-Carlsson's Swedish radio version, from 1962, with Martin's Finland-Swedish radio version from 1989. While having the language, Swedish, in common,[4] the two productions differ considerably.

Characteristic of radio drama is the limited time allowed for presentation; few plays exceed an hour and a half. Transforming stage plays into radio plays therefore usually entails a considerable shortening of the text. Whereas Verner-Carlsson's production has a running time of one hour and twelve minutes, enabling him to cover almost the whole play, Martin's lasts some twelve minutes less.

One of the few omissions in the Swedish version is the brief conversation between the Posh Man and the Dark Lady. The reason for this deletion is undoubtedly that a few lines from these otherwise mute characters would have been disconcerting for the listener. While the omission of this minute subplot – it is cut also in Martin's version – seems altogether warranted, the deletion in the Finland-Swedish version of the fairly long conversation between Johansson and the Student at the end of Act I and most of the Student's speech concluding the play are more questionable. The reason for the latter omission can hardly have been, as in the case of Bergman, that the reference to Buddha would seem too removed from the everyday reality of most listeners, since an earlier reference to this divine figure is retained. Deprived both of the Buddha passage, "The Song of the Sun" and *Toten-Insel* at the end, the Student's prayer that the Lord of Heaven have mercy on the dead Young Lady here comes as an all-too-sudden turnabout after his nihilistic eruption.

Act and scene division in radio drama is usually less explicit than in other presentational forms. Changes of time and place, which may be indicated by musical interludes, often occur rapidly and almost imperceptibly. This is, for example, the case when Martin has a fragment from Beethoven's Op. 70, No. 1 in D major (Ghost Trio) mark the change from Act II to Act III. A more extensive fragment from the first movement, largo assaio ed espressivo, of this sonata accompanies the Student's initial meeting with the Milkmaid, whereas a bit of the furious ride of the valkyries from *The Valkyrie* creates the mood for the Old Man's imposed suicide at the end of Act II as well as an ironic link between him and the opera.

As we have seen, the visual code is exceedingly important in *The Ghost Sonata*, where visions form an integral part of the central thematic pattern: the discrepancy between what seems to be and what is, between appearance and reality. It is therefore a delicate task to adapt the play for the non-visual radio medium.

In any presentation of a drama we need to know, as soon as possible, where we find ourselves. We need, to use the language of film, an initial shot establishing time and place. In the text this is done in the opening stage directions, in a stage version it is done by means of (audio)visual signs. In radio drama it can be done via a narrator, an old-fashioned method; by incorporating the stage directions in the dialogue, much as in Elizabethan drama; or – though this would normally only be a partial solution – by providing informative sound effects.

This is how Verner-Carlsson's radio version opens:

Chiming of several church bells.

OLD MAN. Sunday. Quiet Sunday morning on the little square. I'm sitting here in my wheelchair, keeping watch in front of the house, the respectable house with the round drawing-room at the corner, with marble and brass and laurel trees. Well, well! They are sweeping and polishing. The caretaker's wife. *Laughs.*

Chiming subsides.

I'm waiting. Watching and keeping watch. Sunday. You see, I'm interested in the destinies of people! I observe. What else? Talk about the weather, which we know, ask how we are, which we know? I prefer silence, then you hear thoughts and see the past. Yes, what has been and what shall...

Organ music during the following speeches.

Someone is coming! It's him! It *is* him! The student. At last! Sleepless, unshaven...Of course! He walks straight up to the fountain.

STUDENT *at some distance.* May I borrow the dipper? – Haven't you finished yet?

OLD MAN *to himself.* Who's he talking to? I don't see anyone.

STUDENT. What are you staring at, girl? Do I look so terrible? Well, I didn't get any sleep last night. I suppose you think I was out living it up. Drinking punch, eh? Do I smell of punch?

OLD MAN *to himself.* But who's he talking to? Is he mad?

The need to inform the listener about where the action takes place has here resulted in a somewhat artificial soliloquy on the part of the Old Man, consisting partly of verbalized stage directions, partly of dialogue fragments taken from his speech during the ghost supper. His "you see" implies that he is addressing the listener directly, in the manner of the classical *prologus*. The mighty sound of church bells, logically followed by organ music, suggests that we find ourselves in a city. There is also an attempt to make the listener sense the presence of the mute Milkmaid by having the Student add the word "girl" and by having the Old Man ask himself twice whom the Student is talking to.

Compare this to Martin's opening which is much shorter:

Chiming of church bell, soon mingled with the sound of flowing water.

STUDENT. May I borrow the dipper?

Incidental organ-like music mingles with the chiming and the sound of water.

Haven't you finished soon?

Sound of paper being folded.

OLD MAN. Who's he talking to? I can't see anyone. Is he mad?

Here the listener may easily misinterpret the location. For all he knows, the chiming may originate from a country church. The clatter of horse's hooves heard a little later is at this point certainly an indicator of the time in which the action is set but not of the place. (Later, after we have learnt that the Young Lady is out horse-riding, a somewhat different clatter signifies her return on horseback to the house.) The running water combined with the word "dipper" may indeed tell the listener that the Student is standing by a drinking-fountain. But he will have trouble identifying the "*sound of paper*" as the Old Man's brusque folding of his newspaper, since the newspaper has never been mentioned.

More importantly, like the Old Man he has no clue who the Student is talking to. Like him, he would have the impression that the Student is talking to himself – as a mentally disturbed person might. In other words, the information that is provided to the reader and the spectator – the physical presence of the Milkmaid – is here lacking. Not until later does the listener understand that the Student possesses the ability of second sight.

When Strindberg later in the act notes that "*the blind is raised in the round drawing-room*," Verner-Carlsson as usual transforms this acting direction into dialogue. The Old Man remarks: "Look...look there in the round drawing-room. The blind is being raised." Although somewhat unnatural, the line is certainly informative. Martin, on the other hand, merely reproduces the sound of a blind being raised, a sound which the listener only in retrospect can identify with the help of the Old Man's "Look, there's the Colonel." Martin, in other words, avoids artificiality at the expense of intelligibility.

The ticking of the clock in Act II that is abruptly stopped by the Mummy is an important sound effect. Martin has the clock in this act tick realistically, that is, for a very long time and without any audible change; after a while the sound becomes tiresome and distracting. Verner-Carlsson, on the other hand, uses the sound functionally. The ticking is heard only when it is thematically relevant. It significantly rises to a crescendo just before the Mummy stops the time, indicating that the Old Man's life has come to an end. Sound is followed by silence, as life is followed by death.

Martin's production is generally flawed by an all too frequent use of sound effects, above all of doors opening and closing. The director seems to have had the misguided notion that every entrance and exit must be acoustically accounted for. Take the following passage:

> OLD MAN. Quiet...the Colonel's coming...
>
> MUMMY. Then I'll go in to Adèle...*Pause.* Jacob, think of what you're doing! Spare him...*Pause. She leaves.*

Martin here provides the sound of a door as a sign that the Colonel is coming and again as a sign that the Mummy is leaving. Verner-Carlsson refrains from using doors in both places; the change of configuration is merely indicated through a pause, in which the ticking of the clock is heard. In Martin's Act III we hear various doors opening and closing. The indication is here that the Young Lady takes the Student around in the apartment, a choice that carries little meaning and is in disagreement with the thematically important idea that the Young Lady prefers the escape of her hyacinth room. It is more meaningful when the director lets the Student's outburst be accompanied by the ticking of a clock; the sound here serves to link his eruption with that of the Old Man in Act II.

Without access to the visual code, the listener will often find it difficult to keep track of the various characters and to distinguish their voices from one another. To meet these problems, radio drama favours few roles as well as duologues. In plays comprising large casts – like *The Ghost Sonata* – directors try to dispense with minor characters. As we have seen, the Posh Man and the Dark Lady are absent from both productions.

The greatest problem, naturally, in a non-visual medium is presented by the exclusively visual, pantomimic elements in the play text. Since *The Ghost Sonata* is unusually rich in such elements – besides the two mute ghosts, several other characters are silent for long periods – it follows that the drama text does not lend itself easily to radio adaptation. Obviously, the presence of the silent characters need to be implied somehow. Verner-Carlsson indicates the presence of the Cook by interspersing the comments on her by the Young Lady and the Student with the Cook's loud laughter. Similarly, the Student's verbal 'murder' of the Young Lady is interspersed with her wailing, reminding us of her victimization and preparing us for her death. In a more symbolic way, the director continually indicates the presence of the Young Lady by means of harp music which often seems non-diegetic although it could be diegetically motivated. The instrument links her with the Milkmaid, whose presence is made audible by 'celestial' organ music. When the Milkmaid leaves after her first appearance and the Old Man starts to attract the attention of the Student, the music significantly changes, receives an "*instrumental effect*," as it says in the script, and turns disharmonic.

When a character drastically changes his or her voice, the listener will easily be confused. Thus when the Mummy suddenly abolishes her parrot language and starts speaking "*lucidly and seriously*," the listener of either radio production may have some trouble understanding that it is the Mummy's voice he hears. For quite another reason, he may find it difficult immediately to recognize that it is the Student, who has hardly said a word during Act II, who recites "The Song of the Sun" at the end of this act. When Martin, like Bergman, gives both the role of the Young Lady and that of the Mummy to the same actress, he disregards the difference in presentational mode, the fact that radio drama calls for a greater differentiation of voices than stage drama.

A rather specific problem concerns nonentities, that is, statements about what is *not* seen or heard. What can a director of radio drama do with an acting direction like the following: "*The* BEGGARS *bare their heads, but without cheering.*" In Verner-Carlsson's version they do cheer, be it cheerlessly. Or take the following acting direction: "*He [the* STUDENT] *takes the harp but no sound comes from its strings.*" The lack of sound here contrasts with the miracle later performed when "*the harp's strings begin to rustle.*" In Verner-Carlsson's version the harp does sound when the Student touches it. As a result, his remark "It's deaf and dumb" is not literally true as in the text; it is an approximation, referring to the dull sound coming from the strings. When the harp finally begins to play, the listener in either radio version cannot grasp that it does so by itself, that a miracle is performed. He will either see the harp-chords as emanating from the Student's playing of the harp or, more likely, as non-diegetic, mood-creating music. The only way to save the important acting direction, it seems, is to have the Student verbally explicate the miracle. But such explication would be exceedingly disturbing and both directors have refrained from it.

At the end of Verner-Carlsson's version, after the Young Lady has rung the bell and asked for the death screen, the Student's the-liberator-is-coming speech is accompanied by what in the script is referred to as "*music: the theme of death*," impersonal electronic music. This is replaced by "*humming, unrealistic harp-chords*" when he recites "The Song of the Sun." A final wailing informs us that the Young Lady is giving up her ghost. And the performance is concluded with the Student's intercession for the dead woman, followed by harp-chords which, "*mingled with the sound of bells, swell into a mighty tone block.*"

As already indicated, the three visions of the play – the Milkmaid, the Dead Man, *Toten-Insel* – provide the greatest stumbling-block to anyone adapting *The Ghost Sonata* for the radio. While the directors manage to draw attention to the first two by having the speaking characters comment on them, this is hardly possible in the case of *Toten-Insel*. Strindberg's spectacular conclusion of the play cannot be transmitted to the listener. Instead he is provided with a musical equivalent of the *changement à vue*, informing him of the Young Lady's transference from a painful life to a – hopefully – blissful afterlife. In the final sound effect, the director abstains from Strindberg's "*soft music*" coming from the Isle of the Dead, since this is only functional if the recipient is aware of the isle. Instead the chiming of the bells from the beginning of the performance returns in the concluding tone block but now mingled, not with organ music but with celestial harp-chords – an acoustic circle composition with a significant close.

As appears from the foregoing, Verner-Carlsson's and Martin's productions are very different. Both directors have had the problem of dealing with a play which in some respects, notably the frequent use of visions and panto-mime, is inimical to radio drama. Given this problem, Verner-Carlsson, bene-fitting from some of Sweden's best actors, has on the whole solved his task in a masterly way, whereas Martin has produced a rather flat performance. The difference may have something to do with the fact that Martin, as an Ameri-can, has been working in a language which is not his own. His performance suffers from a hectic tempo and little variation in the actors' phrasing of their lines. But the major reason, I believe, is a difference in sensitivity and aware-ness of what a successful radio presentation entails: a far-reaching reshaping of the text to meet the listener's need both to understand what is happening and to be emotionally influenced by it.

What happens when a play, written for the stage, is presented on television? Transposing a play to the small screen necessarily involves a number of ad-justments originating in the difference between the media. In the theatre we have a fixed seat, from where we can hopefully see the whole stage. The char-acters remain at roughly the same distance from us. A screen version, on the other hand, may well open with a shot of merely a part of the visualized space or even with a close-up of a small object. We are then momentarily at a loss as to where we find ourselves.

The differences between stage and small screen are fundamental and have far-reaching consequences both at the production and the reception end.[5] The most fundamental one, perhaps, is that the stage relies on continuous space, whereas the screen depends on discontinuous space. While in stage drama we remain visually in the same environment within each act/scene, in screen drama the visible surroundings will change with each shot. And while in the 'democratic' stage drama we have, in principle at least, the freedom to focus on whatever we like on the stage, in the more 'authoritarian' screen drama the camera will successively turn our attention to whatever the director wishes us to see. We may hereby note that a screen director has a whole range of choices between rapid cutting and mobile camera at one extreme and long takes and static camera at the other.[6]

Johan Bergenstråhle's Swedish TV production, from 1972, opens as follows (figures left indicate shots):

1   *Fade-in to credits –* THE GHOST SONATA. Chamber Play by August Strindberg – *on patterned wallpaper. Organ music. Dissolve to*

2   *Long shot of a choir dressed in black (six female, four male singers, five on either side of the organ). The organist, his back turned to the spectator, conducts with his L arm. Organ music and singing in the same manner until shot 4.*
    Tilt down to OLD MAN *in light, yellowish summer clothes, hat (with a black ribbon) and black gloves. His face is hidden behind a newspaper. Street drinking-fountain in FG. Splashing of water.*
    Slow zoom-in on OLD MAN, *who lowers his paper and looks up, so that his face can be seen. He wears glasses. Splashing of water.*

3   *Long shot of section of a grey apartment house with high windows, one L with flowers in it (the hyacinth room) and a double bay-window R, covered with white curtains (the round room). Pan R to open front door with laurels in tubs on either side. Window R of door (*FIANCÉE's *window). Inside the door* DARK LADY *is standing, in black with mourning crape over her face.* CARETAKER's WIFE *is scrubbing the floor.*

4   *Medium close-up of* OLD MAN *looking up from his paper, then disappearing again behind it. High organ notes followed by* a capella *female voices and, finally, a single female voice. Dissolve to*

5   *Long shot of* MILKMAID *walking down a stately grey staircase from L to R. She wears a grey dress and beret and carries milk bottles in wire baskets. Turns L when she reaches ground level. Organ music until shot 7. Footsteps.*
    Zoom-in on her as she walks up to drinking-fountain and puts wire baskets next to it. She wipes sweat from her forehead, picks up the dipper, fills it with water from fountain and drinks. Dissolve to

6 Long shot of STUDENT *walking down stately grey staircase (identical with the one in shot 5) from R to L. He wears a Swedish student's cap, black waistcoat and trousers, white shirt with rolled-up sleeves. Footsteps.*

7 Medium close-up of MILKMAID *washing her hands in fountain. Behind her a poster, advertising the program at the Royal Theatre, and part of staircase. She leans on fountain with her arms, mirroring her face in the water. Splashing of water. Chiming of church bell until shot 11.*

8 Medium shot of STUDENT, *with dirty cap and clothes.* May I have the dipper?

9 Medium close-up of MILKMAID *looks at him frightened.*

10 Medium shot of STUDENT. Haven't you finished yet?

11 Medium close-up of OLD MAN, *muttering to himself.* Who's he talking to? *Lowers paper, looks up, turns his head R. To himself.* I can't see anyone. *Turns head back, to himself.* Is he mad?

In Bergenstråhle's scenography there is no indication, as in the play text, of an inward movement. The whole play is acted out in one huge space, in which the high-low dichotomy is essential. The setting is in itself dreamlike in the sense that we do not know whether it is an exterior (a street) or an interior (a church), whether the prop in the foreground is a street drinking-fountain or a baptismal font.

Our first impression, as we see a huge organ with organist and choir, all placed on a raised level in the background and as we hear the music and the singing, is indeed that we are inside a church. In the organ music the director seems to have incorporated Strindberg's ship's bell: the monotonous notes played remind one of the puffing of a steamship chimney. But one may also think of the regular ticking of a clock – relating the sound to the ominous clock in Act II – or the beating of a heart, the Old Man's pangs of conscience. The plaintive, wordless singing from the very beginning intones the mood. We are in a world in which "det är synd om människorna" (meaning both 'humanity is to be pitied' and 'humanity is sinful'), the central line of *A Dream Play*, a drama which looms large in Bergenstråhle's *Ghost Sonata.'* The sound of murmuring water from the fountain – an unrealistic sound – helps to emphasize the biblical connotations of the "fresh water." Bergenstråhle significantly manipulates this sound, turning it especially loud when the Milkmaid, the good Samaritan, in a long take, bathes the Student's eyes.

While in the text we move from (love of) this world to (love of) heaven, from blindness to seeing – at the end we are, as it were, blessed with the Student's second sight – Bergenstråhle makes the heavenly aspect immediately explicit. Instead of a play beginning in a physical reality and ending in a spiritual one, we are faced with a 'medieval,' allegorical construction with heaven above and earth-cum-hell below. The Milkmaid and the Student both enter the ground level (the world) from the organ-loft above (heaven) by virtue of their childlike innocence – much as, in the words of the Student, "Jesus Christ descended into hell. That was his pilgrimage on earth," a line that apparently has been decisive for Bergenstråhle's scenographic solution.

Once we see this, other things fall into place. The dominance of greyness, for example, which indicates not only the drabness of human existence but also the colour of stone, stone being the material with which the Old Man, akin to the biblical Tempter, builds his world. When the camera tilts down from the organist, the praiser of God, to the satanic Old Man,[8] it is a clear statement of the metaphysical polarity.

The Old Man appears in yellowish summer clothes, black mourning ribbon and black gloves. This is a non-realistic costume bringing out his corpse-like nature, his pretence to mourn the Consul, whom he has "murdered," as well as his feeling cold (the gloves), indicative both of his mental coldness and his sense of approaching death. By showing the Old Man first hiding behind his paper, then lowering it so that his face can be seen, Bergenstråhle not only depicts his deceitfulness; he also introduces the central theme of appearance versus reality.

If Bergenstråhle's production is characterized by theatricality, symmetry and a subtle use of colours, Philip Saville's version, transmitted eight years later, is dynamic, cinematic and variegated. Like most British directors dealing with strindberg, Saville relies on Michael Meyer's translation.

Saville's version opens with a pre-credit sequence, based on two events that are related in the play text. The first concerns the collapse of the house the previous night. As long as the illusory child is merely mentioned – as is the case in the text – it fully retains its symbolic significance of child of man. When visualized, as in Saville's version, it can no longer be just a child; it must receive a gender. Saville turns the child into a little girl, dressed in blue. Although the link with the Young Lady is hereby provided, via the blue hyacinth associated with her, the universality indicated in the text – the child as a representative of mankind – is gone.

The collapse of the house is shown in a swift sequence in which Saville crosscuts between the collapsing house and the reactions of the people in and around it. In this way he climactically creates suspense, much as in an adventure film.

Then follows the title of the play, in trembling, ghostlike lettering combined with a picture of a nude young girl who seems to come out of the water only to be pushed back into it. This shot relates to the Old Man's crime against the Milkmaid, revealed at the ghost supper. The shot – out-of-focus, in slow motion – is accompanied by non-diegetic, eerie music. All these unrealistic effects obviously serve to suggest that we are concerned with a nightmarish inner reality: the Old Man's traumatic guilt feelings. In the pre-credits Saville shows us, moreover, two basic actions: the Student saving a little girl from being killed, and the Old Man killing a young girl. Innocence saved versus innocence killed is thus established as the central opposition in the production.

Having devoted a great number of shots to the pre-credit part, Saville begins the teleplay proper as follows:

1   *Curtain raised inside window with shutters, looking out on a square.*

2   DARK LADY *appears inside shutters. Zoom-in on her face. She looks at her nails, then stares out into the square.*

3   *Profile of* OLD MAN *with beard and glasses in FG in a wheelchair, a crutch behind it. He is reading* Dagens Nyheter. *He wears a black coat and a grey shawl and beret and has a grey plaid over his legs.*
    MILKMAID *approaches him from bluish BG with two buckets on a yoke. She wears a white-and-yellow 'folk costume' and a white bonnet. She gains superhuman size and moves off-screen L.*
    OLD MAN *turns round to frontal position. Zoom-out reveals a barrier behind him.*

4   *High angle close-up of drinking-fountain. Reflection of* MILKMAID'S *face in the still water. Water surface splashes as she pumps water into fountain.*

5   *High angle long shot of* OLD MAN. *R FG white-and-red flag of consulate. Stones of square form circular patterns.*

6   STUDENT, *dark-haired, dressed in white, up to pump and* MILKMAID, *who has put her white bonnet on pump. Blue sky behind them.*

7   STUDENT *to* MILKMAID. May I have the cup? *Pan R to* MILKMAID.
    STUDENT *to her.* What are you staring at?

8   STUDENT *to* MILKMAID. Am I so repulsive? Oh, I see. I haven't slept all night, so of course you think

9   *Close-up of* MILKMAID, *frontal.*
    STUDENT *off-screen.* I have been dissipating.

10 *Low angle close-up of* OLD MAN.
    STUDENT *off-screen.* Give me a drink of water, girl – I've earned it. I've been bandaging wounds all night, tending the injured.

11 STUDENT *alone by pump in BG,* OLD MAN *in FG.*
    STUDENT. I was there when the house collapsed yesterday evening. Now you know.

12 MILKMAID *fills cup with water from fountain and reaches it to* STUDENT.
  STUDENT. Thank you.

Although Saville by certain captions – *Bagarbod* (Bakery), *Dagens Nyheter*
(Daily News), *Kungl. Teatern* (the Royal Theatre) – suggests that the action is
set in Sweden, there is little else to verify this. Unlike Bergenstråhle's Student,
Saville's lacks a Swedish student's cap – for natural reasons, since a British audience, unfamiliar with this ethnic phenomenon, would only be confused by
an iconic sign of this kind. The Student's deviating all-white costume, apart
from indicating his purity, may suggest that he is a kind of Samaritan. That
the Milkmaid wears what looks like a German folk costume makes sense but
her yoke and water buckets turn her into a Gretchen of the early nineteenth
century rather than a milkmaid of the early twentieth. Of Strindberg's Milkmaid there remains only a maid; an essential aspect of the figure is lost. Possibly Saville wanted to universalize the play and at the same time indicate the
connection with the Samaritan woman fetching water from Jacob's well.

   Rather than in a street we find ourselves in a square, surrounded by a barrier, which may represent the border between consciousness and subcon-
sciousness. This seems indicated when the drowned Milkmaid grows to
gigantic size behind it, thereby visualizing the Old Man's growing guilt feelings. The grey stones of the square are visually linked with the materialistic
Old Man and contrasted with the blue heaven, against which the Student and
the Milkmaid are silhouetted.

   In a stage performance a director can choose between visualizing or not
visualizing the Milkmaid; in the former case we would share the Student's
point of view, in the latter – which would be quite misleading – the Old
Man's. Since Saville's version was made for the screen, he is able to present a
third alternative. Although the spectator largely shares the Student's optical
point of view – like him we see the Milkmaid – he momentarily (shot 11)
shares the Old Man's point of view. This may seem an asset but since the Student functions as our guide in the play, it is essential that we immediately identify with him. This possibility is disturbed in Saville's version of shifting
optical viewpoints.

   Some notable deviations from the play's stage directions may be due to
Saville's reliance on a target text. Thus while Strindberg's Caretaker's Wife is
"*sweeping the entrance hall,*" Saville's, presumably as a result of Meyer's incorrect rendering, is "*cleaning the front steps.*" And while Strindberg calls for
"*a couple of minutes of silence*" before the Student enters, so that the impression that the Milkmaid is, somehow, linked to the Old Man can sink in,
Saville, possibly misled by the translator's "*a few moments of silence,*" makes
the pause considerably briefer than Bergenstråhle.

In Act II Strindberg's young couple are seen in the hyacinth room in the background. In Bergenstråhle's version they do not appear at this point; instead the white marble statue behind the guests, centre, seems to represent their youthful innocence. As in his version of Act I, the arrangement is highly symmetrical. The director alternates between long shots of the five guests and medium close-ups of the speaker, the Old Man.

Bergenstråhle's production was criticized for its use of old-fashioned language. As a matter of fact, its language is varied in a considered way. Thus when the Old Man adheres to extremely formal language in his monologue – using plural forms of the verbs, for example – the impression is that of pompous solemnity, of a speech rehearsed in advance. To give his condemnation of the others the appearance of objectivity he speaks like a statute book. When his true self later comes to the fore, he reverts to a plain way of speaking. The monologue is delivered in crescendo, with the right arm raised a couple of times – in contrast to the organist who raised his left arm? – reminding us of a certain rhetorical dictator, the prime satanic figure of our time.

The emphasis in Bergenstråhle's version falls on the Mummy's speech of contrition ("we are poor human beings," etc.), delivered with the crucified Christ as background and with a strong back light turning the Mummy's hair into an aureole.

Saville's version demonstrates a very different approach. Unlike Bergenstråhle, he breaks the monologue up into a number of shots, some of which visualize what is on the minds of the characters. This is how the Colonel is revealed:

Close-up of COLONEL *with monocle.* [= mask]

Long shot of COLONEL *naked on stairs, moving away from camera.* [= hiding]

Close-up of COLONEL *looking down.* [= ashamed]

And this is a portrait of the Old Man:

Close-up of OLD MAN *breathing heavily.* [= guilt feelings, thinking of...]

Long shot of MILKMAID, *nude, swimming by a landing-stage, surrounded by green, coming out of water, approaching camera, happily smiling.*

Close-up of OLD MAN.

Long shot of landing-stage, now empty. [= Milkmaid drowned]

The two passages are linked by contrasts: the Colonel's feeling of being ashamed of his nakedness versus the Milkmaid's happy acceptance of it (relating her to the nude marble woman); his environment (stone house, stately staircase) versus her surroundings (simple wooden landing-stage, nature); his movement away from the camera versus her approaching it.

More ambiguous is the following sequence:

Low angle close-up of OLD MAN.

Long shot of YOUNG MAN *in grey suit in green meadow.*

Close-up of FIANCÉE.

Long shot of YOUNG MAN *running towards the camera.*

Close-up of FIANCÉE.

The first shot of the Young Man is inserted between close-ups of the Old Man and the Fiancée, the second one between two close-ups of the Fiancée. This indicates that he represents their remembrance of how the Old Man was once an innocent and attractive young man. Thus viewed, the shots of the Young Man are flashbacks. Alternatively, they may be seen as 'flashforwards,' visualizing the Old Man's dreams of a bright future for the Student and the Young Lady; the shots, it should be noted, accompany his statement about how he has tried to find a friend for her.

During the ghost supper the Old Man is forced to atone for his sins by hanging himself in the closet, where the Mummy has been repenting her adultery for many years. In the text this atonement begins when the Milkmaid *"appears in the hallway door, unseen by all but the* OLD MAN, *who shrinks back in horror."* This happens as the Mummy rings for Bengtsson, the only person who knows about the Old Man's crime against the Milkmaid. Bergenstråhle has the Milkmaid appear on the stairs and sink down there as if she were drowning. Saville has her appear at an earlier point, just before the Old Man imperiously strikes the table with his crutch:

1 *Low angle shot of* OLD MAN, *a big wall clock behind him with a moving pendulum. Ticking of clock. Shadows. Slow zoom-in on* OLD MAN.

2 MILKMAID *in white dress and bonnet in green meadow.*

3 *Hand of clock. Loud ticking.*

4 OLD MAN *raising his crutch.*

5 MILKMAID *coming out of water, out-of-focus, slow motion. Eerie music.*

6 OLD MAN.

7 *Zoom-in to extreme close-up of* MILKMAID, *coming out of water. A hand is pulling her down.*

8   OLD MAN *striking crutch on table.*

In the text, the Old Man's hubris culminates with his striking of the table which he compares to the striking of the clock, thereby equating himself with Fate. With Saville, on the other hand, the striking of the table is an expression of the Old Man's attempt to repress the painful memory of the drowning of the Milkmaid, visualized in shot 7, which is granted key status by being identical with the title shot. Unlike Strindberg, who has Bengtsson reveal that Hummel had the Milkmaid lured "out on to the ice to drown her," Saville offers us a more active, anonymous murderer in a summery setting.

The clock figures prominently in Saville's version, and the Mummy's stopping of it is here clearly the climax of Act II. The reversal of power is indicated by low-angle shots first of Hummel, then of the Mummy. She is dressed like a nun to illustrate her 'nunnery' existence in the wardrobe, her many years of penance.

Towards the end of Act III, as the Student speaks his sombre monologue, Bergenstråhle has him walk up the stairs right, pass in front of the organ and then walk down the stairs left, stopping under way by a mirror, by the choir and by the crucifix. He has made his pilgrimage through life and he now repeats it in quick tempo as he summarizes his negative experience of it. His movement is a spatial counterpart of the coda-like repetition of earlier motifs that his monologue signifies.

Bergenstråhle's Student does not recite "The Song of the Sun" by heart as in Act II but reads it from a book, as though he were distancing himself from it. His concluding prayer for the Young Lady is omitted; death is no "liberator" in this version. The performance ends with a long shot of Bengtsson, in black livery and with clasped hands, in front of the death screen – like a priest officiating in front of the altar. The camera tilts up to the choir and the organist; there is white light from above and plaintive singing. The ending is thus a symmetrical reversal of the opening, Bengtsson (the servant) now taking the place of the Old Man (the master); as it says in the text: "life has its ups and downs."

Saville omits "The Song of the Sun" but retains the Student's prayer. With Bergenstråhle the Student's outburst concerning virginity is uttered as he is standing next to the crucifix; by way of contiguity, "virginity" becomes associated with Christ and, obliquely, with Virgin Mary. Saville places the Student next to the nude marble statue as he utters Meyer's unfortunate rendering of this passage: "Where is virginity to be found? Or beauty? Only in flowers and trees...and in my head when I am dressed in my Sunday clothes." Since the marble statue represents Eve before the Fall, what is here suggested is rather that innocence cannot be found after the Fall. In the text the implied opposition is: nature (innocence) versus human nature (sin). Meyer obscures this with his free rendering "flowers and trees," which may well have inspired Saville to the Eden-like context in which his Student finds himself at this point.

As pointed out earlier, the text does not state that the Young Lady is dying, merely that she "*seems to be dying*," by Meyer tritely rendered as: "*has crumpled in her chair.*" If Saville's way of showing the Young Lady's 'death' seems commonplace, it may have something to do with this.

Saville ends the play by placing the Student, in white, in front of a red death screen, his back to the camera. There is a dissolve to a painting with a white figure in the centre – as though the Student had entered the picture. A zoom-out verifies that the painting is indeed Böcklin's Isle of the Dead, hanging on a wall – as it did during the pre-credits. A sudden crack in the wall causes the painting to fall down. The final shot shows it next to a candelabra on the floor. There is a pan and zoom-in on the little girl in blue whom the Student tried to save from the collapsing house in the pre-credit sequence. The freezing of the frame signals the end of the performance.

By retaining Strindberg's *Toten-Insel*, Saville may seem to follow the text more closely than most directors. Actually, his ending brings a message very different from Strindberg's. In the text it is the white-shrouded corpse in the boat – reminiscent of the white marble statue in the beginning – which represents the recently 'dead' Young Lady; it is she who is taken to a blissful afterlife – at least in the Student's imagination. In Saville's version, it is the Student himself who is taken there – while the little girl in blue (representing the Young Lady) remains among the ruins of the collapsed house. Whereas Strindberg holds the possibility open that the idea of a blessed post-existence is not merely another illusion, Saville dismisses it as just that.

Schematically the differences between the two TV productions may be summarized as follows:

	Bergenstråhle	*Saville*
Text	Source text	Target text
Changes	Slight	Moderate
Scenery	Uniform	Varied
Colour scheme	Sparse	Varied
Sound effects	Sparse	Varied
No. of shots	Low	High
Camera angles	Neutral	Spectacular
Flashbacks	None	Many

The major contrast between the two versions is one between homogeneity (Bergenstråhle) and heterogeneity (Saville). The former is in the Swedish

Molander tradition of heightened or magic realism, with religious overtones and a sparseness of effects. Saville's version – nightmarish, expressionistic, out of touch with recognizable reality – belongs rather in the Reinhardt tradition. It may seem preferable in that it utilizes specific possibilities of the TV medium – as opposed to Bergenstråhle's version. But this is a superficial criterion on a par with statements like: radio plays making the utmost use of sound effects are laudable. Or: films with a minimum of dialogue are preferable. Much more important is the question: Are the visual and verbal elements properly balanced? The lack of visual fireworks in Bergenstråhle's production means that the exceedingly compact and polysemic dialogue receives due attention; we are given time to ponder and feel the effect of the words. In Saville's version the visual elements obtrude, attract too much attention, while the verbal ones are harmed by a sometimes defective translation.

What the two directors have in common is their departure from Strindberg's ending, which neither of them apparently found ideologically attuned to our secularized time and/or to their own conviction.

Epilogue

When the Markers' *A History of Scandinavian Theatre* was published twenty-five years ago, Nora's tarantella from the first production of Ibsen's *A Doll's House* was reproduced on the jacket. When the revised version of this book appeared in 1996, Bengtsson's unmasking of the Old Man at the ghost supper in *The Ghost Sonata*, as recreated in Bergman's 1973 production, was on the front cover. The change is significant. In the twentieth century, realism in the theatre has gradually lost ground. There are many reasons for this, ranging from the impact of psychoanalysis to the arrival of screen media which are superior in reproducing surface reality. Both phenomena promote theatrical interiorization.

It is now clear that along with his earlier plays *To Damascus* and *A Dream Play*, Strindberg's *Ghost Sonata* forms a spearhead of what was to be the major theatrical trend of the century: non-illusionism, inner rather than outer reality or, as Strindberg put it, "half-reality." With *The Ghost Sonata*, Maurice Valency observes,

> Strindberg initiated a style of drama that had not before been attempted, but which had everything in common with the current trends in painting, sculpture, and music, and it presaged a most interesting development of the art of the theatre.[1]

This was, of course, recognized long ago by some of the more sensitive and foresighted people concerned with the arts. Lugné-Poë, for example, declared that "Strindberg has been the first to create this quenching atmosphere of anguish and madness in this magnificent *Ghost Sonata*."[2] He never directed the play, because "at the l'Oeuvre I hesitated in view of the difficulties and yet I loved this disconcerting and seductive piece."[3] In 1915 Rainer Maria Rilke found the play "truly fabulous" when he saw the first production of it in Germany.[4]

As is now generally recognized, Strindberg's so-called dream plays, coinciding with Freudian psychoanalysis, were the great inspiration for the German Expressionists: Hasenclever, Wedekind, Werfel, Toller, Kaiser, and others.[5] In the dream plays, Sokel notes,

> projection and embodiment of psychic forces take the place of imitation of external facts; association of ideas supplants construction of plot based on logical connection of cause and effect. The old structural principle of causal interrelation between character, incident, and action gives way to a new structural pattern, closer to music than to drama – the presentation and variation of a theme.[6]

In 1918 Pär Lagerkvist, along with Hjalmar Bergman the renewer of Swedish drama at the time, in a manifesto debunked Ibsen and declared Strindberg – and he particularly had the late Strindberg in mind – "the greatest playwright of our time."[7] The wounded and crippled characters in Lagerkvist's *The Last Man*, it has been said, "are direct descendants of Strindberg's Mummy, Old Man, etc."[8] A closer parallel is found in the same writer's allegorical *The Secret of Heaven*, where the protagonist, an innocent Young Man, enters the world, in this case literally represented by a part of the earth globe, where he is confronted with a number of human wrecks. He falls in love with an insane Young Woman who is playing the guitar – rather than the harp – and who rejects him in favour of a vulgar Dwarf. Disillusioned with life, the Young Man finally commits suicide by throwing himself from the globe.

When Kjeld Abell, who held a position in Denmark comparable to that of Hjalmar Bergman and Pär Lagerkvist in Sweden, saw Reinhardt's guest performance of *Gespenstersonate* in Copenhagen in 1920, he was "beaten black and blue" after having witnessed his "first 'modern' performance."[9] Its impact can be sensed in his dramaturgy, most clearly perhaps in *The Blue Pekingese*.

Erwin Piscator, who had played the part of the Student in 1919 and who was later to be associated with political multimedia theatre, even made a sketch for a production of *The Ghost Sonata*, published in 1921. In his view, every act should begin with cello music and the play should be acted out behind a transparent gauze. The light in Act I should first be grey and white, then white to yellow, focusing on the Old Man. In Act II there should be white light, with a green-yellow light from in front. The chairs should be unnaturally high with concave legs like those of a spider. In Act III the light should be sun-yellow. In the ending there should be light on Buddha, then darkness: "Und Gott wird abwischen alle Tränen..." (And God shall wipe away all tears). The Student, standing by the footlights, should exit as the curtain falls. Cello.[10]

In America, the leading dramatist, Eugene O'Neill, in 1924 insisted that *The Spook Sonata* be performed at the Provincetown Playhouse and declared in the theatre program:

> All that is enduring in what we loosely call "Expressionism" – all that is artistically valid and sound theater – can be clearly traced back through Wedekind to Strindberg's *The Dream Play, There Are Crimes and Crimes, The Spook Sonata*, etc.
>
> Hence, *The Spook Sonata* at our Playhouse. One of the most difficult of Strindberg's "behind-life" (if I may coin the term) plays to interpret with insight and distinction – but the difficult is properly our special task, or we have no good reason for existing.[11]

If the performance proved difficult for the young cast, it was even more so for the critics who were used to quite different fare. There was also a personal reason for O'Neill's interest in this play. As he later revealed, his semirecluse mother "had reminded him of the Mummy"[12] – which means that this figure has something in common with Mary Tyrone in *Long Day's Journey into Night*.

In 1931 Antonin Artaud, another eager supporter of Strindberg, projected a staging of *The Ghost Sonata*. The plan,[13] which never materialized, has been called "an exercise in the supremacy of the producer over the playwright."[14] In it the characters are supplemented with dolls appearing as their 'ghosts' in "moments of metamorphosis."[15] In Act I,

> three-dimensional freestanding houses lining two streets receding up a hill, but with subtly conflicting perspectives, and details picked out in unnatural clarity. Various objects – the fountain, a cornice, perhaps a window or a pot of flowers – were to function as focal points, highlit with "[-] an intense halo of light. Most would be larger than life [-] the paving stones of the street climbing in the background in sharp relief as in a cinema set."[16]

In Act III,

> the little round salon will be set up, separated from the front of the stage by a large glass comparable to those of windows in department stores, of such a kind that everything which happens behind it will be flat and as if deformed in water; and above all no noise will come from this part of the stage.[17]

The acting "should give at times the impression of slow motion in film." The Cook should be "represented by a mannequin and its speeches projected in an enormous and monotone voice through several loud speakers in such a way that it isn't possible to perceive the source exactly."[18] The ethereal mood in the hyacinth room should be effectuated through small electrical lamps installed among the hyacinths – a method later applied by Molander.

The impact of Strindberg's dream plays did not abate when absurdism became the dominant theatrical trend in the 1950s. In these plays, Esslin states,

> the shift from the objective reality of the world outside, surface appearance to the subjective reality of inner states of consciousness – a shift that marks the watershed between the traditional and the modern, the representational and the Expressionist projection of mental realities – is finally and triumphantly accomplished.[19]

Samuel Beckett saw Roger Blin's production of *The Ghost Sonata*, with Blin himself as the Student, several times in 1950.[20] Five years later Beckett dedicated his play *Endgame* to Blin in the hope that he would direct it which he also did. Although Beckett denied that he had been influenced by Strindberg, critics have found striking correspondences between Hummel and Hamm in *Endgame*.[21]

Friedrich Dürrenmatt, the author of *Play Strindberg*, considered the 1952 Zürich production of *The Ghost Sonata* "the high point of the season" and found that the play had "its strongest impact in the mythical quality of its figures."[22] Six years later he declared: "The modern theatre emanates from Strindberg: the second act of *The Ghost Sonata* has never been transcended."[23] Ward finds a striking resemblance between the first act of *The Ghost Sonata* and Dürrenmatt's *The Visit*.[24]

More striking than any of these correspondences are those between Strindberg's chamber play and some of Ingmar Bergman's films. Thus there is a nearly silent character in THE SEVENTH SEAL (the Girl) and in CRIES AND WHISPERS (Anna); like the mute Milkmaid they both incarnate what in a medieval morality play would have been called Good Deeds.[25] The setting of CRIES AND WHISPERS is a stately manor and its owner, Agnes, strikingly resembles the Young Lady. Part of the Chaplain's intercession for her once she has died has much in common with the Student's intercession for the recently dead Young Lady.[26] According to Sjöman, Bergman's planned film "The Great Picture Book" was to begin with "an old man-woman who is soon to die," and "the Old Man in the wheelchair" is still found in the script for THE SILENCE.[27] Just as *The Ghost Sonata* ends with a 'coda' – a swift recapitulation of earlier themes and an execution: the faith in a benevolent God which is a prerequisite for the Student's intercession for the Young Lady – so THROUGH A GLASS DARKLY ends with a "divine proof" – the idea that God is love – and this forms, says Bergman, "the actual *coda* in the last movement."[28] The paradisaic final visions of WILD STRAWBERRIES and CRIES AND WHISPERS relate closely to the Student's vision of a blessed Isle of the Dead. And so on.

The most interesting affinity, perhaps, concerns Bergman's interest in the formal aspects of the Strindbergian chamber play, an interest significantly coinciding with his marriage to the renowned concert pianist Käbi Laretei. "Ever since he discovered how suited the film is for what Strindberg calls 'the intimate procedure,'" Sjöman notes, "he has become the most energetic pursuer of the Strindbergian chamber play tradition."[29] And Bergman himself has declared:

> THROUGH A GLASS DARKLY and WINTER LIGHT and THE SILENCE and PERSONA I have called chamber plays. They are chamber music. That is, you cultivate a number of motifs with an extremely limited number of voices and characters. You extract the backgrounds. You place them in a kind of haze. You create a distillation.[30]

To this we might add AUTUMN SONATA which, like Strindberg's play, by its very title implies a relationship with the sonata form. In his so-called film trilogy, it has been said, the settings are Strindbergian in the sense that they "define the mental states of those who inhabit them."[31]

Bergman's life-long concern with *The Ghost Sonata* – "to me it's among the greatest works in the history of drama," he remarked in 1946[32] – is based not only on the text but also on Molander's productions, which made an indelible impression on him. In the program for his 1945 performance of *The Pelican*, he clearly stated his indebtedness to Molander, who

> has made us see the magic in Strindberg's plays. [-] Molander gives us Strindberg without additions and directorial visions, tunes in to the text, and leaves it at that. He makes us hear a poet's anguished, feverish pulse. [-] We listen to a strange, muted chamber music. [-]
>
> First it was *The Dream Play*. Night after night I stood in the wings and sobbed and never really knew why. After that came *To Damascus*, *The Saga of the Folkungs*, and *The Ghost Sonata*. It is the sort of thing you never forget and never leave behind, especially not if you happen to become a director and least of all if you, as one, direct a Strindberg drama.[33]

What was so remarkable with Molander, he later explained, was that he

> did not make any symbolic, mysterious tricks or scenographic juggleries but that he was drillingly, etchingly concrete. Whereby he conquered the magic of the Strindbergian word, the Strindbergian stage language.[34]

Whereas his own, second production of *The Ghost Sonata* was a conscious attempt to build further upon Molander's 1942 production, the third meant an independent development in a new direction:

> Then I tried to do away with the scenery as much as possible [-] eventually I thought that Molander built the stage too full. He crowded it so that it was difficult for the actors to accomplish this conspiracy between themselves and the stage.[35]

After nearly a hundred years, we can now see that irrespective of whether we think of the text or of productions based on the text, "the influence of *The Ghost Sonata* on the drama of the 20th century is boundless."[36] To understand why this is so, we need only think of the play's 'musical' structure, that is, the intricate interweaving of various thematic strands; its combination of verbal, visual and aural (musical) elements; its symbolically unsurveyable plot; its archetypal use of ages or phases in life; its employment of visionary characters; its use of questions without any clear answers; of characters as vi-

sual metaphors (the Mummy, the Cook); of pantomimic characters and si-
lences; of a character-reporter (the Old Man). In particular we may think of
its breaking down the generic barrier between novel and drama by making use
of a subjective observer and implied narratator (the Student), whose gradual
involvement in and eventual unmasking of life we are invited to share.

In his program note for this play some seventy-five years ago, O'Neill declared that "Strindberg still remains among the most modern of moderns, the
greatest interpreter in the theater of the characteristic spiritual conflicts which
constitute the drama – the blood – of our lives today."[37] He still does.

Appendix 1: Configuration chart of Strindberg's drama text

Abbreviations

DL	The Dark Lady
CW	The Caretaker's Wife
OM	The Old Man, Jacob Hummel
M	The Milkmaid (a vision)
S	The Student, Arkenholz
C	The Colonel
F	The Fiancée, Beate von Holsteinkrona
YL	The Young Lady, Adèle
D	The Dead Man (a vision)
J	Johansson
PM	The Posh Man, called Baron Skanskorg
B	The Beggars
MA	The Maid
BE	Bengtsson
MU	The Mummy, Amalia
CO	The Cook

Small letters in chart indicate silent characters.

[Act]	Conf.	SV 58	On stage
I	A	163:1	*The house façade*
	1	163:23	dl cw om
	2	163:29	dl cw om m
	3	164:7	dl cw OM m S
	4	166:8	dl cw OM S
	5	171:11	dl cw om
	6	171:13	dl cw OM S
	7	172:15	dl cw OM S c
	8	174:8	dl OM S c
	9	175:11	dl OM S c f
	10	175:28	dl cw OM S c f
	11	178:5	dl cw om s c f yl
	12	178:9	dl cw OM S c f ma
	13	179:20	dl cw OM S c f yl
	14	180:6	dl cw OM S c f yl d
	15	180:23	dl cw OM S c f yl

```
   16   181:10  dl cw OM     s c f yl          j
   17   181:27  dl cw        s c f yl
   18   182:1   DL cw        s c f yl                PM
   19   182:14  dl cw        S c f yl          J pm
   20   186:3   dl cw OM     s c f yl          j pm b
   21   186:17  dl cw OM     s c f yl ma       j pm b
   22   186:27  dl cw OM m   S c f yl ma       J pm b


II  B   188:1   The round drawing-room
   23   188:6               c  yl
   24   188:8               c  yl      J       BE
   25   190:1               c  yl      J       BE MU
   26   190:26              c  yl      J       BE
   27   192:11     OM       c  yl      J       BE
   28   193:13     OM       c  yl      j
   29   193:23     OM       c  yl
   30   194:20     OM       c  yl                MU
   31   198:20     OM       C  yl
   32   202:22     OM   S   C  yl
   33   203:24     OM   s   C f yl
   34   204:12     OM   s   C f yl      pm
   35   204:24     OM   s   C f yl      pm       MU
   36   208:3      om m s   c f yl      pm       mu
   37   208:4      om   s   c f yl      pm    BE MU
   38   208:27     OM   s   c f yl    j pm    be MU
   39   209:22          S   C F yl    J PM    BE MU


III C   211:1   The hyacinth room
   40   211:6          S c    YL                mu
   41   216:17         S c    YL                mu CO
   42   217:1          S c    YL                mu
   43   220:3          S c    YL                mu CO
   44   220:22         S c    YL                mu
   45   224:32         s c    YL             be mu
   46   224:33         s c    yl                mu
   47   224:34         s c    yl             be mu
   48   225:1          s c                      mu
   49   225:27  Böcklin's Toten-Insel
```

The following entrances (ma in 12, f in 33) and exits (S in 4, cw in 7, ma in 12, be in 45 and 46, S in 48) are not indicated in Strindberg's acting directions.

Appendix 2: Configuration chart of Bergman's 1973 production

For abbreviations, see Appendix 1.

Act	Conf.	On stage							
I	A	*The house façade*							
	1	om							
	2	om	m						
	3	om	m	c					
	4	om	m	c	dl				
	5	om	m	c	dl	cw			
	6	om	m	c	dl				
	7	om	m	c	dl		f		
	8	OM	m	c	dl		f	S	
	9	om	m		dl		f	S	
	10	OM			dl		f	S	
	11	om					f	S	
	12	OM						S	
	13	OM				cw		S	
	14	om			dl	cw			
	15	om				cw			
	16	OM				cw		S	
	17	OM			dl	cw		s	
	18	OM		c	dl	cw		S	
	19	OM		c		cw		S	
	20	OM		c	dl	cw		S	
	21	OM		c	dl			S	
	22	OM		c	dl		f	s	
	23	OM			dl		f	s	
	24	OM			dl	cw	f	S	
	25	OM			dl		f	s	
	26	OM			dl	cw	f	S	
	27	OM			dl	cw		S	
	28	OM					f	S	
	29	om				cw	f	s	
	30	OM				cw	f	S	yl
	31	om				cw	f	S	
	32	OM					f	S	

#	OM	m	c	dl/DL	cw	f	s/S	yl	d	j/J	pm/PM	b	BE	MU
33	OM					f	s	yl						
34	OM		c			f	s	yl						
35	OM					f	S	yl						
36	OM					f	S	yl	d					
37	OM					f	S	yl						
38	OM					f	s	yl		j				
39	OM			dl		f	s	yl		j				
40	OM			dl		f	s	yl		j	pm			
41	OM			dl		f	s	yl		j				
42				dl		f	s	yl						
43				DL		f	s	yl			PM			
44						f	s	yl		J				
45				dl		f	S	yl		J	pm			
46						f	S	yl		J				
47						f	S			J				
48							S			J				
49	OM						s			j		b		
50	OM				cw	f	s			j		b		
51	OM				cw	f	s	yl		j		b		
52	OM		c		cw	f	s	yl		j		b		
53	om	m	c		cw	f	s	yl		j		b		
54	om		c		cw	f	s	yl		j		b		
55	om						s	yl		j		b		
56	OM						s	yl		j				
57	OM						s			j				
58							s	yl						
59							S			J				

II   B   *The round drawing-room*

#	OM	c	yl	j/J	BE	MU
60			yl	j		
61			yl	J	BE	
62			yl	J	BE	MU
63			yl	J	BE	
64	OM		yl	J	BE	
65	OM		yl	j		
66	OM		yl			
67	OM		yl			MU
68	OM		yl			
69	OM		yl			MU
70	om	C	yl			
71	OM	C	yl			mu

```
72    om    C          S yl              mu
73    om    C          S yl    j      be mu
74    OM    C          s yl              mu
75    OM    C        f s yl
76    OM    C        f s yl      pm
77    om    C        f s yl    j pm    be
78    OM    C        f s yl    j pm    be mu
79    OM    C        f s yl      pm       mu
80    OM m c        f s yl      pm       mu
81    om m c        f s yl    j pm    BE MU
82    OM   c        f s yl    j pm    be MU
83         C        F   yl    j PM    BE MU
84                    s yl    j
85                    S yl
```

III   C   *The hyacinth room*

```
86          c          S YL              mu
87          c          S YL              mu CO
88          c          S YL              mu
89          c          S YL              mu CO
90          c          s yl           BE mu CO
91          c          S YL              mu
92          c          S YL
93          c          S yl              mu
94          C            yl              MU
```

Appendix 3: Short rehearsal diary of Ingmar Bergman's 1973 production

The information below is based on notes made during the rehearsal period, supplemented by Bergman's statements in my interview with him on 5 Jan. 1973.

31 October

First meeting between director and cast. Everybody is present in rehearsal room No. 1 on the fifth floor of Dramaten. Bergman appears in the dress he is to wear during the whole rehearsal period: brown trousers and loafers, sports shirt, dark brown, loose, knitted jacket with a collar, glasses hanging on his breast. Although now 54, he is as vital as a twenty-year-old, and has a way of infecting people around him with enthusiasm for the task at hand.

The situation is unusual. *The Ghost Sonata* has been produced on Swedish television the evening before, under the direction of Johan Bergenstråhle. Two days earlier a Marxist critic, Maria Bergom-Larsson, published a socio-political analysis of the play in *Dagens Nyheter*, Sweden's leading paper. Although some critics have found the article in agreement with the production, there is actually little evidence of this – for natural reasons, since it seems almost impossible to make the class struggle a central issue of this drama. The leading critics have been enthusiastic, and a few weeks later, Bergenstråhle is awarded the prize for the best Swedish 1972 teleplay production in colour.

What effect will the TV production have on Bergman's production in January? Will people stay away from Dramaten feeling that they have seen the play already? Or will they be curious to see another approach? The general feeling is that TV, which is not sensitive to competition the way regular theatres are, should have waited to produce this play until Bergman's stage version had been running for some time. As it is, the TV version will serve as a challenge.

Practical questions dominate the early part of the meeting. A complete rehearsal schedule has been made up in advance, but some minor changes are necessary. There will be rehearsals three or four hours a day five days a week for some ten weeks; after about six weeks the rehearsals will be public. (This will be the fifth production by Bergman to which the audience is invited at the end of the rehearsal period.)

In the second part of the meeting, Bergman gives some indication of what he will be aiming at in his production. Act III, he points out, has always been a stumbling-block on stage, not least in in his own earlier productions. Bergman:

> We must relate it organically to the preceding acts. The whole play is a dream – fairly realistic in the beginning, but growing more and more grotesque as the action develops. It is not a dream of any one of the characters, although in my Malmö production the assumption was that the Student was the dreamer – but that didn't make sense, because he is not always on the stage. No, it is the dream of Strindberg himself. Notice how we move inwards in the play from the street to the round room and from there to the hyacinth room. Strindberg takes us by the hand and we enter deeper and deeper into the dream.
>
> Everything in this production must be close to us, immediate, naked, simple. Simple costumes, hardly any make-up. The characters are not monsters but human beings. And if some of them – the Cook for example – are evil, this does not mean that they need to look evil. The point is that they are evil to the characters on the stage, and we must sense their evil nature through the reactions of these characters. We must never underestimate the audience's sensitivity to the reactions of the characters.

1 November

The scenographer, Marik Vos, has built a model of the stage. Bergman:

> One of the problems in Act I has always been that Hummel and the Student have to turn away from the audience every time the Old Man tells the Student about the people in the house. And so we don't see much of their faces, of their reactions. In this production we shall place the house – the imaginary house, that is – in the auditorium, so that Hummel and the Student constantly keep facing the audience.
>
> The people in the house will appear at either side of the proscenium arch. At the back of the stage will be two huge white concave screens, with an opening in the middle – a pair of tongs, an embrace, a womb. On these screens we shall project the scenery and the properties: houses of the turn-of-the-century type at first, later the marble statue, the clock, and so on. These things appear when they are needed, then fade out again. For the Milkmaid's appearances – she was lured out onto the ice in Hamburg – we shall project a snowfall. The stage itself will be practically empty, slightly slanting. Even the advertisement kiosk I have managed to get rid of. There must be nothing to block the action and make it heavy-going.

Later Bergman tells me: "We have few properties, very few things, nothing that can distract from the faces. The important thing is what happens to the bodies. They must make a choreographic pattern which must be completely disengaged from the room and from the scenery."

Linking the Young Lady's illness with the first symptoms of the cancer of the stomach that five years later was to end Strindberg's life, Bergman reiterates his fundamental view of the play: "The whole play [-] is a feverish dream, the product of a man with a little poisonous spot inside him which, like a foetus, slowly keeps growing – a man burning with vitality, not at all a madman, but on the contrary, an unusually wise man with a tremendous experience of life."

7 November

Act I. Screens about eight feet high have been put up. The drinking-fountain, right, is the only property. Today and the next two days everybody must get a basic idea of the blocking: stage positions, entrances, exits. Bergman gives some initial instructions from his director's chair but after a few minutes he is on the stage, demonstrating positions, movements and gestures to the actors. He likes to work very close to them, to establish a rapport with them. He will frequently put his right arm around their shoulders and walk them across the stage, while talking to them about "the spiritual blocking" of a particular passage. Rather than analyse various parts of the play, he gives short, suggestive indications.

Later, Bergman gives me his view of the relationship between director and actors:

> [-] actors are independent people, exceedingly creative, and they fare best and feel happiest if they get a chance to be creative themselves – get ideas, find out, formulate. This is a creative process of enormous importance. If the director, who has spent several months on the play before the rehearsals start, pours all his ideas about it over the actors, he paralyzes their creative faculties. If he feels that the actors themselves are about to express what he himself has intended from the beginning, he only needs to grab hold of their ideas and perhaps develop them further. If he feels that his intentions are not expressed, he can inject them through a piece of stage business or some such thing. It is very important that the actors feel that they are independently creative, and that the director is there primarily to record, to create a sense of security, to stimulate and to guarantee a certain homogeneity.

Bergman is highly disciplined, frowning on any actor who turns up even a minute late for rehearsal. And so this hardly ever happens. He demands much of his actors but even more of himself. Generally speaking, he gives much instruction during the early part of the rehersal period. Later the actors are left more to themselves. He is one of the relatively few directors who always gets a production ready in time. During rehearsals he frequently asks for silence. A faint whisper can irritate him no end. Once his assistant was even asked not to use the eraser because it might disturb the actors.

His approach is not unlike that of a conductor or a choreographer. He divides the speeches up into minute parts and indicates to the actors how each part should be intoned, so that the whole speech becomes, in effect, a varied 'melody,' rich in psychological nuances.

When the lines "OLD MAN. Are you a sportsman. STUDENT. That's my misfortune" are being rehearsed, Bergman repeats the Student's line, limping across the stage, adding: "This is my third production of the play, but I've never understood those lines."

When the Dark Lady makes inaudible conversation with the Caretaker's Wife, Strindberg does not tell us what the two are talking about. To tell the actresses to improvise some small talk would be to ignore the dramatic possibilities of their conversation. "After all," Bergman explains, "the Dark Lady is waiting in vain for a man who has made her pregnant. She is desperate. And the Caretaker's Wife, her mother, is trying to calm her."

What about the costumes? Marik Vos wants to make her designs as soon as possible, so that the seamstresses can get them ready in time. But Bergman is evasive. Instead he asks Marik to make slides for the projections, so that they can be tried out on the model stage. Bergman: "Since we can't use back projections, we must be careful that the actors do not cast shadows. They will have to keep well away from the screens. Well, we'll have to try it all out."

8 November

Act II. Four chairs are on the stage, to the right a vertical piece of wood representing the marble statue. Gertrud Fridh, who yesterday did the part of the Young Lady, now plays the Mummy, while a stand-in – a ballet dancer – does the silent part of the Young Lady. Bergman:

> The fact that the Young Lady is slowly turning into another Mummy is a fundamental idea in my production. That is what is so horrifying in the whole situation. My original idea was that the actors doing the Mummy and Hummel should play the parts of the Young Lady and the Student in the last act, but that proved technically impossible.

One of the pre-absurdist effects of the play is the parrot language spoken by the Mummy. "This language," Bergman explains, "is but an extreme form of the kind of endearing nonsense talk that you can often find between married partners. The Mummy has been brought up to please her husband, to pose before him."

"Another Nora," Gertrud exclaims. Bergman: "Exactly."

For the famous ghost supper Bergman gives the following memo:

When Hummel, in his long speech, reveals the secret signs of everyone present, the audience must be able to feel how he grows and grows, like a frog blowing himself up, while the others keep shrinking. Then comes the counter-attack from the Mummy. She gives Hummel three pricks. Now it is his turn to shrink. When he has just received the third prick, he thinks: all right, I can stand all this, just don't you start talking about the Milkmaid I've murdered. At this point the Milkmaid appears. Produced by Hummel's anguish.

For the harp accompaniment at the end of this and the following act, Bergman gives Daniel Bell, who is responsible for the sound effects, the following hint: "E flat major, only incidental notes, no melody."

9 November

Act III. From the very beginning it has been clear that Bergman wants to build the action towards this final act, so that it becomes a true climax, instead of the anti-climax it has usually been on the stage. "And this we must remember," he tells the actors,

that the Student kills the Young Lady. And that it is a frightening, horrifying scene of unmasking and murder. It corresponds to the Mummy's unmasking of Hummel in the second act, but here the scene is shorn of nearly every remnant of reality. In the second act we still have the rope with which Hummel is to hang himself. We still have the idea of apoplexy. Here it is only the fact that the Student attacks the Young Lady with frightening words, that he grabs hold of her, that he tears her dress off. And this kills her.

Bergman is describing his own version of the Student's action; with Strindberg the Lady's dress stays in place.

The change from hyacinth poetry at the beginning of the act to household worries in the middle of it is underlined in gesture, movement and intonation. The Young Lady is gradually mummified, the Student finds it increasingly hard to breathe. Bergman outlines an ending which differs from Strindberg's. Instead of having the Student express compassion for the dead girl (as in the play text), he has the Colonel and the Mummy voice their sympathy for her by giving the final part of the Student's monologue to them.

In Act II the Mummy speaks the following lines, highly central to the play as a whole: "We are poor human beings, we know that. We have erred, we have sinned, like everyone else. We are not what we seem, for at heart we are better than ourselves, since we dislike our faults." This is a speech breathing compassion for mankind. We recognize the leitmotif of *A Dream Play*: "Mankind is pitiable." Since the final lines of the play are in much the same spirit, it seems natural that these too be spoken by the Mummy. Commenting on this, Bergman tells me: "In the end, I have stressed the fact that the only thing that can give man any kind of salvation – a secular one – is the grace and compassion which come out of himself."

14 November

Act I. When Hummel takes the Student's hand, he is acting the part of a vampire, sucking the Student's blood. Bergman: "The movements must be soft, slow here – as in a dream. A quiet atrocity."

15 November

Act II. Hummel's monologue is profiled. Bergman as yet gives little instruction to Toivo Pawlo, who takes Hummel's part, but concentrates on how the other actors should react to his speech. Their heads should slowly keep sinking as he unmasks them. They should look like ashamed little children. When Hummel finally collapses, the Fiancée should titter, while the Posh Man should smile maliciously. The Mummy's "It is finished" should come as a relief to them. The final "Amen," hitherto spoken in unison, is now spoken individually. Bergman: "It mustn't be too ritualistic."

16 November

Act III. Bergman: "There must be a tension between the Student and the Young Lady from the very beginning. The first part of the act must be at once soft and charged. No physical contact between the two in the beginning, everything light, fragile."

The actress playing the part of the gigantic Cook, one of the grotesque elements of the play, is instructed: "You must work your way out of the wall terribly slowly, first a hand, then a shoulder, finally a bottom." In this way Bergman seeks to indicate the nightmarish character of the Cook, her dream reality.

In the fifteen-minute break, usually devoted to small talk about theatre experiences, Bergman indicates his idea for the colouring of the three acts: in the first, only black and grey; darkish colours in the second – "it must bleed" – and a blue haze in the third.

17 November

Rehearsal of the whole play with few interferences. Bergman wants this kind of rehearsal once a week, so that the actors can experience the play in its entirety, and feel where their acting breaks or bends.

Since yesterday he has been considering how to shape the Student's monologue at the end. When Mathias Henrikson comes to the line "To think that the most beautiful flowers are so poisonous," Bergman demonstrates to the actor how he might pull the Young Lady from her chair, drag her to the front stage, and brutally take her face between his hands while she, anguished, sinks down on her knees.

Marik Vos shows her costume designs. Bergman is playing with the idea of putting a Semitic mask on Hummel, the Mummy and the Young Lady – to indicate their blood relationship. But how will a post-Nazi audience interpret the fact that the most mephistophelian character in the play looks Jewish? Indeed, by providing Hummel with a Semitic mask – in the final production he merely wore a Jewish skull-cap – Bergman could stress his resemblance to a punishing Jehovah as well as his position as a revengeful outcast in society. Bergman later tells me: "I think it would have been more embarrassing if one did *not* dare to turn Hummel into a Jew. He is a kind of Shylock – conceived, as is Shakespeare's Jew, with a strange kind of compassion and a deep aversion at the same time."

18 November

Act III. One of the Cook's speeches – "You suck the strength out of us and we out of you" – is divided up between her and Bengtsson. In this way the class struggle, inherent in the speech, is stressed. Later, two more characters, hidden behind the screens, are to echo these lines, so that a nightmarish effect is gained: the fear among the upper classes, here represented by the Student and the Young Lady, of the revenge of the suppressed. But this experiment is soon abandoned.

19 November

Act I. So far the Caretaker's Wife has been sprinkling real spruce twigs in front of the house in the background as a token that the Consul has just died. Now she sprigs merely imaginary spruce twigs.

The beginning of the act is still problematic, still too expository. The conversation between Hummel and the Student, Bergman points out, must not be merely informative. "You must be more active, Toivo. Remember, you're a spider spinning that little fly, the Student, into your web."

23 November

Johansson's part is examined. Bergman: "When Johansson talks to the Student, he swells with self-importance. He hates his master (Hummel), but here he identifies himself with him, uses him as a weapon against the Student." To make the actor get the right feel of this, Bergman has him momentarily say "I" every time there is a "he" (referring to Hummel) in his speeches.

29 November

Act I. The Student's report about the collapse of the house the day before is shaped. Bergman: "This is an important passage. Here we have a kind of dream atmosphere." The actors who are on the stage during this passage are instructed to freeze their positions. Later the dream atmosphere is indicated also by a softening of the light around the Student. General memo from the director: "Remember, we don't play psychological theatre but something higher. The rhythm of the play is tremendously important. There are no intermediate joints here, as in Ibsen's plays, which are much easier to do."

Later Bergman points out to me that the characters in *The Ghost Sonata* abruptly oscillate between their social roles and their true human nature, between mask and face, and that this must be brought out in production: "[-] in many contexts they behave extremely grotesquely. Society and they themselves have imposed these roles on them. [-] As I experience it, we don't make caricatures of them. We combine all the time the human aspect with the grotesque one."

30 November

Bergman finds the actor doing the part of Bengtsson a little too friendly towards Johansson, his younger colleague. His advice to the actor is: "Look at his forehead, don't let your eyes sink to meet his glance."

1 December

Bergman specifies the lighting for the third act: a blue haze gradually changing into a shadowy, dead grey light. The change of light is obviously meant to visualize the Young Lady's gradual mummification.

5 December

How should the Student recite "The Song of the Sun" at the end of Act II and III? Traditionally, the actor playing the Student recites the poem in much the same way in both acts: tenderly, idealistically. Bergman wants to reserve this manner for the second act. At the end of the play the poem must be recited quite differently. "You must try to read *against* the rhythm of the poem, break up the verse," he tells Mathias Henrikson. Commenting on the poem Bergman later points out to me: "What nonsense to a modern audience, which every day witnesses how true criminals don't harbour any fear at all, and how the innocent must suffer. If the Student the second time he reads the poem feels that it turns to dust, then it seems to me meaningful."

Johansson's language is discussed. Bergman wants him to speak Stockholm slang – with all the gestures and facial expressions of a wise guy that go with it.

6 December

Act II. The scene between Hummel and the Colonel is rehearsed. Hummel's unmasking of the Colonel is purely verbal in the text. Bergman wants it, in addition, acted out. After all, we are dealing with a dream, a nightmare. Thus when the Colonel tries to call for his servant Bengtsson, Hummel throws him down onto the floor and forces him to unmask himself. (The expression "shave off your moustache" is accordingly changed into "tear off your moustache.") By this device, the scene becomes much more dynamic. Moreover, the view of the Colonel trembling, stripped of his outer paraphernalia, prostrate on the floor, provides an effective contrast to the mask – his scarlet uniform – he hides behind before and after this sequence.

7 December

Act III. At the end of the play, the Student, referring to the Young Lady, asks: "[-] where is virginity?" Is the Young Lady a virgin? The text is vague on this point. Bergman suggests the following interpretation: "His question is, intellectually, preposterous. But if you regard it as a shameful gesture, expressing the urge of a man to rape the girl he desires but who refuses him, then it makes sense." In accordance with this, Bergman has the Student violently part the Lady's thighs and put his hand against her pudenda as he asks this question.

12 December

Marik Vos is looking for an eye – possibly Strindberg's own – to be projected on the curtain between Acts II and III. The idea was, Bergman later tells me, that the eye should gradually be enlarged, so that finally the black of the eye would cover the whole curtain – "as though you were walking into some mysterious room." But the idea was given up. "I found it too arty."

Instead, a 'snowfall' – white spots moving upwards and downwards – was later projected on the curtain. "When you have looked at it for a while you get dizzy, and I thought that was rather nice."

14 December

First rehearsal on the big stage of Dramaten.

16 December

The crowd of beggars surrounding Hummel in Act II is complete. Apart from the two men who have been present all along, there are now four more men, a woman, and a little girl. The beggars are strongly differentiated.

30 December

First public rehearsal. No costumes, no make-up, no projections, only working light. But sound effects – church bells in the beginning, barrel-organ when the Dark Lady appears together with the Posh Man. This last sound, Bergman later tells me, is a little present to Harriet Andersson in remembrance of his film SAWDUST AND TINSEL, where he used the same instrument and tune and where Harriet played a lead. The Milkmaid's later appearances are accompanied by a thunder-like sound referred to as 'piano bang.' During the second act there is the stubborn tick-tock of the clock accentuating the silence.

Before the play begins, Bergman gives a short speech: "For a performance three things are necessary: a play, actors, and an audience. A performance is to an unusual extent a question of give and take. It is in your hearts, in your imagination, that this performance should take place. It takes one hour and forty minutes. It is an unusually horrid play. Have a nice time."

2 January

Lighting rehearsal. Being also a filmmaker, Bergman is more aware than most directors of the possibilities of creating special effects by means of light in the theatre. Especially in a production so devoid of scenery as this.

3 January

Costume rehearsal. Bergman is not quite satisfied with some of the costumes for Act II. "They must be more saturated, have more mystery about them. Give the sense of beetles. It's a world of insects, this!"

4 January

Photo call. Pictures of the production must be distributed well in advance of the opening.

6 January

First performance with an audience. The production is virtually finalized. During the week that remains until opening night only minor adjustments are made, and there are public performances every day. After each one Bergman, the actors and the other persons involved in the production gather in the green room to discuss the performance of that particular day. Everybody seems to have faith in this production.

Appendix 4: Transcription of Bergman's 1973 production

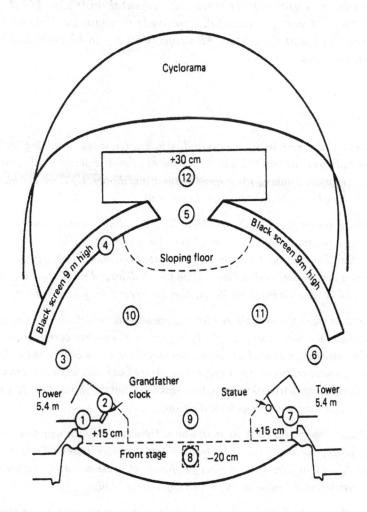

Scenery

All three acts share a scenery consisting of two black screens (4), forming a semicircle, with an opening between them (5). Behind the screens, visible through the opening, a black cyclorama. These three surfaces are used for projections. Between the screens a raised floor sloping towards the sides and the auditorium. On either side of the proscenium a raised platform. Behind these platforms black screens, set at an angle, enabling inconspicuous entrances and exits (1, 7). L a small door – the closet in Act II (2) – and two more openings

(3, 4), the latter used only once (by the OLD MAN*). R another opening (6). The floor is covered with a thick, soft, dark grey carpet. On the front stage which is lower than the main stage a trapdoor (8). Four acting areas (9-12) are marked. In FG L a grandfather clock with oriental motifs, in FG R a white marble statue of a young, beautiful, semi-nude woman. Projections of palm twigs on the clock and the statue. All projections are in black-and-white and slightly out of focus.*

Act I

A   *Projection on the screens of a beautiful, white* art nouveau *building and on the cyclorama of part of a church. L and R (at 3 and 6) a banister of silver-coloured brass. R (at 11) a grey street drinking-fountain with pump and dipper. L FG (at 1) a black chair. White working light. Dull chiming of church bells.*

1   OLD MAN *is sitting in his black wheelchair at 10 reading a newspaper. He has white hair, moustache and beard and wears glasses. He is dressed in a black overcoat with a velvet collar, black striped trousers, black button-up boots with light grey gaiters, black-green neckerchief with a diamond tie-pin. A diamond ring is on his little finger. On his head he wears a black skull-cap, over his knees a grey, checked rug.*

2   MILKMAID *in from 5 with milk bottles in wire baskets, which she puts down by the drinking-fountain. She wears a simple, light grey, small-checked cotton dress, a peaked cap of the same material, a white apron, grey stockings, black boots, and a black purse by the belt. She wears her hair in a single plait.* OLD MAN *looks anxiously around, tucks the rug around him.* MILKMAID *up to the drinking-fountain, mirrors her face in its water, takes off her cap and hangs it on the pump.*

3   COLONEL *in from 7, his back to auditorium. He wears a black wig and a black silk dressing-gown, reaching down to his feet. He pats statue on its behind and starts scrutinizing it.* MILKMAID *dries sweat from her forehead, washes her hands, arranges her hair, mirroring herself in water, then puts cap on her head.*

4   DARK LADY *in from 5, walks back and forth in upstage opening, looks around. She wears a dark-grey, almost black silk coat, underneath it a high-collared dark grey chiffon dress, a huge hat with roses and crape, dark-grey gloves, and a black parasol. When she moves, the hem of a bright red petticoat can be glimpsed. Her hair is chestnut red.*

5   CARETAKER'S WIFE *in from 3 with a laurel bush. She is poorly dressed in a grey skirt, grey blouse, grey-black knitted vest, a black kerchief on her head, slippers. She stops, looks at* DARK LADY, *out at 5.*

6   MILKMAID *presses pump, drinks from dipper.*

7   FIANCÉE *in from 1, sits down on chair, looks at an imaginary gossip mirror, starts to knit. She wears a black-lilac silk dress of the 1880s, a black thin lace shawl and a small black lace cap. Her hair is grey.*

8   STUDENT *in from 5. He has a reddish blond moustache and beard, glasses. He wears a light-grey linen jacket, grey striped waistcoat, a white, open shirt, grey canvas shoes, everything somewhat torn and dirty. His L hand is bandaged. He lacks headgear. He walks straight up to drinking-fountain.*

STUDENT. May I have the dipper? OLD MAN *startles, looks R.*

MILKMAID *hugs dipper to her.* Haven't you finished yet?

She looks terrified at him.

OLD MAN *to himself.* Who's he talking to?

STUDENT. What are you staring at?...Do I look so terrible?

OLD MAN *to himself* Fh.,.I can't see anyone.

STUDENT. Well, I didn't get any sleep last night. I suppose you think I was out living it up. MILKMAID *as before.* Drinking punch, eh?

OLD MAN. Is he mad?

STUDENT *breathes on* MILKMAID. Do I *smell* of punch? MILKMAID *as before.* I haven't shaved, I know. *Touches his chin.* MILKMAID *looks down.* Give me a drink of water, girl. I deserve it. OLD MAN *takes off his glasses.* MILKMAID *is immobile.* Well. Then I'll have to tell you that I've been binding up wounds. MILKMAID *looks up.* COLONEL out at 7.

9   STUDENT. and keeping watch over the sick all night. I was there, you see, when the house collapsed last night...Now you know. OLD MAN *puts back his glasses.* MILK-MAID *presses pump, fills dipper and hands it to* STUDENT. Thanks! *Drinks, hands dipper back to* MILKMAID. Will you do me a big favour? *Pause.* The thing is, my eyes are inflamed, as you can see. *Takes off his glasses.* I've been handling the injured and the dead. So I can't safely touch my eyes. Would you take my clean handkerchief, moisten it in the fresh water and...bathe my poor eyes?...Would you?...Would you be my good Samaritan? *Sits down on fountain.* MILKMAID *smiles cautiously, takes handkerchief from his pocket, holds it under pump, bathes his eyes, and puts back his glasses.* Thank you, my friend. *Takes out a coin and gives it to her.* MILKMAID *shakes her head, takes a step back. The chiming subsides.* For...forgive my thoughtlessness but MILKMAID *curtsies.* I'm not quite awake. MILKMAID *takes up wire baskets, puts on cap and exits at 6.*

10 STUDENT *looks after her, takes out handkerchief and dries his hands.*

OLD MAN. Excuse my intrusion. I heard you were caught up in the accident last night. I've just been reading about it in the paper.

STUDENT. Is it in already?

OLD MAN. Yes, the whole thing. Your picture too. But they regret they didn't learn the name of the brave student.

STUDENT *rises*. Really? *Up to* OLD MAN, *looks at portrait*. Yes. That's me. Well?

OLD MAN. Whom were you talking to just now?

STUDENT *moves away from* OLD MAN. Eh...Didn't you see?

OLD MAN. Is it STUDENT *stops*. impertinent to ask...get to know...your name?

STUDENT. What's the point? I don't like publicity. No sooner do they praise you than they find fault with you. Yes, the art of belittling has been developed to such a magnitude...besides, I don't ask for any reward. *Further away from* OLD MAN.

OLD MAN. Wealthy perhaps? DARK LADY *out L at 5*.

11 STUDENT *stops*. Not at all. Quite the contrary. I'm extremely poor. *Is about to leave*. FIANCÉE *out at 1*.

12 OLD MAN. One moment! STUDENT *stops*. I think I've heard that voice before. I had a friend when I was young who couldn't say window but always said...winder. I've only met one person with that pronunciation and that was him. And now you. Are you related to Mr Arkenholz, the merchant, by any chance?

STUDENT. He was my father.

OLD MAN. The ways of fate are strange. I saw you as a little child, in exceedingly difficult circumstances.

STUDENT. Yes, they say I came into the world in the midst of a bankruptcy.

OLD MAN. Quite so.

STUDENT *irritated*. May I ask *your* name?

OLD MAN. I'm Hummel, Company Director.

STUDENT. Are you...? *Looks away, sulkily*. Then I remember.

OLD MAN. You've often heard my name mentioned in your family, have you?

STUDENT. Yes!

OLD MAN *nods*. Perhaps mentioned with a certain disapproval? STUDENT *remains silent*. OLD MAN *laughs*. Yes, I can imagine. I can...I suppose they said I was the one who ruined your father? All those who've ruined themselves with foolish speculations always find themselves ruined by the person they couldn't fool. *Harshly.* But the fact is that your father deprived me of 17,000 crowns, my total savings at the time.

STUDENT. It's strange how stories can be told in two such contrary ways.

OLD MAN. You surely don't think I'm lying?

STUDENT *aggressively.* What am I to think? My father didn't lie!

OLD MAN *harshly.* That's very true. A father never lies. *Softly.* But I'm a father, too. Consequently...

STUDENT *suspiciously.* What are you driving at?

OLD MAN. I saved your father from destitution. He repaid me with all the terrible hatred that debt of gratitude breeds. He taught his family to slander me.

STUDENT. But perhaps you made him ungrateful by poisoning your help with unnecessary humiliation.

OLD MAN. Well...all help is humiliating, young man.

STUDENT. What do you want of *me*?

OLD MAN. No, no, no...I do not demand the money. But if you'll do me some small favours, I'll be well repaid. You see *Pointing to his legs.* I'm a cripple. Some say it's my own fault. Others blame my parents. I myself tend to believe that it is life itself with all its snares. For if you avoid one snare, you walk right into the next. However...I can't run up stairs, can't ring doorbells. So I say to you...help me!

STUDENT. What can I do?

OLD MAN. First of all, push my chair so I can read the playbills. I want to see what they're putting on tonight.

STUDENT *takes a step towards* OLD MAN, *then stops.* Don't you have a man with you?

OLD MAN. Yes, but he's running an errand. He'll soon be back. *Snaps his fingers.* STUDENT *up to* OLD MAN, *pushes wheelchair towards the drinking-fountain.* Are you a medical student?

STUDENT. No, I study languages, but actually I don't know what I'm going to be.

OLD MAN. Oh. Do you know mathematics?

STUDENT. Yes, reasonably. *They have arrived at an imaginary advertising column at 6.*

OLD MAN. That's good! Would you want a job, perhaps?

STUDENT. Yes, why not?

13 CARETAKER'S WIFE *in from 6 with a black watering-can which she fills at pump.*

OLD MAN Good! *Snaps his fingers, delightedly.* They're giving *The Valkyrie* as a matinée. *Turns wheelchair and rolls it towards 10.* Then the colonel and his daughter will be there. And since he always sits at the end of the sixth row, I'll put you next to him. Go into that telephone kiosk, *Points R.* will you, and book a ticket for row six, number 82!

STUDENT *surprised and delighted.* Am I to go to the opera this afternoon?

OLD MAN. Yes! And if you obey me, you'll fare well! I want you to be happy...rich...and honoured. Your début yesterday as the brave rescuer will make you famous tomorrow. Then your name will be worth a great deal.

STUDENT *goes to telephone kiosk, merrily.* What a strange adventure.

OLD MAN. Are you a sportsman?

STUDENT. Yes, that's my misfortune.

OLD MAN *pointing knowingly.* It will become your fortune! Telephone now! STUDENT *out at 6.*

14 DARK LADY *in from 5, goes up to* CARETAKER'S WIFE *at fountain. They whisper to one another.* DARK LADY *takes out a handkerchief.* OLD MAN *turns wheelchair around, begins to read paper, takes up a cigarette and starts to smoke.*

Faint barrel-organ music. DARK LADY *crying out at 5.*

15 CARETAKER'S WIFE *remains at fountain, then begins to water laurels in front of house in BG.*

16 STUDENT *in from 6, sits down on fountain, takes off his glasses.*

OLD MAN *laughing heartily.* Ha, ha, ha...Done?

STUDENT. It's done. *Wipes his eyes with handkerchief.*

OLD MAN *looking upwards towards auditorium.* Do you see this house? *Barrel-organ music fades away.*

STUDENT *looking upwards towards auditorium, dreamily.* Yes, I've certainly noticed it. I walked by here yesterday when the sun shone in the windows. Imagining all the beauty and luxury inside, I said to my companion: "Fancy having an apartment there four flights up, a beautiful young wife, two pretty little children...And a private income of 20,000 crowns."

OLD MAN *delighted, sentimentally.* Did you say that? Did you say that? There you are! I too love this house.

STUDENT *suspiciously*. Do you speculate in houses?

OLD MAN. Well...yes! But not in the way you think.

STUDENT. Do you know those who live there?

17 DARK LADY *in from 5, with a handkerchief in her hand. She has a whispering conversation with* CARETAKER'S WIFE *upstage*.

OLD MAN. All of them. At my age, you know everybody, their fathers and forefathers. You're always related to them in some way. I just turned eighty, *Meaningfully*. but no one knows me...really.

18 COLONEL *in from 7. He is dressed in a black-brown frock coat and black trousers and carries a riding-whip. He keeps polishing his nails*.

OLD MAN. I take an interest in people's destinies. *Lightly*. Look, there's the Colonel whom you'll be sitting next to this afternoon.

STUDENT. Is that the Colonel? I don't understand any of this, but it's like a fairy tale. COLONEL *puts nail-file away*.

OLD MAN. My whole life is a book of fairy tales, young man. COLONEL *turns towards statue, bows to it*. Though the tales are different, they all hang together on a thread, and the leitmotif recurs regularly.

STUDENT *up to* OLD MAN. But...who's the marble statue in there?

OLD MAN. It's his wife, of course. DARK LADY *out at 5*.

19 STUDENT. Was she that wonderful?

OLD MAN. Well...yes...Yes!

STUDENT. Tell me! COLONEL *ties a handkerchief to his riding-whip*.

OLD MAN. We can't judge a human being, my dear boy! COLONEL *dusts statue with handkerchief*. But if I tell you that he beat her, that she left him, came back, remarried him, and that she is now sitting in there like a mummy and worships her own statue...then you'll no doubt think I'm crazy.

STUDENT. I don't understand. COLONEL *shakes handkerchief*.

20 DARK LADY *in from 5, has a whispering conversation with* CARETAKER'S WIFE *upstage*.

OLD MAN. I imagine not. COLONEL *turns towards auditorium, puts down his handkerchief*. There *Points*. is the hyacinth window. That's where his daughter lives...She's out riding but will soon be back home. COLONEL *circumstantially produces a letter*.

STUDENT *walks around wheelchair.* But...who's the dark lady talking with the care-taker's wife?

OLD MAN. Well, that's a little complicated, but it has to do with the dead man. You see *Points.* the white sheets up there.

STUDENT. Who was he? COLONEL *reads letter.*

OLD MAN. He was a human being...like us...*Aggressively.* But what was most obvious was his vanity...If you were a Sunday child, you'd soon see him come out of that door *Points to 3.* to look at the consulate's flag at half mast. He was a consul, you see. He liked crowns, lions, plumed hats, and coloured ribbons. CARETAKER'S WIFE *out at 3.*

21 DARK LADY *stands immobile upstage.*

STUDENT *walks back to wheelchair.* You mentioned Sunday child. Well, they say *I* was born on a Sunday. *Pause.*

OLD MAN. Really!...You are? COLONEL *puts down letter.* I almost knew. I saw it in the colour of your eyes. Then you can see what others can't. Have you noticed that?

STUDENT. I don't know what others see, but sometimes...*Covers his eyes with his hand.* Well, one doesn't talk about that.

OLD MAN *eagerly whispering.* Yes, yes, yes, yes, yes, yes. I was almost sure! COLONEL *stands immobile, with crossed arms.* But you can tell me...because I...I understand such things. *White working light fades away. Cold light on* STUDENT.

STUDENT. Yesterday, for example. I was drawn to that obscure little back street where the house later collapsed...I got there and stopped in front of the building, which I had never seen before...Then I noticed a crack in the wall, heard the joists creak. I ran for-ward and grabbed hold of a little child who was walking below the wall...The next moment the house collapsed...*I* was safe but...in my arms where I thought I had the child...*Sighs.* was nothing.

OLD MAN *whispers.* Well, I must say...Indeed I...thought that... *Beckons to* STUDENT, *pulls him close.* Te...tell me. Why did you gesture just now at the fountain? And talk to yourself?

STUDENT. Didn't you see the milkmaid I was talking to? OLD MAN *startles. Pause.*

OLD MAN *quietly.* Milkmaid?

STUDENT. Of course. The one who handed me the dipper. *Moves away from* OLD MAN.

OLD MAN. Really? So that's how it is?

22 FIANCÉE *in from 1.*

OLD MAN. Well, I can't see. *Threateningly.* But I can do other things. FIANCÉE *sits down on chair.* STUDENT *moves further away from* OLD MAN. COLONEL *out at 7.*

23 *White working light.*

OLD MAN *delighted.* But lo...look at the old woman in the window! STUDENT *up to* OLD MAN. DARK LADY *takes a few steps back and forth.* Do you see her?...Good! She was my fiancée once, sixty years ago...I was twenty then...Don't be afraid. She doesn't recognize me. *Nods smiling towards* FIANCÉE. We see each other *every* day FIANCÉE *smiles back.* but that doesn't affect me, not in the least. Even though we vowed eternal faithfulness to each other then. Eternal!

STUDENT *cheerfully.* Oh how foolish you were in those days! We don't talk about things like that with our girls nowadays.

OLD MAN *mildly ironical.* Forgive us, young man. We didn't know any better...Can you see that that old woman once was young and beautiful?

STUDENT. It doesn't show. But yes, she has an attractive way of looking. OLD MAN *takes up a cigarette case.*

24 CARETAKER'S WIFE *in from 3 with a basket, moves R.*

STUDENT. I don't see her eyes.   *Who's!? What is happening?*

OLD MAN. The caretaker's wife. CARETAKER'S WIFE *out at 6.*

25 OLD MAN. The dark lady over there, that's her daughter by the dead man. And that's why her husband got his job as caretaker. *Takes up a cigarette.*   *Dark Lady is the daughter of the caretaker's wife*

26 CARETAKER'S WIFE *in from 6 with duster and polish, starts to polish brass banister R.*

OLD MAN *delighted.* But the dark lady has a suitor who's posh and expects to get rich. He's about to get divorced, you see, from his wife, who offers him a stone house to get rid of him. And the posh suitor is the son-in-law of the dead man, whose bedclothes you can see being aired up there on the balcony...Complicated, isn't it?

STUDENT. Yes, it's terribly complicated.

OLD MAN. Yes, so it is, inwardly and outwardly. Though it looks simple.

STUDENT. But who was the dead man then?

OLD MAN. You asked just now, and I answered. If you could look around the corner *Points towards 6.* to the service entrance... mm...you'd see a crowd of poor people that he helped...when he felt like it.

STUDENT. He was a charitable man then? DARK LADY *out at 5.*

27 *Strong white sunlight on front stage.*

OLD MAN. Yes...sometimes. *Lights cigarette.*

STUDENT. Not always?

OLD MAN. No!...People are like that! CARETAKER'S WIFE *out at 6.*

28 OLD MAN *blows out match, feebly.* Ah...push my chair...so it gets into the sun...I'm terribly cold. STUDENT *pushes wheelchair to 9.* When you're never...up and about, your blood congeals. *Nonchalantly.* I'll die soon. That I know. *Ominously.* But before that, I have a few things to do. *Stubs cigarette, appealingly.* Take my hand and feel how cold I am.

STUDENT *takes* OLD MAN'S *hand.* That's extraordinary! I...*Backs away.*

OLD MAN *quietly, passionately, with a feeble look at* STUDENT. Don't leave me. I'm tired. I'm alone. I haven't always been like this...you understand? I have an endless life behind me...endless!...I have made people unhappy *Spitefully.* but they have made me unhappy...the one will cancel out the other. *Leans towards* STUDENT. But before I die, I want to see *you* happy. Our destinies are entwined through your father...and other things.

STUDENT *anguished, feebly.* Let go of my hand! You're...you're taking my strength away! You're freezing me! OLD MAN *lets his hand loose.*

STUDENT *looks at his hand.* What do you want?

29 CARETAKER'S WIFE *in from 3.*

30 YOUNG LADY *in from 5. She has rich, beautiful black hair. She is dressed in a light-grey riding habit (with a skirt), top hat in light-grey velvet, grey-white blouse with a soft bow, gloves, riding-whip.*

OLD MAN *still looking at* STUDENT. Patience. You'll see and understand. *White working light.* There comes the young lady.

CARETAKER'S WIFE *and* YOUNG LADY *whisper with one another at 10.* STUDENT *approaches* YOUNG LADY. The colonel's daughter.

OLD MAN. Daughter? Do you see her?...Have you ever seen such a masterpiece?

STUDENT *pointing.* She's like the marble statue in there.

OLD MAN *indifferently.* Yes, of course, that's her mother. YOUNG LADY *leaves* CARETAKER'S WIFE, *walks towards 6.* CARETAKER'S WIFE *curtsies.* YOUNG LADY *walks past* STUDENT, *glances quickly at him.*

STUDENT. You're right. *Follows* YOUNG LADY *with his glance.* YOUNG LADY *out at 6.*

31 STUDENT. Never did I see such a woman of woman born. CARETAKER'S WIFE *out at 5.*

32 STUDENT. Happy the man who may lead her to altar and home. *Puts his hands to his face, crying.*

OLD MAN *nods. You* can see it...Not everyone sees her beauty...Well, so it is written...*Mildly.* Are you crying?

STUDENT *sobbing.* Before what's hopeless there's only despair!

OLD MAN *whispers passionately.* But I can open doors and hearts, if only I have an arm to do my will...Serve me, and you shall have power!

STUDENT *lowers his hands.* Is this a pact? Am I to sell my soul?

OLD MAN. Sell nothing!...*With quiet passion.* You see, I have taken all my life. Now I have a longing to give, give, give! But no one wants to receive!...I'm rich, very rich. I have no heir. *Spitefully.* Yes, one rascal who torments the life out of me. *Gropes for* STUDENT, *appealingly.* Be like a son to me. Inherit me while I'm alive. Enjoy life so I see it...at least from a distance!

STUDENT. What shall I do?

OLD MAN. First, go and hear *The Valkyrie!*

STUDENT. That is already settled. What else?

OLD MAN. Tonight you'll be sitting *Points.* in there in the round room.

STUDENT. How am I going to get in there?

OLD MAN. Through *The Valkyrie!*

STUDENT. But why have you chosen me of all people as your medium? Did you know me before?

33 YOUNG LADY *in from 7. She wears a hyacinth-blue, high-collared chiffon dress, a gold bracelet and a necklace with a crucifix. Her hair is loosely plaited. She is breathing at imaginary hyacinths.* STUDENT *up to* YOUNG LADY, *looks at her.*

OLD MAN *laughing.* Yes, of course! I've had my eyes on you for a long time...*Looks at* YOUNG LADY. Ah look, there *is* my little girl. Look at her, ha-ha! She's talking to the flowers. Isn't she like the blue hyacinth herself? YOUNG LADY *is watering imaginary hyacinths with an imaginary watering-can.* Now she gives them a drink, only pure water. They transform the water into colours and fragrance.

34 COLONEL *in from 7 with a newspaper.*

OLD MAN. Here comes the Colonel with the paper! COLONEL *and* YOUNG LADY *read paper.* He's showing her the collapsed house. *Cold light on 3.* He's pointing to your picture. YOUNG LADY *takes paper, looks at picture, looks at* STUDENT, *turns to* COLONEL. *Delighted.* Aah...She is not indifferent... She's reading about your achievement. COLONEL *and* YOUNG LADY *smile at each other. Worriedly.* I think it's getting cloudy. What if it should rain? Then I'd be in a nice mess if Johansson doesn't get back soon. COLONEL *gets paper back, caresses* YOUNG LADY'S *cheek, out at 7.*

35 YOUNG LADY *looks again at* STUDENT, *then resumes her business with imaginary hyacinths.* FIANCÉE *rises and closes her imaginary window.*

OLD MAN. Now my fiancée's closing her window...Seventy-nine years old...The gossip mirror's the only mirror she uses, because in that she doesn't see herself, only the outside world, and in two directions. But the world can see *her.* She hasn't thought of that. STUDENT *turns away from* YOUNG LADY. *She and* FIANCÉE *freeze their positions.* A beautiful little old woman, for that matter. *Dull chiming of church bells.*

STUDENT *looks terrified towards 3, backs R.* Good God! What do I see?

OLD MAN *looking at* STUDENT. *What* do you see?

STUDENT *whispers terrified.* Don't you see in the doorway?...The dead man!

OLD MAN *looks towards 3.* I see nothing. But I expected this. Tell me!

36 DEAD MAN *in from 3. He is grey-haired, has unnaturally red cheeks, wears tails with many gaudy medals.*

STUDENT. He's going out into the street. DEAD MAN *stops at 10, turns to auditorium, his glance turned upwards.* Now he's turning his head and looking at the flag.

OLD MAN. What did I say? He'll count the wreaths too. And read the calling cards. DEAD MAN *takes up a monocle.* Woe to anyone who's missing!

STUDENT. Now he walks towards the corner. DEAD MAN *out at 6.*

37 FIANCÉE *sits down again.* YOUNG LADY *begins to rake in imaginary flower plots.*

OLD MAN. He's going to count the poor ones at the service entrance...The poor are very decorative: "Accompanied by the blessings of many." *Chiming subsides. Aggressively.* But he won't get my blessing! Between you and me, he was a big scoundrel.

STUDENT. But charitable.

OLD MAN *aggressively.* A charitable scoundrel, who was always thinking of a beautiful funeral...When he felt the end approaching, he cheated the state of *Pounces his hand on arm of chair.* 50,000 crowns!

38 JOHANSSON *swiftly in from 5, stops at 10. He wears a brown moustache and is dressed in a threadbare black suit, ditto striped waistcoat, lace-up boots, and bowler hat. A dirty bandana is in his rear pocket.*

OLD MAN. And now his daughter's involved in another man's marriage and is wondering about the inheritance...And he, the scoundrel, hears everything we say. Serves him right! JOHANSSON *dries his forehead and sweat-band of his hat, clears his throat.* Ah well, there *is* Johansson!...Report. STUDENT *and* YOUNG LADY *look at each other.* JOHANSSON *whispers during following speech in* OLD MAN's *ear.* Not at home? Well, *Puts his elbow against* JOHANSSON. you're a fool!...The telegraph?

39 DARK LADY *in from 5, stands immobile upstage.* Nothing!...Go on!...Six o'clock tonight? That's excellent! Special edition too? JOHANSSON *hands him special edition, takes up a notebook.* Oh yes. Let's see. *Holds a magnifying glass in front of paper.* Let's see...let's see. *Laughs.* Ha-ha-ha-ha! With his full name! Arken...born... parents.... It's excellent, quite excellent this! YOUNG LADY *puts her hand to her face, resumes her business with hyacinths.* I think it's beginning to rain....Didn't he want to?

40 POSH MAN *in from 3. He wears an elegant, grey-black overcoat, black top hat with a crape band, white neckerchief, pointed button-up boots, black gloves.*

OLD MAN. Well, then he must! *Ironically.* There comes the posh man! Push me around the corner, Johansson JOHANSSON *puts his hat on.* POSH MAN *out at 3.*

41 OLD MAN. so I can hear what the poor people are saying...Hurry up now! Hurry up! JOHANSSON *starts pushing wheelchair.* OLD MAN *slaps* STUDENT, *pointing.* And Arkenholz, you wait for me here! Understand! *Faint barrel-organ music.* Hurry up now! JOHANSSON *pushes* OLD MAN *out at 6.*

42 STUDENT *stands looking at* YOUNG LADY, *who smiles and quietly hums to tune of barrel-organ.*

43 POSH MAN *in from 5 L, passes by* DARK LADY, *stops at 10, takes out a watch.* DARK LADY *follows him. They hold a whispering conversation for a moment.*

POSH MAN *irritated.* Well, what can we do about that?...We'll have to wait.

DARK LADY. I can't wait!

POSH MAN. Is that the way it is? Then go to the country!

DARK LADY *screaming.* No I don't want to. *Crying.*

POSH MAN. Come this way! *Seizes her arm.* Or they'll hear what we're saying. POSH MAN *and* DARK LADY *out at 3.*

Is this the first anyone besides Student + Old Man have actually spoken?

44 JOHANSSON *in from 6, making notes. Goes to fountain, clears his throat. To* STUDENT. My master asked you, sir, not to forget that other matter!

45 POSH MAN *and* DARK LADY *in from 5, stop upstage, whisper inaudibly to one another.*

STUDENT. Listen! JOHANSSON *turns to* STUDENT. Tell me first, who *is* your master?

JOHANSSON. Well, he's an awful lot...And has been everything.

STUDENT. Is he sane?

JOHANSSON. Well, what's *that*?...All his life he has been looking for a...Sunday child...he *says*, but...that need not be true.

STUDENT. What does he want? Is he greedy?

JOHANSSON. He wants power. YOUNG LADY *begins to collect imaginary withered flowers in her hand.* JOHANSSON *up to* STUDENT. All day long he rides about in his waggon like...the god Thor. *Laughs.* He looks at houses, tears them down, opens up streets, settles squares...this and that. But...he breaks into houses too. He creeps in through windows, plays havoc with people's fates, kills his enemies, and never forgives. *Seizes* STUDENT'S *arm and leads him to 9. Confidentially.* Can...mm...you imagine, sir, that the limping little fellow has been a Don Juan POSH MAN *and* DARK LADY *out at 5 R.*

46 JOHANSSON. even though he has always lost his women?

STUDENT. How can that be?

JOHANSSON. Well, he's so sly he gets them to leave when he's got tired of them. *Grinning.* He-he-he. However *Looks worriedly around.* he's like a horse thief in the human market. He steals people *Points meaningfully.* in many ways...Well, well...He has stolen me literally out of the hands of justice. *Takes off his hat, dries sweat-band with his bandana.* Well, I'd made a blunder...see...which only he knew about. And instead of having me locked up, he made me his slave. Yes, I slave for my food...which isn't the best.

STUDENT. What does he want to do in this house?

JOHANSSON. Well, I don't want to say! It's so complicated.

STUDENT *moving towards 5.* I think I walk away from all this.

YOUNG LADY *drops her bracelet through imaginary window.*

JOHANSSON *takes a few steps back.* Look, the young lady dropped her bracelet through the window! YOUNG LADY *sighs.* STUDENT *slowly up to her.* JOHANSSON *puts his hat on his head and a cigar butt in his mouth.* STUDENT, *kneeling, picks up bracelet and hands it to* YOUNG LADY. *Their hands touch for a moment.* YOUNG LADY *quickly out at 7.*

47 JOHANSSON *up to* STUDENT. So...You're thinking of leaving...Well, that isn't as easy as you think once *he* has his net over your head. FIANCÉE *out at 1*.

48 JOHANSSON. And he fears nothing between heaven and earth...Yes, one thing, or rather...one person.

STUDENT. Who? Maybe I know!

JOHANSSON. How can *you* know?

STUDENT. I guess!...Is it a little milkmaid he's afraid of?

JOHANSSON *to himself*. He always turns away when he meets a milk cart...And he talks in his sleep. It seems he was in Hamburg once.

STUDENT. Can you believe this man?

JOHANSSON. You can believe everything and anything...about him!

STUDENT. What's he doing *Pointing*. round the corner now?

JOHANSSON *slowly walking towards the fountain*. He's listening to the poor people...Sows a little word, picks out one stone at a time until the house collapses...figuratively speaking...You see, I'm an educated man and have been a bookseller. *Takes off one shoe and dips his foot in fountain*. STUDENT *moves towards 5*. You going now?

STUDENT *to 10*. I don't want to be ungrateful...This man saved my father once. And now...well now he's only asking a small favour in return.

JOHANSSON. Oh, what's that?

STUDENT. I'm to see *The Valkyrie*.

JOHANSSON. He-he. I don't understand that at all...But he's always up to something...Look...now he's talking to that policeman. *Dries his foot with bandana*. Yes, he always keeps in with the police. He...makes use of them. He...gets them involved, binds them with false promises and prospects. While pumping them...You'll see he'll be received in the round room before nightfall. *Rises*.

STUDENT. What does he want there? What is there between him and the colonel?

JOHANSSON. Well. I can guess, but I don't know! You'll no doubt find out when you get there! *Takes up a pocket-watch and looks at it*.

STUDENT *walks past* JOHANSSON. I'll never get in there!

JOHANSSON. That depends on you! *Puts pocket-watch back*. Go to *The Valkyrie*.

STUDENT. Is that the way?

JOHANSSON. Yes, since *he* said so. *Moves to 10, pointing towards 5.* Look at him, look at him, in his battle waggon, drawn in triumph by the beggars, who won't get a penny as reward, just a hint of something nice at his funeral! *Slaps* STUDENT *on his behind, cuts a caper, laughs spitefully.*

49 OLD MAN *in from 5, kneeling in his wheelchair, drawn by two* BEGGARS, *accompanied by six others, up to 9.* BEGGARS *all wear grey-black clothes. Among them can be distinguished a discharged accountant, an Italian with a barrel-organ on his back, a longshoreman, an invalid, a female street singer, and a little girl.* JOHANSSON *straightens up and venerably takes off his hat.* STUDENT *backs R.* OLD MAN *throws out a lot of silver coins.* BEGGARS *try desperately to collect as many as possible for themselves.*

OLD MAN. Hail to the noble youth STUDENT, *embarrassed, protests.*

50 FIANCÉE *in from 1.* CARETAKER'S WIFE *in from 3.*

OLD MAN. who, in spite of danger to his own life, saved many

51 YOUNG LADY *in from 7.*

OLD MAN. during yesterday's disaster! Hail Arkenholz! JOHANSSON *animates* BEGGARS.

52 COLONEL *in from 7.*

OLD MAN *claps his hands.* Clap your hands, citizens! OLD MAN, YOUNG LADY, FIANCÉE, CARETAKER'S WIFE, *and* BEGGARS *raise right arm.*

COLONEL *raises his hands as though to clap.* JOHANSSON *raises his bowler hat.* It's Sunday, of course, but the ass in the pit and the ear in the field absolve us. *White light disappears. Cold light on* OLD MAN *and* STUDENT. *Façade projections grow dark.* And though I'm no Sunday child ALL *begin to lower their arms.* I possess both the spirit of prophecy *Dull chiming of church bells.* and the gift of healing, for I once summoned a drowned person back to life...It was in Hamburg...one Sunday morning like this one. *Projection of a stone wall on screens and on cyclorama. Cold light on 8. Dull 'thunder clap.'*

53 MILKMAID *up from 8. Turning her face towards* OLD MAN, *she raises her arms like a drowning person, then turns around and sinks back down, her face now turned to auditorium. Her eyes and mouth are wide open. Dull 'thunder clap.'* OLD MAN *turns his glance downwards towards* MILKMAID. *When he tries to seize her, he loses his crutches.* ALL, *immobile, watch* OLD MAN.

54 *Wall projection disappears. Façade of the house and church are again projected on screens and on cyclorama but now enlarged. White working light. Dull 'thunder clap.'* FIANCÉE *out at 1.* CARETAKER'S WIFE *out at 3.* COLONEL *out at 7.*

55 OLD MAN *collapses anguished in his wheelchair.* JOHANSSON *pushes* BEGGARS *away, and tries to turn* OLD MAN *upright in his wheelchair.* BEGGARS *out at 5.*

56 OLD MAN *faintly.* Take me away, Johansson...Quickly! YOUNG LADY *out at 7.*

57 OLD MAN *shouting.* Arkenholz! Don't forget *The Valkyrie! Screams with anguish.* JOHANSSON *pushes him out at 5.*

58 YOUNG LADY *quickly in from 7.* STUDENT *quickly up to* YOUNG LADY. *They look at each other.* YOUNG LADY *out at 7.*

59 JOHANSSON *runs in from 5, picks up one of* OLD MAN'S *crutches.*

STUDENT *up to* JOHANSSON, *grabs him, admonishingly.* What is all this?

JOHANSSON *mystifyingly.* We'll see....We'll see! *Out at 5.*

STUDENT *out at 3. Chiming of church bells subsides. Black-out.*

Projection of a dense, moving 'snowfall' on a black curtain. Prolonged 'thunder' followed by occasional ghostlike bars.

Act II

B *On screens is projected a turn-of-the-century round drawing-room, on cyclorama a tall, narrow window with a pleated curtain arrangement. In area behind screens (12), representing hyacinth room, a harp in white and gold and two slender white chairs. In FG L (at 3) a folding-screen, covered by black silk and with Japanese nature and bird motifs painted in gold on it. In middle of stage two black chairs with intensely red velvet seats, one at 10, the other at 11. Next to former chair a small round black table with a bell. Cold light. Grandfather clock strikes five, ticks.*

60 YOUNG LADY *sits turned away on chair L in hyacinth room reading a book. She wears same hyacinth-blue dress as in Act I.* JOHANSSON *at 9, turned towards auditorium and wearing ill-fitting black tails and a moderately clean starched collar and shirt-front, is busy putting on a pair of dirty white gloves in front of an imaginary mirror. He then grooms his eyebrows.*

61 BENGTSSON *in from 3. He is dressed in a somewhat worn and faded wine-red livery with gold stripes, black-striped waistcoat, white gloves. On his livery he wears patriotic medal. He is white-haired and leans on a black cane. To* JOHANSSON, *clearing his throat.* You're to serve now...while I take their coats. *Condescendingly.* Have you...done this before?

JOHANSSON Well, I...spend the days pushing a battle waggon around, as you know, but...in the evenings I usually wait at parties BENGTSSON *brushes off* JOHANSSON'S *lapel.* and it has always been my dream to get into this house. *Looks around.* Queer bunch?

BENGTSSON. Oh, ay, a little unusual, you might say.

JOHANSSON. Is it going to be a musical evening *Pointing with his thumb towards harp.* or what?

BENGTSSON. It's the usual ghost supper...as we call it. They drink tea and don't say a word, or the colonel talks all by himself. Then they nibble their biscuits, all at the same time, so it sounds like rats in an attic.

JOHANSSON. Why...is it called ghost supper?

BENGTSSON. They look like ghosts....And they've kept this up for twenty years, always the same people saying the same things. Or they keep silent...to avoid feeling ashamed.

JOHANSSON *looks around.* Isn't there a lady of the house too?

BENGTSSON. Oh yes, but she's crazy. She sits in a closet because her eyes can't stand the light...She is sitting in here. *Points towards* 2.

JOHANSSON. In there?

BENGTSSON. Yes, I told you they're a little unusual.

JOHANSSON. What does *she* look like?

BENGTSSON. Like a mummy...Do you want to see her? *Opens the closet door.* Look...there she is!

JOHANSSON *carefully up to closet, backs away.* Jesus Chr...

62 MUMMY *like a parrot.* Why do you open the dawer? Didn't I twell you to keep it cwosed!

BENGTSSON *squatting in front of closet.* Ta, ta, ta, ta, ta, ta! Ittle lolly must be nice now, then...then she'll get a sweetie! *Offers her something.* Pretty Polly!

MUMMY *like a parrot.* Prrretty Polly! An Jacob is there. Currrre!

BENGTSSON. She...she thinks she's a parrot, and maybe she is...*Gives a meaningful sign to* JOHANSSON. *To* MUMMY. Polly, whistle something for us! MUMMY *softly whistles "Toreador aria" from* Carmen.

JOHANSSON *to himself.* I've seen a lot, but nothing to match this!

BENGTSSON. You see, when a house gets old...it gets mouldy. And when people sit together for a long time, tormenting each other, they go crazy. This lady of the house...Quiet, Polly! MUMMY *becomes silent*. This mummy has been sitting here for forty years. The same husband, the same furniture, the same relatives, the same friends. MUMMY *begins to whistle again, this time "Greensleaves."*

63 BENGTSSON *closes closet door*. MUMMY *stops whistling*.

BENGTSSON *with a somber expression*. And what has occurred in this house...*I hardly know. Passes closely by* JOHANSSON *as though he did not see him. Points with his cane at statue*. JOHANSSON *backs away*. Look at that statue...It's the lady...as a young woman!

JOHANSSON. Good heavens!...Is that *Nod at statue, gesture to closet*. the mummy?

BENGTSSON. Yes!...It's enough to make you weep...But through the power of imagination or something else, this lady has adopted some of the peculiarities of that talkative bird. She can't stand cripples and sick people...She can't stand her own daughter...because she's ill.

JOHANSSON. Is the young lady ill?

BENGTSSON *sharply*. Didn't you know?

JOHANSSON. No!...And the colonel, who is he?

BENGTSSON. You'll see!

JOHANSSON *points eagerly to statue, ingratiatingly*. It's...it's terrible to imagine...*Pointing with his thumb to closet*. How old is the lady now?

BENGTSSON. No one knows...But they say that when she was thirty-five, she looked as if she were nineteen and that she made the colonel believe she was. JOHANSSON *laughs silently*.

BENGTSSON *to himself*. In this house...*Looks around*. Do you know what *Points to 3*. that black Japanese screen is for, the one next to the couch?...It's called the death screen and is put up when someone's going to die, just as in the hospital.

JOHANSSON. It's a terrible house, this one...And the student wished to get into it as though it was...Paradise.

BENGTSSON. What student? Oh, the one who's coming here tonight...The colonel and the young lady met him at the opera and were both taken with *Beckons* JOHANSSON *to come to 9*. him.

64 OLD MAN *on black crutches quickly and silently in from 4. He wears a frock coat, trousers and top hat of intensely emerald-green velvet. Black-green neckerchief with a diamond tie-pin and boots as in Act I.*

BENGTSSON. But now it's my turn to ask. Who's your master? The company director in the wheelchair.

JOHANSSON. Well, well, well. Is he coming too?

BENGTSSON. He hasn't been invited.

JOHANSSON. That one comes uninvited...if need be!

BENGTSSON. He's a regular old rascal, eh?

JOHANSSON. Full-blown!

BENGTSSON. He looks like Old Nick himself!

JOHANSSON. And he's a magician, too, it seems...for he goes through locked doors.

OLD MAN *up behind* JOHANSSON, *takes him by ear.*

JOHANSSON *screaming.* Ow! *Is thrown off his feet and lands on floor near 2.*

OLD MAN. You scoundrel! *With an admonishing forefinger.* Watch out! *To* BENGTSSON. Announce me to the Colonel! *Hands him his hat, while keeping his face turned away.*

BENGTSSON *condescendingly.* Yes but...we're expecting guests.

OLD MAN. I know! But my visit is *almost* expected, if not longed for.

BENGTSSON *stiffly.* Oh! What's the name? OLD MAN *turns his face towards* BENGTSSON. *Terrified.* Mr Hummel? *Stands as though petrified.* JOHANSSON *rises, dusts off his trousers.*

OLD MAN *smiling.* Quite so. BENGTSSON *bows, out at 6.*

65 OLD MAN *to* JOHANSSON. Get out! JOHANSSON *moves over to 11, walks around chair and takes a few steps towards* OLD MAN. *Hissing.* Get out! JOHANSSON *out at 6.*

66 OLD MAN *up to 9. Facing auditorium, he smooths his hair in front of an imaginary mirror.*

67 MUMMY *from inside closet, like a parrot.* Prrrretty Polly.

OLD MAN *startled.* What's that? Is there a parrot in the room? I don't see any.

MUMMY *like a parrot.* Is Jacob there?

OLD MAN, *his hand on his heart.* The place is haunted.

MUMMY *like a parrot.* Jacob!

OLD MAN. I'm frightened!...*Looks terrified around.* So that's the kind of secrets they have in this house? *Up to statue, startles, whispers.* Amalia! MUMMY *leaps forward from 3. She wears a dress with bustle and train, lace cap and half-gloves. Lace cap and upper part of dress are grey-yellow-white. Dress turns into red below and lowest part of it and train are intensely red. Whole dress is dirty and torn, silk and lace hanging in flakes. She turns around as soon as she sees* OLD MAN, *and exits at 3.*

68 OLD MAN *moved.* Amalia!...It is she!...It...is...she! *Stands close to statue, kisses it.*

69 MUMMY *in from 2. She dries her peering eyes, sighs, coughs. Then jumps, like a parrot, wildly smiling up to* OLD MAN, *tears at his wig and screams.* Currrre! Is it Currrre?

OLD MAN *turns terrified around, backs to 9.* Eternal God in heaven! *Looks at* MUMMY. Who is it?

MUMMY *with a 'parrot gesture'(her hands put together under her chin) in normal voice.* Is it you, Jacob?

OLD MAN. My name is indeed Jacob.

MUMMY *moved.* And mine is Amalia.

OLD MAN *compassionately.* No...No, no, no...Oh, Jesus Christ.

MUMMY. How I look. Yes...And *have* looked *Nod at statue.* like that! *Sarcastically.* We learn a lot through living. *Bitterly informative.* I live mostly in the closet, both to avoid seeing and being seen...But you, Jacob, what are *you* seeking here?

OLD MAN. My child. Our child.

MUMMY *nod at 12.* She's sitting there.

OLD MAN. Where?

MUMMY. There...in the hyacinth room.

OLD MAN *regards* YOUNG LADY. Yes, it's she. *Pause.* What does her father say? MUMMY *looks puzzled. Ironically, hissing.* The Colonel? Your husband?

MUMMY *ashamed.* I was angry with him once, and then I told him everything.

OLD MAN. Well?

MUMMY. He didn't believe me but answered: "That's what all wives say when they want to murder their husband." *Repentantly.* All the same it was a terrible crime. His whole life has been falsified, his family tree too. I sometimes read in the book of peerage, and then I think: "She's got a false birth certificate like a servant girl, and for that you're sent to a reformatory."

OLD MAN. Many do. I seem to remember yours was false.

MUMMY *apologetically*. My mother taught me that...It wasn't *my* fault! *Spitefully, with 'parrot gesture' and a few steps towards* OLD MAN. But you were most to blame for our crime.

OLD MAN *agitated*. No!...Your husband provoked the crime when he took my fiancée from me!...My nature's such I can't forgive before I have punished!...I regarded it as an imperative duty...and I still do!

MUMMY *softly but aggressively*. What do you seek in this house? What do you want?...Is it my daughter?...If you touch her, you must die!

OLD MAN. I want what's best for her.

MUMMY. But you must spare her father!

OLD MAN. No!

MUMMY *with a 'parrot movement,' spitefully up to* OLD MAN. Then you must die. In this room! *Walks around* OLD MAN. Behind this screen! *Points to 3*.

OLD MAN. Maybe...but I can't let go once I have my teeth in someone!

MUMMY *aggressively*. You want to marry her off to the student. Why? He is nothing and has nothing.

OLD MAN *aggressively*. He'll *get* rich...through me!

MUMMY *aggressively*. Were *you* invited here...tonight?

OLD MAN *aggressively*. No, but I intend to *have* myself invited to the ghost supper this evening!

MUMMY *contemptuously*. Do you know who's coming?

OLD MAN *ironically*. Not exactly.

MUMMY. The baron...who lives upstairs and whose father-in-law was buried this afternoon.

OLD MAN *sarcastically*. The one who's getting divorced to marry the caretaker's daughter...The one who once was your lover.

MUMMY *sarcastically*. And then there's your former fiancée *Sadly*. who was seduced by my husband.

OLD MAN *ironically*. A fine bunch.

MUMMY. God, *On verge of tears.* if we could die! *If we could die!*

OLD MAN *angrily.* Why do you get together then?

MUMMY *sobbing remorsefully.* Crimes and secrets and guilt bind us together. We have broken up and gone our ways infinitely many times, but...we're drawn together again.

OLD MAN. Quiet...The colonel's coming.

MUMMY *in 'parrot position,' turns away from* OLD MAN. Then I'll go in to Adèle. *Turns to* OLD MAN, *whispers.* Jacob. *Strokes his hair.* Think of what you're doing! *Takes a step away, looks appealingly at* OLD MAN, *who keeps his head lowered.* Spare him! *Remains for a moment helplessly hesitant, then out at 3.*

70 COLONEL *in from 6. He wears a gold-braided, somewhat worn ruby-red uniform, black elasticated boots, riding-whip, and monocle.* OLD MAN *adjusts his trousers.* COLONEL *whips his leg with riding-whip. They bow reservedly to each other.*

COLONEL *pointing with his riding-whip to chair R, coldly, reservedly.* Please be seated! *White light on the two black-and-red chairs.* OLD MAN *slowly sits down on chair at 11.*

COLONEL *stares at* OLD MAN's *disabled body, walks to chair at 10, takes up a letter.* You're the gentleman...who wrote this letter? *Ticking of clock subsides.*

71 MUMMY *enters 12 and sits down on chair R of harp.*

OLD MAN. Yes.

COLONEL. Your name is *Puts monocle to his eye.* Hummel?

OLD MAN. Yes!

COLONEL *sits down.* Since I know you've bought up all my outstanding notes of hand, *Projected interiors fade out as light on two chairs midstage successively increases.* it follows that I'm at your mercy. What do you want *now*?

OLD MAN. I want to be paid...in one way or another.

COLONEL. Yes, but in what way?

OLD MAN. Very simply.

COLONEL. Oh?

OLD MAN. Let's not talk about the money. Just bear with me in your house...as a guest.

COLONEL. Well...if you'll be satisfied with so little. *Laughs falteringly.*

OLD MAN. Thanks.

COLONEL. What else?

OLD MAN. Dismiss Bengtsson!

COLONEL. Why should I? My faithful servant, who has been with me all his life, who has...the patriotic medal for faithful service. Why should I? *Laughs falteringly.*

OLD MAN. All these beautiful things he possesses only in your imagination...He is not what he seems to be!

COLONEL. Who is?

OLD MAN. True!...But Bengtsson must go!

COLONEL *faintly protesting*. Are *you* to run my house?

OLD MAN. Yes! Since I own everything you can see here: furniture, curtains, china, linen cupboard...*etcetera*.

COLONEL. What other things?

OLD MAN. Everything! Everything you see. It's mine!

COLONEL. All right, it's yours. But my coat of arms and my good name will still be mine!

OLD MAN. No, not even that!...You're not a nobleman!

COLONEL *agitated*. Shame on you!

OLD MAN *takes out a piece of paper*. If you read this excerpt from the College of Arms, you'll see that the family whose name *you* bear has been extinct for a hundred years.

COLONEL *puts riding-whip aside, anxiously*. I've heard rumours like that, *Up to* OLD MAN. but I inherited my name from my father. OLD MAN *hands him paper*. COLONEL *reads*. That's right. *You* are right. *Lowers hand in which he holds paper.* OLD MAN *grabs paper*. COLONEL *to himself*. I'm not...a nobleman. Not even that!...Then I'll take off my signet ring. *Looks at it, again conscious of* OLD MAN's *presence*. It's true. It belongs to you...Here you are! *Hands* OLD MAN *ring, walks back towards his chair*.

OLD MAN *pockets ring*. Now we'll continue! COLONEL *stops*. You aren't a colonel either!

COLONEL *helplessly*. Aren't I?

OLD MAN. No! You *were* an acting colonel in the American *volunteer* force, but after the Cuban war and the reorganization of the army, all earlier titles have been abolished.

COLONEL. Is that true?

OLD MAN *gesturing to his pocket*. Do you want to read?

Colonel *loudly protesting.* No, that's not *necessary*! *Backs frightenedly.* Who *are* you...that have the right to strip me like this?

Old Man. Time will tell!...But talking of stripping *Points with his crutch at* Colonel, *vehemently.* do you know who *you* are? Colonel *up from chair, approaches* Old Man *with raised riding-whip.* Have you no shame?

Old Man *leaps up, pushes* Colonel *down on chair which overturns, landing him on floor.* Take off your hair!

Colonel *on his knees, groans, and obeys.* Have *Points.* a look at yourself in the mirror! Take out your teeth at once! Tear off your moustache! Colonel *obeys.* Old Man *thrusts him over to L.* Let Bengtsson *Slits up* Colonel's *uniform so that a corset is exposed.* unlace your metal corset Colonel *closes his eyes.* and we'll see if footman XYZ won't recognize himself! The one who sponged food in a certain kitchen-maid's room. Colonel *takes hold of bell on table and rings.* Old Man *grasps* Colonel *by neck and pushes him so that he falls forward on floor.* Don't touch that bell! Don't call for Bengtsson, or I'll have him arrested! *Clock strikes six.* Old Man *strikes* Colonel *with his crutch.* The guests are coming!...Keep calm, now, and we'll go on playing our old roles.

Colonel *on his knees up to table, puts on his wig, moustache and false teeth again. Terrified.* Who *are* you? I recognize your look...and your voice. *Buttons his uniform.*

Old Man *commanding.* Don't ask! Be quiet...just obey! *Lets ring fall on table.* Colonel *takes ring and puts it back on his finger, gets up.*

72 Student *in from 6. He wears same light summer clothes as in Act I but they are now neat and clean. Bandage is gone. In his hand he holds a book with red covers. He bows deeply to* Colonel. Colonel!

Colonel *up to* Student *at 11.* Welcome to my house...young man! *Takes* Student's *hand and puts his other hand on* Student's *shoulder.*

73 Bengtsson *and* Johansson *in from 6. The latter carries two chairs, identical with the ones already found in round room.* Johansson *puts chairs down in middle of room.*

Colonel. Your noble behaviour...at the great disaster...has put your name on everyone's lips...and I count it an honour to receive you in my home. Bengtsson *raises chair that has fallen and orders* Johansson *to fetch a chair from 3 and to move table to middle of room.* Johansson *obeys.*

Student. Colonel...my humble origins, Colonel *pats him benevolently on shoulder.* your illustrious name...your noble birth...

COLONEL. May I introduce: Mr Arkenholz, Mr...Hummel...*To* STUDENT. Would you be so good as to join the ladies? *Takes* STUDENT *towards 12.* I must finish a talk with Mr Hummel.

BENGTSSON *and* JOHANSSON *out at 6.*

74 STUDENT *enters 12, where he kisses hands of* MUMMY *and* YOUNG LADY. *He remains standing next to harp, shyly and inaudibly conversing with the ladies.*

COLONEL *returns.* A superb young man...musical, sings, oh yes, writes poetry. *Up to* OLD MAN *in front of 10.* If he were a nobleman and...our equal, I'd have nothing against...well...

OLD MAN. What?

COLONEL. My daughter.

OLD MAN. *Your* daughter!...By the way, why is she always sitting in there?

COLONEL *guiltily.* She has to sit in the hyacinth room when she's not out. It's a peculiarity of hers.

MUMMY *out from 12 L.*

STUDENT *takes her place on the chair R.*

75 FIANCÉE *trips in from 6. She wears a dress with bustle and train of shimmering green-black silk with trimmings in emerald-green, black lace cape, and feathers in her hair.*

COLONEL *to* OLD MAN. Here comes Miss Beate von Holsteinkrona...a charming woman...*Whispers.* a secular canoness with an income appropriate to her rank and circumstances.

OLD MAN *to himself.* My former fiancée. *Sighs.*

COLONEL *kisses hand of* FIANCÉE, *introduces.* Miss Holsteinkrona, Mr...Hummel. FIANCÉE *curtsies briefly.* OLD MAN *bows reservedly.*

76 POSH MAN *in from 6, looks delighted. He wears a frock coat and trousers of an intense dark-violet velvet, black-violet neckerchief with a shimmering violet tie-pin, pointed elasticated boots, a carnation in his buttonhole.*

COLONEL *takes hand of* POSH MAN. And Baron Skanskorg! POSH MAN *and* OLD MAN *bow reservedly to each other.*

OLD MAN *to himself.* Well if it isn't the jewel thief. POSH MAN *kisses* FIANCÉE'S *hands.* COLONEL *hums a few bars.* OLD MAN *up to* COLONEL. Bring in the mummy and the collection's complete!

77 BENGTSSON *with a teapot and* JOHANSSON *with a tray in from 6. They remain standing behind 11.*

COLONEL. Poll!...Poll!...*Beats chair L with his riding-whip.* Polly!...Polly, Poll...Poll-Poll...Poll-Poll...*Opens closet door.*

78 MUMMY *peeps out behind folding-screen.* Currrrre! FIANCÉE *giggles.* POSH MAN *laughs loudly.* COLONEL *offers* MUMMY *his arm and leads her to guests.* MUMMY *greets* OLD MAN, *who kisses her hand; then* FIANCÉE : *they giggle and kiss each other on cheeks. She smiles invitingly to* POSH MAN, *who kisses her high up on her hand, to her great satisfaction. She then spreads her arms as a sign that everyone may sit down.* ALL *sit down except* OLD MAN, *who takes out a notebook and puts on his glasses.*

COLONEL *glancing at* OLD MAN. Shall we have the young people come in too?

OLD MAN. No! Not the young people!

COLONEL. Right.

OLD MAN. They're to be spared.

COLONEL. Yes, yes...May we serve the tea ? *Ticking of grandfather clock.*

OLD MAN. What for? No one likes tea? *Looks around.* POSH MAN *protests faintly.* Why play the hypocrite then. COLONEL *gives a sign with his riding-whip that* BENGTSSON *and* JOHANSSON *may leave. They exit at 6.*

79 OLD MAN *sits down.*

COLONEL. Shall we converse then?

OLD MAN. Talk about the weather...which we know. Ask how we are, which we know...I prefer silence. Then you hear thoughts...and see the past. Silence can conceal nothing...which words can. *Pause.* MUMMY *closes her eyes.* OLD MAN *takes out his cigarette case, lights a cigarette.* I read the other day that the difference between languages really arose among primitive peoples in order to conceal the secrets of one tribe from the others. Languages are consequently codes, and he who finds the key understands all the languages of the world. But...there are secrets which can be revealed without a key. Especially when paternity has to be proved. MUMMY *looks anxiously at* OLD MAN. But proof in court is something else. Two false witnesses *Looks at* POSH MAN. make full proof...provided they are in full agreement. But in the kind of errand I have in mind...one does not take any witnesses along. *Leans towards* FIANCÉE. Nature herself has endowed man with a kind of...shame FIANCÉE *lowers her glance.* which tries to conceal what should be concealed. MUMMY *lowers her glance.* Still...we glide into situations without wanting to, and opportunities sometimes arise, when what is most secret must be revealed, when *Looks at* COLONEL. the mask is torn from the deceiver, when

Looks at POSH MAN. the villain is exposed. *Dries his mouth with his handkerchief. Pause.* ALL *look stiffly in front of them.* How quiet it became. *Pause. Projected interiors fade out.* In this respectable house, in this lovely home, where *Looks at* MUMMY. beauty, *Looks at* POSH MAN. culture, and *Looks at* COLONEL. wealth *Stone wall is projected on screens and cyclorama.* have been united. COLONEL, FIANCÉE, POSH MAN *and* MUMMY *slowly begin to droop, lowering their heads.* MUMMY *purses her mouth harshly.* We know who we are...don't we?...I don't need to tell you. *Vehemently.* You know who I am...although you *pretend* ignorance...In there *Points towards* 12. my daughter is sitting...*Mine!* MUMMY *clasps* COLONEL's *hand.* You know that too. *Violently.* She had lost the desire to live, without knowing why...But she withered in this air which breathed crime, deception...and every other kind of falsehood. *Calmly.* That's why I sought a friend for her in whose presence she could experience the light and feel the warmth of a noble deed. *Violently.* This was my mission in this house: to root out the weeds, expose the crimes...settle past accounts, so that the young people may have a fresh start in this home, which *I* have given them! *Wipes his nose, matter-of-factly.* Now I grant you leave to go...each of you...in turn and order. Whoever stays...I'll have arrested! MUMMY *looks spitefully at* OLD MAN. POSH MAN *is about to rise from his chair. Pause.* Listen to the ticking of the clock...like the death-watch beetle in the wall. Do you hear what it says? *Whispers.* "The time...The time." When it strikes, in a little while, *then* your time is up. POSH MAN *half-rises from his chair. Violently.* Then you may go! POSH MAN *sits down again.* Not before! *Pause.* But it threatens first *Takes up one crutch.* before it strikes!...Listen! *Clock mechanism is heard.* Now it's warning you. *Whispers.* "The clock can strike." *Pause.* I too can strike. *Strikes crutch against table.* COLONEL *puts his arms protectively over his head.* POSH MAN *ducks as if he were beaten. Quietly.* Do you hear?

MUMMY *sensibly and seriously.* But *I* can stop time in its course. *I* can wipe out the past, *Looks at* COLONEL. undo what has been done. COLONEL, FIANCÉE *and* POSH MAN *raise their glances and look at* MUMMY. *She goes to grandfather clock, puts her hand on its hand. Ticking subsides.* Not with bribes, not with threats. But through suffering...and repentance. *Wall projection darkens.* MUMMY *up behind* COLONEL, *her arms around him, looks at* OLD MAN. COLONEL *takes hold of one of her hands.* We *are* poor human beings, we know that. We *have* erred, we *have* sinned, like everyone else. We *are* not what we seem, for at heart we are better than ourselves, when we dislike our faults. *Up behind* OLD MAN. *Repressing her tears, spitefully.* But that you, Jacob Hummel, with your false name COLONEL, FIANCÉE *and* POSH MAN *begin to raise their heads.* can sit here in judgement on us, that shows that you are worse *Wall projection disappears. Chairs in round room are strongly lit.* than we miserable creatures. You...you...you aren't either the one you seem to be. You're a stealer of souls! You stole me once with false promises. You murdered the Consul who was buried here today. You strangled him with notes of hand. You stole the student by binding him with an imaginary debt of his father's who never owed you a penny...But there is a black spot

80 MILKMAID *in from 2, places herself in front of grandfather clock, stares at* OLD MAN *who startles and stares back.*

MUMMY. in your life I don't quite know, but I have my suspicions. I think Bengtsson knows about it.

OLD MAN. No, not Bengtsson! Not that one! *Falls backwards in his chair.*

MUMMY. Aha...*he* knows! *Beckons* BENGTSSON *to enter.*

81 BENGTSSON *in from 6.* JOHANSSON *in from 3.*

MUMMY. Do you know this man, Bengtsson?

BENGTSSON *calmly.* Yes...I know him and he knows me. Life has its ups and downs...as we know. And I've served him, and he has served me. He was, for example, a sponger in the room of my kitchen maid for two whole years. Since he had to leave at three, dinner was ready at two. *With rising agitation.* And the family had to eat food warmed up after *Raises his hand as if to strike* OLD MAN. that ox! *Kneeling next to* OLD MAN. He also drank juice from the meat *Violently seizes* OLD MAN's *lapel,* which then had to be eked out with water. And he sat out there like a vampire sucking all the goodness out of the house so that we became like skeletons. *Sobbing.* And...and he nearly got us into prison...when we called the cook a thief. *Covers his head with his hands. Rises. Matter-of-factly.* Later...I came across this man...in Hamburg MILKMAID *begins to raise her arms.* under another name. He was then a usurer, a bloodsucker. But he was also accused there...of having lured a girl out on to the ice...to drown her...because she had witnessed a crime...he feared would be discovered. *Dull 'thunder clap.'* OLD MAN *voices a stifled cry.* MILKMAID *lowers her arms, out at 2.*

82 MUMMY *moves her hands across* OLD MAN's *face as if unmasking him.* That *Dull 'thunder clap.'* is you! *Dull 'thunder clap.'* Now let's have those notes of hand and the will! *Takes* OLD MAN's *hand which desperately holds on to crutch, moves it towards his inside pocket and forces him to hand over papers to* COLONEL. *Behind* OLD MAN, *her head close to his, with her parrot's voice.* Currrre! Polly! Is Jacob there? *Long pause.*

OLD MAN *half-lying in his chair, with voice of a parrot.* Ja-cob is there!...Cacadora! FIANCÉE *giggles.* POSH MAN *smiles maliciously.* Dora!

MUMMY *like a parrot.* Currrrre! Can the clock strike?

OLD MAN *clucks.* The clock can strike. *Imitates a cuckoo clock.* Cuck-oo, cuck-oo, cuck-oo, cuck-

MUMMY *puts her hand over* OLD MAN's *mouth, seriously.* Now the clock has struck...Get up, go into the closet where I have been sitting for twenty years weeping over our misdeed! *Puts her hand over* OLD MAN'S *eyes*. There's a rope in there…that can represent the one you strangled the Consul with up there, and with which you in-tended to strangle your benefactor. *Sharply.* Go! POSH MAN *smiles triumphantly.* OLD MAN *takes a few steps forward without his crutches, falls, rolls floundering across floor to R, while voicing various unintelligible sounds.* JOHANSSON *brutally falls upon* OLD MAN, *drags him out at 2 and closes door.*

83 JOHANSSON *walks over to the grandfather clock and leans against wall there.*

MUMMY. Bengtsson! Put the screen in front! *Cold light on stage. Projected interiors re-turn.* The death screen! BENGTSSON *puts screen up and places himself behind it. A bang, followed by a rattle is heard from closet.* JOHANSSON *lowers his head.* MUMMY *up to 2, opens closet door, looks inside, calmly.* It is finished. *Admonishes by her glance the oth-ers to come forward.* COLONEL, FIANCÉE *and* POSH MAN *up to 2.* God have mercy on his soul!

COLONEL. Amen.

FIANCÉE *curtsies*. Amen.

BENGTSSON. Amen.

POSH MAN *very lightly*. Amen. *They exit silently at 3 as follows:* MUMMY, FIANCÉE, BENGTSSON, POSH MAN, COLONEL.

84 *Only hyacinth room is lit. Interior projections dim while window projection upstage sharpens. Occasional harp notes until end of act, as follows:*

JOHANSSON *over to R, stops in middle of stage, turns towards open closet, puts his hands in his pockets, out at 6.*

85 STUDENT *standing by harp, with red book in his hands, recites to* YOUNG LADY.

> I saw the sun. To me it seemed
> that I beheld the Hidden.
> Men must reap what they have sown,
> blest is he whose deeds are good.
> Deeds which you have wrought in fury,
> cannot in evil find redress.
> Comfort him you have distressed

> with loving-kindness – this will heal.
> No fear has he who does no ill.
> Sweet is innocence.

Projection of the the aged Strindberg's face covered by a dense, moving 'snowfall' on a black curtain. Prolonged 'thunder,' followed by occasional musical notes.

Act III

C *Downstage hyacinth room, upstage (12) round drawing-room. L in FG (in front of 3) Japanese folding screen. At 10 one white chair, at 11, next to harp, another. At 12 two chairs identical with ones seen in round room in Act II but now with black upholstery. On screens and cyclorama projections of high narrow windows with pleated curtain arrangements.*

86 MUMMY *is sitting on chair left in 12, half turned away, somewhat bent, idle. She wears a dress of about same fashion as that in Act II, but it is now almost colourless – grey-white-yellow – and very torn and stained.* COLONEL *is sitting on chair R in 12, half turned to auditorium, his hands on a newspaper in his lap. He wears a shirt buttoned up at neck, an old worn grey velvet dressing-gown and slippers. A few grey hairs on his almost bald head.* STUDENT *is standing by harp. He is dressed as in Act II but no longer wears glasses.* YOUNG LADY *is standing midstage with one hand covering her face. She wears a hyacinth-blue, high-collared dress with cream-coloured, lace sleeves. Around neck she wears, as before, a small crucifix.*

YOUNG LADY *lowers her hand, smiles, mildly.* Sing now for my flowers! *Up to 9, busies herself with imaginary hyacinths.*

STUDENT. Is this the flower of your soul?

YOUNG LADY. The one and only. Do *you* love the hyacinth?

STUDENT *up to* YOUNG LADY. I love *that* above all others...its virginal form which...straight and slender...rises from the bulb, rests on the water and sinks its pure white roots into the colourless liquid. I love its colours: the innocent pure snow-white, the honey-sweet yellow, the youthful pink, the mature red...but above all...the blue, YOUNG LADY *takes a step away from* STUDENT, *smiles.* the dewy-blue, the deep-eyed, the faithful. I love them more than gold and pearls. I have loved them since I was a child, have admired them, since they possess all the fine qualities I lack...But

YOUNG LADY. What?

STUDENT. my love is unrequited, for these beautiful flowers hate me.

YOUNG LADY. How?

STUDENT. Their fragrance, strong and pure from the first winds of spring which have passed over melting snow, it...it confuses my senses, deafens me, blinds me, drives me out of the room, assails me with poisonous arrows that make...make my heart sad *Closes his eyes, one hand to his heart, the other to his head.* and my...my head hot. YOUNG LADY *up to* STUDENT, *raises her hands towards him as if to caress him, then retires R and raises one hand avertingly while smiling.* Don't *you* know the story of this flower?

YOUNG LADY. Tell it.

STUDENT *smiling.* But first its meaning. *Turns towards imaginary hyacinths on front stage, carefully picks one, clasps it with both hands.* The bulb is the earth, which rests on the water YOUNG LADY *turns away, moved.* or lies in the soil. Now...the stalk shoots up, straight as the axis of the earth, and at the top are the six-pointed starflowers.

YOUNG LADY *turns to* STUDENT *again.* Above the earth the stars. Oh it is magnificent. *Where* did you learn that? *How* did you see that?

STUDENT *up to* YOUNG LADY. Let me think...In your eyes!

YOUNG LADY. Whose thought was that?

STUDENT. Yours!

YOUNG LADY. Yours! Yours! *They stand close together without touching one another.*

STUDENT. Ours!

YOUNG LADY *whispers eagerly.* Yours! Yours!

STUDENT. We have given birth to something together!...We are married.

YOUNG LADY *takes a step back, sadly.* Not yet.

STUDENT. What remains?

YOUNG LADY *takes a few more steps away from* STUDENT, *tenderly, sadly.* The waiting, the trials, the patience.

STUDENT *assuredly.* Good. Try me! YOUNG LADY *up to* STUDENT, *kisses him on forehead, takes him by hand and leads him to chair at 10, puts her hand on his shoulder. Seated.* Tell me...why do your parents sit so silent in there...without saying a word?

YOUNG LADY. Because they've nothing to say to each other, because...neither believes what the other says.

87 *Hand of* COOK *is seen at 7.*

YOUNG LADY. My father once put it like this:

COLONEL. What's the point of talking? We can't...fool each other anyway.

STUDENT. That's horrible!

YOUNG LADY *tired*. Here *comes* the cook. Look at her, how big and fat she is!

STUDENT. What does *she* want?

YOUNG LADY. She wants to ask me about dinner. COOK *extremely slowly in from 7. She is big and very fat. She is dressed in a long skirt, a simple blouse, and a large apron – everything of linen – wrinkly stockings, slippers, kerchief on her head, all of it in grey-yellow-white.* I'm looking after the house, you see, during my mother's illness.

STUDENT. Do *we* have to deal with the *kitchen*?

YOUNG LADY *moving to midstage*. Well, we have to eat. *Moves towards* COOK. Look at the cook! I *can't* bear to see her. *Turns away from* COOK, *her hand covering her eyes.*

STUDENT. Who *is* this giant woman?

YOUNG LADY. She belongs to the Hummel family of vampires. *Anguished.* She's devouring us!

STUDENT. Why isn't she dismissed?

YOUNG LADY. She won't go. We can't manage her. *Kneeling before* STUDENT. We've got her for our sins. Can't you see we're wasting, pining away? *Holds her lean hands up to* STUDENT.

STUDENT. Don't you get anything to eat then?

YOUNG LADY. Yes, we get many dishes but all the strength is gone. *Whispers quickly, breathing more and more heavily.* She boils the meat and gives us the sinews and the water while she drinks the stock herself. And when there's a roast...she first cooks the juice out of it, eats the sauce and drinks the broth. Whatever she touches loses its juice. *Looks at* COOK. It's as if she *sucked* it out with her eyes. We get the dregs after she's drunk the coffee. She drinks the wine and fills the bottles with water.

STUDENT *whispers powerlessly*. Send her away!

YOUNG LADY *plaintively*. We can't.

STUDENT. Why not?

YOUNG LADY. We don't know. She won't go. No one can manage her! *Screams powerlessly.* She's taken our strength away!

STUDENT. May *I* get rid of her?

YOUNG LADY. No, no...no! *Resigned, slowly.* I think it's meant to be the way it is. *Gets up.* COOK *advances one step.* Here she is now. She'll ask what we'll have for dinner. I'll tell her this and that. She'll object. And it'll be the way she wants.

STUDENT. Let her decide for herself then.

YOUNG LADY. That she doesn't want.

STUDENT. What a strange house. It's bewitched! COOK *turns around but remains where she was.*

YOUNG LADY. Yes...But now she turned around when she saw you.

COOK. No...That wasn't why. STUDENT *up from his chair, furious.*

YOUNG LADY *backs away, frightened.*

STUDENT *shouts.* Get out, woman!

COOK *calmly.* When I feel like it. STUDENT *sits down again.* Now I feel like it. *Slowly out at 7.*

88 YOUNG LADY *grabs hold of* STUDENT. Don't get upset!... Practise patience. She's one of the trials we have to endure here in this house. *With slight mummy intonation and parrot gesture.* There's also a maid. Whom we have to clean up after.

STUDENT. Now I'm sinking. Cor in aethere. *Sits down.* Song!

YOUNG LADY *covers her face with her hand.* Wait!

STUDENT *passionately, desperately.* Song!

YOUNG LADY *lowers her hand.* Patience... *Matter-of-factly.* This is called the room of trial. It's beautiful to look at but full of imperfections.

STUDENT. Incredible. But you have to overlook that. It's beautiful...but a bit cold. Why don't you have a fire going?

YOUNG LADY. Because it smokes.

STUDENT. Can't the chimney be swept?

YOUNG LADY. That doesn't help. *Points to auditorium.* Do you see the writing desk over there?

STUDENT. Exceedingly beautiful.

YOUNG LADY. But it wobbles. *Window projections fade.* Every day I put a piece of cork under the leg, but the maid takes it away when she sweeps and I have to cut a new one. The penholder is inky *every* morning, and the writing utensils, too. I have to clean them after her *every* blessed day. *Turns to* STUDENT, *thumb in mouth, whispering.* What do you dislike most?

STUDENT *whispers*. Counting laundry.

YOUNG LADY. That...is my job.

STUDENT. What else?

YOUNG LADY. Being disturbed in your sleep at night when you have to get up to fasten the catch on the window...the one the maid's forgotten.

STUDENT. What else?

YOUNG LADY. Climbing a ladder and mending the cord on the damper after the maid has torn it off.

STUDENT. What else!

YOUNG LADY *shrilly, with increasing speed*. Sweeping after her, dusting after her, making a fire in the stove after her. She just puts in the logs! *Slowly begins to turn around.* Watching the dampers, wiping the glasses, relaying the table, uncorking the bottles, opening the windows and airing the rooms, remaking my bed, rinsing the water decanter *Slower tempo with increasing mummy intonation.* when it gets green with algae, buying matches and soap that we're always out of, wiping the lamps and trimming the wicks, so the lamps won't smoke, and so the lamps won't go out. When we have guests I have to fill them myself.

STUDENT *with a desperate look walks up to harp, takes hold of it with both hands, shouts*. Song!

YOUNG LADY *cries out*. Wait!...*Helplessly*. First the drudgery...the drudgery of keeping the impurity of life at bay.

STUDENT. But you're wealthy, after all. You have...two servants.

YOUNG LADY. It wouldn't help, even if we had three. *Up to chair at 10, sits down leaning forward, straddling, struggles out of her shoes, sighs.* Living is hard, and I *am* tired sometimes...Imagine having a nursery as well.

STUDENT. The greatest of joys!

YOUNG LADY. The most expensive! *Bitterly.* Is life worth that much trouble?

STUDENT. It all depends on the reward you expect for your drudgery. *Up to* YOUNG LADY, *kneels before her*. I'd stop at nothing to win your hand!

YOUNG LADY *looks at him, irritated*. Don't talk like that. *Covers her face with her hand, removes her hand, sadly*. I can never be yours.

STUDENT *desperately*. Why not?

YOUNG LADY *calmly*. That you mustn't ask. *Raises one leg as if to protect her womb.* *Pause.*

STUDENT *gets up, takes her L arm, looks at it*. You dropped your bracelet through the window.

YOUNG LADY *looks at him*. Because my hand has grown so thin. *Pulls back her hand.* *Pause.*

89 COOK *is seen at 1 with a soya bottle in her hand.*

YOUNG LADY. There's the one who's devouring me...and all of us.

STUDENT. What's she got in her hand?

YOUNG LADY. That's the colouring bottle with scorpion letters on it. That's the soya which turns water into bouillon, which replaces gravy,

90 BENGTSSON *in from 7. He wears shirt, trousers, a large linen apron and slippers, all in same grey-yellow-white colouring as* COOK. *On his apron hangs patriotic medal.*

YOUNG LADY. in which one cooks cabbage and of which one makes turtle soup.

STUDENT *yells to* COOK. Get out!

COOK *calmly*. *You* suck the strength out of us, and *we* out of you.

BENGTSSON *calmly*. *We* take the blood...and *you* get the water in return

COOK *calmly*. with colouring. It is colouring.

COOK *and* BENGTSSON *look at each other. He whispers something inaudible to her. She nods back.*

COOK *calmly*. Now we'll go

BENGTSSON *calmly*. but we'll stay just the same

COOK. as long as we want. *Out at 1.* BENGTSSON *out at 7. Pause.*

91 STUDENT *up to 9*. Why does Bengtsson have a medal?

YOUNG LADY. Because of his great merits.

STUDENT. Has he no faults?

YOUNG LADY. Yes, big ones, but you don't get a medal for those. *Smiles.*

STUDENT *snorts, walks towards 5, turns to* YOUNG LADY. You have many secrets in this house.

YOUNG LADY *curtly*. Like everyone else. Let us keep ours! *Pause*.

STUDENT. Do you like frankness?

YOUNG LADY *coldly*. Yes, in moderation. *Pause*.

STUDENT *sits down on chair at 11, violently*. Sometimes I get a furious urge to say everything I think. But I know the world would collapse if you were absolutely frank. YOUNG LADY *laughs coldly. Pause*. STUDENT *puts one leg across the other*. I was at a funeral the other day...in church. It was very solemn and beautiful.

YOUNG LADY *reservedly, politely smiling*. It was Mr Hummel's.

STUDENT. My false benefactor's, yes...At the head of the coffin stood an elderly friend of the dead man. He carried the funeral mace. The minister impressed me especially with...his dignified manner and his moving words. *Short laughter*. I wept, we all wept...Afterwards we went to a restaurant...There I learned that...the mace bearer had loved the dead man's son. *Puts his finger to his mouth*. YOUNG LADY *looks puzzled at him*. And that the dead man had borrowed money from his son's...admirer...The next day the minister was arrested because he had embezzled the church funds. *Sarcastically*. Pretty, isn't it!

YOUNG LADY *sighs tormentedly*. No! *Pause*. STUDENT *turns violently to her. She startles*.

STUDENT *pointing to her*. Do you know what I think about you now?

YOUNG LADY *appealingly*. Don't tell me or I'll die.

STUDENT *violently*. I must...or I shall die!

YOUNG LADY *whispers*. In the asylum you say everything you think.

STUDENT *violently*. Quite so!...My father ended up in a madhouse.

YOUNG LADY *compassionately*. Was he ill?

STUDENT *violently*. No, he was sane! *Cold light increases. Matter-of-factly*. But he was crazy. *Up to midstage*. Well, it broke out once under the following circumstances. *Sarcastically*. Like all of us he was surrounded by a circle of acquaintances whom he called friends for short. They were a bunch of wretches, of course, like most people but...he had to have some companions since he couldn't sit there all by himself. *Up to* YOUNG LADY, *violently*. Well, you don't normally tell people what you think of them, *Behind* YOUNG LADY. and he didn't either! He knew, though, how...false they were. He knew their treachery thoroughly! *Quietly, moved*. But he was a wise man and...well brought up, so he was...always polite. *Away from* YOUNG LADY. One day he gave a party. It was in the evening. And he was tired after the day's work, and from the effort on the one hand of keeping still, on the other of talking shit with his guests.

YOUNG LADY *sighs tormentedly*. No!

STUDENT. Well. *Up to* YOUNG LADY. At the table he taps for silence, raises his glass to give a speech. *Very close to* YOUNG LADY. Then the brakes let go...and in a long address he stripped the whole company bare, one after the other, and told them all their...falseness! *Moves away from* YOUNG LADY. Then, weary, he sat down right on the table and told them to go to hell! YOUNG LADY *gasps for breath*. STUDENT *helplessly*. I was there. I'll never forget what happened next...Father and mother came to blows. The guests ran for the door. And father was taken to the madhouse...where he died. *Window projection is replaced by a faint projection of stone wall. With increasing aggressiveness.* Keeping silent too long creates a pool of stagnant water which rots! Well, that's how it is in this house too! *Violently seizes* YOUNG LADY's *arm*. MUMMY *begins to droop*. There's something very rotten here! COLONEL *begins to observe the action in hyacinth room*. And I thought it was paradise when I first saw you enter here! Then I stood there on a Sunday morning looking in. I saw a colonel who was not a colonel! I had a noble benefactor who was a crook and had to hang himself! I saw a mummy who was no mummy! And a virgin...! *Brutally separates* YOUNG LADY's *thighs and puts his hand against her womb. She falls back on her chair.* Speaking of which, where is virginity? *Cuts air with his hand. Turned away from* YOUNG LADY, *vehemently*. Where is beauty? *Quietly.* In fairy tales and children's plays! Where are honour...and faith? In nature...and in my mind when it's in its Sunday best. YOUNG LADY's *hand covering her face*. And where...where is anything that keeps what it promises?...In my imagination! *Takes* YOUNG LADY *violently under her chin, vehemently*. Now your flowers have poisoned me...and I have poisoned you in return! YOUNG LADY *about to go towards 12. Kneeling beside her, takes her hand, on verge of tears*. I asked you to be my wife in a home. YOUNG LADY *compassionately shakes her head*. We indulged in fancies, we sang, and we played music. *Moves her hand to his forehead.* And then the cook appeared...Try...try once more to strike fire and purple from the golden harp. Try, I beg you...yes, I implore you on my knees!...Well, then I'll do it myself. *Up to harp, plucks strings which do not sound.* Mm...it's deaf and...dumb. *Strong white light on 9. Seizes* YOUNG LADY *and drags her to 9, desperately and bitterly*. To think that the most beautiful flowers are so poisonous, are the most poisonous. *Vehemently.* The curse rests on all creation and on life! *As* YOUNG LADY *collapses on floor, her dress is torn apart and falls off her and she loses her crucifix. Underneath her dress she wears a torn and dirty, high-collared grey-white petticoat with red stains close to womb and at hem.* MUMMY *out at 12 L.*

92 STUDENT *kneeling beside* YOUNG LADY, *violently*. Why...why wouldn't you be my bride? Because you're...you're sick at the source of life! *Pushes her away. Dull 'thunder clap.'* YOUNG LADY, *her hands against her womb, creeps plaintively back to chair at 10,*

huddles up on it. STUDENT *remains sitting on floor at 9, to himself.* Now I feel *Dull 'thunder clap.'* the vampire in the kitchen beginning to suck my blood. I believe it's a lamia giving suck to children, for it's always...in the kitchen-maid's room that the children are nipped in the bud. Unless it happens in the bedroom. *Rubs his eyes, then lowers his hands.* COLONEL *gets up.* There are poisons that take away sight...and poisons that open eyes. I seem to be born with the latter kind. I...I can't see the ugly as beautiful, or call evil good. I can't! *Finds crucifix, whispers.* What? *Picks it up, looks at it, gets up, walks over to R.* Jesus Christ...descended into hell. That was his pilgrimage on earth...this madhouse, this prison, this charnel-house the earth. YOUNG LADY *slowly rises.* COLONEL *slowly in from 12, stops upstage.* And the madmen killed him when he wanted to set them free. But the bandit was released. The bandit always gets the sympathy! Alas...alas for us all. Saviour of the World...save us...for we perish!

YOUNG LADY *standing close to 3, faintly, helplessly.* Bring the screen...Quickly. I'm dying. *Wall projection fades away. Faint, mild light on stage. Then strong beamed light from above.*

COLONEL *up to* YOUNG LADY, *puts his arm around her shoulder, mildly.* The liberator is coming. Welcome...you pale and gentle one. *Moves her behind folding screen, which he places so that it hides her. One of her hands falls outside screen. He sits down on floor next to screen, seizes her hand.* Sleep, you beautiful...unhappy, innocent creature, who bear no blame for your suffering. Sleep without dreams. And when you awake again...may you be greeted by a sun...that does not burn...in a home without dust...by friends without faults...by a love...without flaw.

STUDENT *standing at 7 recites tonelessly, turned to auditorium.*

> I saw the sun. To me it seemed
> that I beheld the Hidden.
> Men must reap what they have sown,
> blest is he whose deeds are good.
> Deeds which you have wrought in fury,
> cannot in evil find redress.
> Comfort him you have distressed
> with loving-kindness – this will heal.
> No fear has he who does no ill. *Looks at* COLONEL.
> No fear has he who does no ill.
> Sweet is innocence.

93 MUMMY *enters 12 from L.*

STUDENT. Sweet is innocence...innocence? *He shakes his head, out at 7.*

94 MUMMY *slowly in from 12, up to folding screen, pulls it aside, sits down on chair next to it, regards* YOUNG LADY *who is lying on floor, puts one hand on* COLONEL's *shoul-*

40

der. You poor little child, *Beamed light increases. Occasional harp notes during the following according to pattern at end of Act II.* child of this world of illusion, guilt, suffering and death, this world of endless change, disappointment and pain. May the Lord of Heaven...have mercy on you on your journey. *A final harp note. Slow black-out. Curtain.*

Select annotated list of productions

T = Translation, D = Direction, S = Scenography, M = Music.
OM = Old Man, S = Student, M = Mummy, YL = Young Lady.

1908   21 Jan. *Spöksonaten*. Intima Teatern, Stockholm. D August Falck. *OM* Johan Ljungquist, *S* Helge Wahlgren, *M* Svea Åhman, *YL* Anna Flygare.

1915   1 May. *Gespenstersonate*. Kammerspiele, München. D Otto Falckenberg. *S* Erwin Kalser, *M* Emilie Unda.
        Acting area barely 26 feet wide and without depth. Expressionist production in which physical details were exaggerated. The Cook carried an oversized ladle and soya bottle and the clock dwarfed the characters. Ecstatic acting style. (Innes, 44-45, 74)

1916   20 Oct. Kammerspiele, Berlin. T Emil Schering. D Max Reinhardt. S Gustav Knina. *OM* Paul Wegener, *S* Paul Hartmann, *M* Gertrud Eysoldt, *YL* Roma Bahn.

1919   Das Tribunal, Königsberg. S Erwin Piscator.

1921   13 Oct. *Spøkelse-sonaten*. Centralteatret, Oslo. D Gyda Christensen. *OM* J.A. Holst-Jensen, *M* Gyda Christensen.

1922   Autumn. Svandas Theatre, Prague. D Jan Bor.

1923   April. *La sonata degli spettri*. Bragaglia Theatre, Rome.

1923   *Tondite sonaat*. Theatre School, Tallinn. D P. Sepp. M A. Vedro. *OM* Karl Otto, *S* Felix Moor/Alexis Ormusson, *M* Hilda Vernik, *YL* Ly Lasner.

1924   3 Jan. *The Spook Sonata*. Provincetown Playhouse, New York. T Edwin Björkman. D Robert Edmond Jones/James Light. S Robert Edmond Jones/Cleon Throckmorton. Masks James Light. *OM* Stanley Howlett, *S* Walter Abel, *M* Clare Eames, *YL* Helen Freeman.
        Eugene O'Neill, attached to the group, had selected the play for performance – with masks. Jones disliked the play. Rehearsals did not go smoothly. Kyra Markham, the costume designer, felt that O'Neill's ideas were lost and that Jones wrecked the play. The critics were baffled and derisive. The play closed after three weeks.

(Sheaffer, 123-24)

Pictures from the production in Stockenström (1988) xi.

1924   Akademietheater, Wien. D Albert Heine. S Alfred Roller.

1926   Summer. Zakopane, Poland.

1927   Globe Theatre/Strand Theatre, London. D J.B. Fagan. OM Allan Jeayes.

1931   24 Feb. Opera. M Julius Weissmann. D Walter Felsenstein. S Carl Kolter ten Hoonte. OM Sigmund Matuszewski, S Dago Meybert, M Pauline Strehl, YL Johanna von John.

1933   23 Feb. *La Sonate des Spectres*. Théâtre de l'Avenue, Paris. T Maurice Rémon. D Marcel Herrand. S Jacques Dupont. M Henri Sauguet. OM Guy Favières, S Marcel Herrand, M Germaine Géranne, YL Anne-Marie Rochaud.

1941   Autumn. Sagoteatern, Medborgarhuset, Stockholm. D Ingmar Bergman. S Gunnar Lindblad. OM Erland Colliander, S Peter Lindgren, M Dagny Lind, YL Karin Lannby.

1942   16 Oct. Dramaten, Stockholm. D Olof Molander. S Sven-Erik Skawonius. OM Lars Hanson, S Frank Sundström, M Märta Ekström, YL Inga Tidblad.

1946   14 Sep. Göteborgs stadsteater. D Olof Molander. S Sven-Erik Skawonius. M Ture Rangström. OM Sven Miliander, S Claes Thelander, M Maria Schildknecht, YL Gertrud Fridh.

1948   18 Feb. *Spøgelsessonaten*. Det kgl. Teater, Copenhagen. T Tom Kristensen. D Olof Molander. OM Thorkild Roose, S Jørgen Reenberg, M Clara Pontoppidan, YL Ingeborg Brams.

     The new translation was praised. No intermission between Acts II and III. "No one smiled. Molander does not permit that." (Frederik Schyberg in *Politiken* 19 Feb.)

1949   22 Jan. *Aavesonaatti*. Kansanteatteri, Helsinki. D Edvin Laine. S Jussi Kari. M Yngve Ingman. OM Sasu Haapanen, S Martti Katajistos, M Elsa Turakainen, YL Aino Mantsas.

     Abstract-expressionistic scenery, the house façade in green and black. Entrances of the two dead characters marked by violin tremolandi. Böcklin's *Toten-Insel* at the end seemed meaningless since not many know the name of the painting which was hardly visible. (N.L-ou in *Nya Pressen* 24 Jan.)

Hummel seemed likeable rather than terrifying, the opposite of what the author has intended. (Hans Kutter in *Hufvudstadsbladet* 26 Jan.)

1949   25 Oct. Gaité-Montparnasse, Paris. T Maurice Rémon. D Roger Blin. S Thanos Tsingos. M Jeannine de Waleyne. OM O'Brady, S Roger Blin, M Christine Tsingos, YL Nina Peinado.

Translation via Schering's German translation. About a hundred performances but only some fifteen spectators each time. A shallow stage with cardboard wings. The Student, appearing in a student's cap and frock coat, moved automatically and spoke monotonously as though he was sleep-walking. The Milkmaid in a German-looking folk costume. (Tidström, 78-79)

The Old Man "moved disturbingly in his wheelchair," Johansson "moved as little as possible and limited gestures to his right hand," and the Student "allowed himself few gestures." The production "suggested subterranean currents, halftones." (Aslan, 20)

1950   21 Jan. *The Ghost Sonata*. Yale University Theatre, New Haven, Conn. T Elisabeth Sprigge. D John Sydow.

1952   June. Schauspielhaus Zürich. T Willi Reich. D Frank-Patrich Steckel. OM Walter Richter, S Schmidt, M Traute Carlsen, YL Gisela Mattishent.

1953   8 Oct. *Spøk-Sonaten*. Det Norske Teatret, Oslo. T Ragnvald Skrede. D Olof Molander. S Sven-Erik Skawonius /Arne Walentin. OM Lars Tvinde, S Pål Bucher Skjønberg, M Lydia Opøien, YL Urda Arneberg.

1954   5 March. Malmö stadsteater. D Ingmar Bergman. S Martin Ahlbom. OM Benkt-Åke Benktsson, S Folke Sundquist, M Naima Wifstrand, YL Gaby Stenberg.

1955   23 Oct. BBC. Radio.

1956   Städtische Bühne, Frankfurt am Main. D Lothar Müthel. S Paul Haferung.

1961   6 Oct. *Sonata widm.* Teatr Polskiego Radia, Warszawa. T Zygmunt Łanowski. D Z. Kopalko.

1961   *De spooksonate.* Dutch Television. D Ton Lensink. OM Albert van Dalsum, M Ida Wasserman.

1962   7 Feb. Genève. Théâtre de Carouge. D Philippe Mentha. *OM* François Simon, *S* Philippe Mentha.

1962   16 March. British Television. T Michael Meyer. D Stuart Burge. S Clifford Hatts. *OM* Robert Helpmann, *S* Jeremy Brett, *M* Beatrix Lehmann, *YL* Ann Bell.

The 70 minutes allowed for the performance necessitated some deletions which made the plot unclear. (K.G. Bolander in *Svenska Dagbladet* 19 March)

Maurice Richard in *The Observer* was enthusiastic. The reviewer of *The Times* regretted that Ingmar Bergman did not direct the play, as originally intended. He praised the actors but criticized the restless camera work in Act I as well as the lighting. (Ossia Trilling in *Berlingske Aftenavis* 26 March)

1962   6 May. Swedish Radio. D Per Verner-Carlsson. M Bengt Hambræus. *OM* Allan Edwall, *S* Lars Lind, *M* Margareta Krook, *YL* Christina Schollin.

1962   11 May. Dramaten, Stockholm. D Olof Molander. S Sven-Erik Skawonius. M Ture Rangström. *OM* Anders Henrikson, *S* Allan Edwall, *M* Birgitta Valberg, *YL* Barbro Larsson.

1964   4 Jan. Toneelgroep Theater, Nijmegen. T Remco Campert. D Ton Lensink. S Wim Vesseur/Ton Lensink. M Hans van Sweeden. *OM* Hans Tiemeijer, *S* Willem Nijholt, *M* Jacqueline Royaards-Sandberg, *YL* Nienke Sikkema.

The assumption behind the production was that Strindberg has portrayed himself both in Hummel and in the Student, who "ultimately seems condemned – out of self-preservation – to become another company director Hummel." (Ton Lensink in theatre program)

1964   9 Feb. Teatr T-38, Kraków. T Zygmunt Łanowski. D Jerzy Paszula. S Jan Kaiser. *OM* Andrzej Skupień, *S* Andrzej Niketyński, *M* and *YL* Barbara Jasińska.

The stage picture, representing a mortuary, symbolized a world full of crimes and lies, dictatorially ruled by "the God of Falsehood." Between Him and the people a privileged class consisting of "the rulers of the kitchen." Hummel was portrayed as the leader of the suppressed people symbolized by the Student. But Hummel's motives proved to be false. The production was a satire on the policy of the Polish leaders during the Stalin era. (Uggla, 73-74)

1965   19 June. *Sonata widm*. Teatr Polski, Warszawa. T Zygmunt
Łanowski. D Jerzy Kreczmar. S Jan Kosiński. *OM* Bronisław Pawlik,
S Wacław Szklarski, *M* Barbara Ludwiżanka, *YL* Hanna Stankówna.

In Act III, the Colonel and the Mummy were represented by two
dolls, and the dead Hummel, played by a young actor, appeared behind the death screen. Scenery and costumes were in black, grey and
white. The round room was surrounded by grey curtains looking like
spiderwebs. The director aimed at distance to the spectators. (Uggla,
87-88)

1965   Aug. Finnish Television.

1965   26 Nov. Finnish Radio. In Swedish. D Eddie Stenberg. *OM* Erik
Lindström, S Gösta Bredefeldt, *M* Kerstin Nylander, *YL* Ulla-Britt
Boström.

1966   11 April. Danish Television. D Leon Feder.

1967   8 Feb. Riksteatern/Svenska teatern, Växjö. D Sandro Malmquist.
OM Gösta Cederlund, S Lennart Tollén, *M* Fylgia Zadig, *YL* Lena
Gumælius.

Esthetic performance in violet, brown and white. In Act II the tile
stove with the candles and the white covers on the furniture gave an
impression of altar and mortuary in tune with the meaning of the
play. (Hanserik Hjertén in *Svenska Dagbladet* 9 Feb.)

1967   21 Nov. Théâtre de l'Alliance française (L'Autre Théâtre), Paris. T
Arthur Adamov/Carl-Gustaf Bjurström. D Jean Gillibert. S Claude
Auclair. *OM* Marcel Cuvelier, S Bruno Sermonne, *M* Tania
Balachova, *YL* Josette Boulva.

Movements, gestures and mimicry unintelligible, all this in a
tempo of about one word a minute. "I left the theatre [–] a ghost myself, killed by boredom." (Jean Dutourd in *France-Soir* 22 Nov.)

"Totally uninintelligible because of the abstraction and the impenetrable symbolism." (Jean-Jacques Gautier in *Le Figaro* 22 Nov.)

1968   15 Oct. *Sonata di spettri*. Italian Television. T Luciano Codignola.

1968   11 April. Danish Television. D Leon Feder. S Jørgen Espen-Hansen.
OM Elith Pio, S Niels Hinrichsen, *M* Else Højgaard, *YL* Ulla-Britt
Borksand.

The 'invisible' characters in the beginning presented difficulties but
the scene where the Milkmaid is drowned by Hummel was well shot.
(Erik Ulrichsen in *Berlingske Aftenavis* 13 Apr.)

Magic and poetry lacking. The performance did not move. The

drowning Milkmaid was seen sinking down to the bottom of the sea. (Svend Kragh-Jacobsen in *Berlingske Tidende* 13 Apr.)

1969   4 March. Linköpings stadsteater, Sweden. D Lars-Erik Liedholm. S Jost Assman. OM Runar Schauman, S Lars Elfvin, M Kerstin Rabe, YL Ann Falk.

   The house in Act I was a white villa silhouetted against a bright blue sky. Act II was set in a silk-black room, visualizing the secret crimes of the bourgeoisie behind their light façades. Well designed, absurd effects but lacking in deeper originality. (Leif Zern in *Dagens Nyheter* 6 March)

1969   25 March. Gävle stadsteater, Sweden. D Stig Ossian Ericson. S Helge Refn. OM Fredrik Ohlsson, S Palle Granditzky, M Elsa Prawitz, YL Bodil Mannheimer.

   Musical structure of play emphasized. Performance interspersed with Beethoven's Piano Sonata Op. 31 No. 2. Intermissions between the 'movements.' Each one had its own characteristics, the first playfully improvisational, the second dramatic, the third lyrical-elegiac. The actor doing Hummel was only 30; this worked well. (Åke Janzon in *Svenska Dagbladet* 26 March)

1969   Autumn. Finnish Radio.

1971   Feb. Stuttgart. D Hans Neuenfels. OM Hans Mahnke, S Ulrich Wildgruber, M Edith Heerdegen, YL Ilse Ritter.

   A complicated production utilizing psychoanalysis, surrealism, silent film technique and commenting loudspeaker voices. The Student pushed Hummel's wheelchair walking on his knees. (Gunnar Ollén in *Meddelanden från Strindbergssällskapet*, 47/48, 8)

1972   30 Oct. Swedish Television. D Johan Bergenstråhle. S Bo Lindgren. OM Allan Edwall, S Stefan Ekman, M Ulla Sjöblom, YL Marie Göranzon.

1972   Nationaltheatret, Oslo. T Carl Fredrik Engelstad. D Stein Winge. S Lubos Hruza. OM Georg Løkkeberg, S Erik Hivju, M Ella Hval, YL Monna Tandberg.

1972   24 Nov. Polish Television.

1973   13 Jan. Dramaten, Stockholm. D Ingmar Bergman. S Marik Vos. M Daniel Bell. OM Toivo Pawlo, S Mathias Henrikson, M and YL Gertrud Fridh.

1975   18 Sep. Théâtre Oblique, Paris. Hubert Jappelle et ses marionettes.

1975   25 Nov. L'Odéon (Théâtre Oblique), Paris. T Arthur Adamov/Carl-
        Gustaf Bjurström. D Henri Ronse. S Béni Montrésor. OM François
        Chaumette, S Bruno Devoldère, M Catherine Samie, YL Fanny
        Delbrice.
            Played on a big stage. Scenography in baroque style, with marble
        and gold, an Italian drinking-fountain, costumes in silk brocade, ev-
        erything seen through tulle draperies as in turn of the century sym-
        bolist theatre. The table for the ghost supper placed on an elevated
        piece of stone, was reached via stairs. Ornamented pillars and high
        coloured windows as in a cathedral. Theatrical positions and ges-
        tures. Music by Wagner. (Tidström, 87)

1977   7 Jan. Gate Theatre, London. T Inga-Stina Ewbank. D Georgina van
        Welie. S Jackie Brooks. OM Alan MacNaughtan, S Mark Letheren,
        M Diana Fairfax, YL Josephine Butler.

1977   18 June. Grudziadz, Poland.

1977   Yale Repertory Theater, New Haven, Conn.
            Favourable reviews by Jack Kroll in *Newsweek* 24 Oct. and Har-
        old Clurman in *The Nation* 5 Nov.

1978   5 Feb. Opole, Poland.

1978   25 Jan. *Sonata di fantasmi*. Quattro Cantoni, Rome.

1980   23 March, British Television. T Michael Meyer. D Philip Saville. S
        Barrie Dobbins. M Peter Howell. OM Donald Pleasance, S Clive
        Arrindell, M Lily Kedrova, YL Nina Zuckerman.

1981   12 Sep. Göteborgs stadsteater. D Claes Lundberg. S Olle Montelius.
        OM Roland Söderberg, S Bengt Järnblad, M Lena Brogren, YL
        Mariann Rudberg.
            Black auditorium with walls draped with white sheets. On the
        stage a clock with a hand turning round and round. For the rest
        empty except for a red ladder, a fire-place and a pillar with an Egyp-
        tian cat as ornament. Silent faces projected on the backdrop. The sur-
        realist dream world, here anguished. No nuances in dialogue, only
        grotesque smiles. Hummel presented as the failing dictator with me-
        galomania. He looked straight into the auditorium. The mental Stu-
        dent-Hummel connection emphasized. (Bengt Jahnsson in *Dagens
        Nyheter* 21 Sep.)

1982   13 Kasum [?]. *Hayaletler sonati.* National Theatre, Istanbul. T Güngör Dilmen. D Levend Öktem. S Refik Eren. OM Muammer Esi, M Tülin Oral Boratap.

1982   April. Classic Stage Company, New York. D Christopher Martin/Karen Sunde. S Christopher Martin. OM Noble Shropshire, S Tom Spackman, M Carol Schultz, YL Ginger Grace.

   Setting was like a Chirico landscape with still objects oddly juxtaposed on a surrealistic, checkerboarded plane: a torso of a woman with her head draped, a tall clock that acted as a casket for the Mummy, empty shrouded chairs. (Mel Gussow in *The New York Times* 21 Apr.)

1984   25 Sep. Opera. Hebbel-Theater, Berlin. T Aribert Reimann/Uwe Schendel. M Aribert Reimann. D Heinz Lukas-Kindermann. S Dietrich Schoras. OM Hans Günter Noecker, S David Knutson, M Martha Moedl.

   A chamber orchestra of 12 musicians. An oblique glass roof was peopled by the inhabitants of the house. Their movements were seen from below – as were they in an aquarium – also by Hummel and the Student who were on the stage floor. What happened there was mirrored in the glass ceiling, so that the characters mingled in an hallucinatory manner. Dark sounds for Hummel, strings for the burgeoning love, "moth-eaten notes" from a chamber organ for the Mummy. (Leif Aare in *Dagens Nyheter* 4 Oct.)

1986   6 Sep. Aarhus Teater. D Hans Rosenquist. S Finn Erik Bendixen. OM Aksel Erhardtsen, S Lars Høy, M Karen Lis Ahrenkiels, YL Merete Voldstedlund.

   A high-tech façade of glass and steel. The nobly grizzled Hummel wore a fashionable suit of the 1980s. (Jan Hedegaard in *Jyllands-Posten* 7 Sept.)

1988   Feb. Opera. Prinzregententheater/Bayrische Staatsoper. M Aribert Reimann. D Helmuth Lehberger. S Ulrich Franz. OM Hans Günter Noecker.

1988   May. Akademietheater, Wien. T Florian Brandstätter. D Cesare Lievi. S Daniele Lievi. OM Walther Reyer, S Christoph Waltz, M Gusti Wolf, YL Josefin Platt.

   In Act I, a narrow strip in front represented the street; behind it the characters in the house, in slow motion, gave the impression of being dream projections. In Act II the house became transparent. As the Young Lady was dying, blood was running down her right leg. At the end the room opened up to a cloudscape. (Reinhard Baumgart in *Die Zeit* 20 May)

1989   20 Feb. Opera. Queen Elizabeth Hall, London. M Aribert Reimann. D David Freeman. S David Roger. *OM* Richard Stuart, *S* David Aldred, *M* Nigel Robson, *YL* Helen Charnock.

Much of the naturalistic detail was cut. Two major sections of text were added for the Mummy and the Dark Lady in order to give them more musical profile. "The Song of the Sun" was given to the Young Lady at the beginning of Act III. She became in a sense the teacher, which led to quite a different ending. (David Freeman in theatre program)

1989   23 Feb. Queen Elizabeth Hall, London. T Gregory Motton. D David Freeman. S David Roger. *OM* Jerome Willis, *S* Adam Kotz, *M* Linda Marlowe, *YL* Caroline Bliss.

"Freeman has chosen to mount opera and play in the same short season; but where the opera is a triumph, the play is a disaster." (Richard Allen Cave in *The Times Higher Educational Supplement*, 10 March)

1989   15 March. Teater 9, Stockholm. D Bo Dahlberg and Stefan Johansson. S Eva-Katarina Ekermann. *OM* Stefan Hallin, *S* Michael Olsén, *M* Gunnel Broström, *YL* Saara Salminen.

The audience, separated from the stage through veils, was sitting on three sides around the stage, at the back of which a staircase led to a front door high up on the wall. The performance began with a wedding. When the Milkmaid appeared, this was interrupted and she was killed in the middle of a Holy Communion. The Colonel wore a Strindbergian 'mask.' The Old Man and the Cook were played by the same actor. The frail, beautiful Mummy was not mad; she had just escaped from life. (Richard Bark in *Strindbergiana*, 6, 157)

1989   24 Sep. Betty Nansen Teatret, Copenhagen. T Svend Lange. D Staffan Valdemar Holm. S Bente Lykke Møller. *OM* Ove Sprogøe, *S* Thomas Mork, *M* Lily Weiding, *YL* Pia Stangerup.

As the audience got seated, the Student walked around in the auditorium with a white rose in his hand. Then the collapse of a house the previous night was acted out. The Student tried to save a child but fainted. When he woke up again, the Milkmaid poured milk over his face. The characters lived high up in a windowless building. There was a movement inward and upwards, via stairs. When unmasked, the Old Man became a little child; he stood in cruciform with a

happy smile on his lips before he went into the closet. The Young
Lady's movements gradually became resemblant of the Mummy's.
When the Student verbally attacked her, he pushed his hand between
her legs. The closing lines were divided between different characters.
At the end the recently dead Young Lady and the Milkmaid climbed
the stairs upstage in a bright white light. After the iron curtain was
lowered, the Student's hand was seen, trying in vain to reach the
white rose on the forestage. (Richard Bark in *Strindbergiana*, 6, 166-
68)

1989   Finnish Radio. D Christopher Martin. OM Tom Wentzel, S Robert
Enckell, M and YL Elina Salo. (Broadcast by the Swedish Radio 22
January 1990.)

1991   20 Jan. Park Square Theatre Company, Saint Paul, Minnesota. T
Evert Sprinchorn. D Richard Cook. M Michael J. Croswell. OM David Ward Melmer, S Craig Johnson, M Sara Jane Olson.
    In order to create the atmosphere of Kama-Loka that he wanted to
superimpose on the realistic setting, Cook added a brief prelude inspired by Munch's paintings of death scenes, in which the mourners
seem related to one another, yet isolated in their suffering. Organ,
church bells and harp were incorporated in the music. At the end the
Student transcended to a higher realm, where he was comforted by
the nurturing female figure of the Milkmaid. (Barbara Lide in *Theatre Review*, 1991, 111)

1991   8 Feb. Uppsala stadsteater, Sweden. D Ulf Fredriksson. S Gunnar
Steneby. OM Tommy Nilsson, S Lars Wik, M Ulla Blomstrand, YL
Tytte Johnsson.
    A huge, realistic grey façade dominated the stage. To the left a high
glass wall, behind which the Milkmaid drowned. (Richard Bark in
Strindbergiana, 9, 138)

1992   13 March. Folkteatern, Gävle, Sweden. D Ulf Fembro. S Gunnar
Ekman. OM Lasse Karlsson, S Pontus Stenshäll, M Sara Svanberg,
YL Susanna Fredriksson.
    The audience walked into the auditorium through a ghostly tun-
nel. Rock music from the loudspeakers. The house façade consisted
of a piece of drapery which when drawn aside revealed the round
room. The hyacinth room opened up at the end and the light broke
through. (Richard Bark in *Strindbergiana*, 9, 145)

1992   11 April. Strindbergsmuséet, Stockholm. D Mattias Lafolie. OM
Thomas Olsson, S Dag Lindberg, M Pia Landgren, YL Tuvalisa

Rangström.

The scenery consisted of curtains which, when lit, showed the characters as shadowy figures. Grotesqueness prevailed over psychological analysis. (Richard Bark in *Strindbergiana*, 9, 145)

1992   27 May. Sturdy Beggars Theatre Company. New End Theatre, Hampstead. T/D Jonas Finley. S Andrew Marsland. *OM* Stephen Jameson, *S* Nicholas Gilbrook, *M* Elisabeth McGrath, *YL* Alison Redford.

1992   7 Nov. Marionetteatern, Stockholm. D/S Roman Paska. M Richard Termini. Dolls Arne Högsander, Karin Magnusson. Doll players Helena Nilson, Pär Heimdal, Jorge Onofri.

A praised performance directed by a leading puppeteer. The tension between the dolls, in Japanese buraku style, and the doll players, visible in their dark hats, was fully utilized. The music was specially composed by an American rock musician. (Charlotte Wendt in *Svenska Dagbladet* 6 Nov.)

The gate to heaven or to the big house was framed by two oars, "possibly lent by Charon." In its middle the black back of a man in a top hat and with an umbrella, a "Magritte painting" or "the turned-away person's eternal effort to take a step beyond." (Pia Huss in *Svenska Dagbladet* 21 Nov.)

1993   Polish Radio. D Andrzej Wajda.

1994   26 Feb. Dramaten, Stockholm. D Andrzej Wajda. S Krystyna Zachwatowicz. M Stanislaw Radwan. *OM* Max von Sydow, *S* Benny Haag, *M* Margaretha Krook, *YL* Stina Ekblad.

Chopin's Piano Sonata Op. 35 was played live. The Funeral March accompanied the ghost supper. Upstage a 'rolling' silvery black plastic cover, the boundless "sea of death." The transparent closet and the hyacinth room formed framing constructions. (Carlhåkan Larsén in *Sydsvenska Dagbladet* 27 Feb.)

What is the point of moving the ingenious first act to a sunny, glittering sea – with the Milkmaid's zinc desk (the fountain) as only scenographic element? (Jens Kistrup in *Berlingske Tidende* 27 Feb.)

Does the Cook [played by a black actress] symbolize the third world which now demands back what has been stolen from it? And are the Caretaker's Wife and her daughter prostitutes and the Posh Man a pimp, and is the idea that the West is still impoverishing black countries? (Gunnar Lindén in *Nerikes Allehanda* 28 Feb.)

1994   12 March. *Spoku sonate*. Riga. T Solveiga Elsberga. D Ints
        Sedlenieks. S Andris Freibergs. M Andris Maskats. OM Janis
        Samauskis, S Girts Kesteris, M Nina Leimane/Skaidrite Putnina, YL
        Nora Bidere.

1995   16 Sep. *Sonáta duchu*. Divadlo Komedie, Prague. T Radko Kejzlar. D
        Jan Nebeský. S Jana Preková. OM Milos Mejzlík, S Sasa Rasilov, M
        Zdena Hdrbolcová, YL Petra Lustigová.

1998   26 Feb. Opera. Australian National University Arts Centre. M Judith
        Crispin-Creswell. D David Atfield. S David Longmuir. OM Tom
        Layton, S Kent McIntosh, M Erika Tolano.

2000   22 jan. Swedish Radio (P1). D Åsa Melldahl. OM Jan Malmsjö, S
        Jonas Malmsjö, M Marie Göranzon, YL Elin Klinga.

2000   12 Feb. Dramaten, Stockholm. D Ingmar Bergman. S Göran Wass-
        berg. OM Jan Malmsjö, S Jonas Malmsjö, M Gunnel Lindblom, YL
        Elin KLinga.

Notes

Notes to Prologue

1   Letter to Adolf Paul 6 Jan. 1907, in Strindberg (1992) 734.

2   Falck, 81-82.

3   The name given by theosophists to the first stage which the soul enters after death.

4   Letter 27 March 1907, in Strindberg (1992) 735. Robinson in this letter calls the play *A Spook Sonata*.

5   The Piano Sonata Op. 31 No. 2, and the Piano Trio Op. 70 No. 1, traditionally known as The Ghost Trio.

6   Letter 1 April 1907, in Strindberg (1992) 736. Unlike Robinson, I have retained Strindberg's German terms.

7   Letter 7 April 1907, in Strindberg (1992) 738.

8   Letter 26 April 1907, in Strindberg (1992) 741.

9   Bergman (1966) 283.

10   Strindberg (1959) 19.

11   Letter 2 April 1907 in Strindberg (1992) 736-37, with a slight change: for Sw. "diktat," I prefer "fiction" to Robinson's "poetry."

12   Lamm (1926) 393, 395.

13   *Göteborgs-Posten* 12 Sep. 1946. The relevant passage is reprinted in Törnqvist (1973) 19. Brandell (1989, 319) questions Molander's assumption.

14   Falck, 41-42, 74. According to Lindström in Strindberg (1963, 102), the Buddha statuette was found on the mantlepiece in the dining room – below a plaster cast of Beethoven's death-mask.

15   Ollén (1961) 469.

16   Falck, 84-85. Lindström (1979), however, points out that Hirsch did not become an invalid until after Strindberg's death. Instead he argues convincingly (28-31) for another model: the rich and reckless businessman, theatre director and collector Christian Hammer. Sprinchorn (1976, 16-17) interestingly points to a literary source, Herr Hyazinth in Heinrich Heine's *The Baths of Lucca*.

17   Ollén (1961) 469.

18   Ibid., 333.

19   *Dagens Nyheter* 11 April 1954. See further Törnqvist (1973) 21.

20   Ollén (1982) 518.

21   For Strindberg's acquaintance with Hoffmann's work, see Lindström (1977) 87, 137 and (1990) 121.

22   Letter to Henning Berger ca. 10 Dec. 1906, in Strindberg (1976) 326.

23   Lindström in Strindberg (1963) 97-98.

24   Ibid., 99-101.

25   Strindberg (1959) 98.

26   For further correspondences between *Hamlet* and *The Ghost Sonata*, see Lindström (1958) and Törnqvist (1969). Lindström (1956, 91) sees a parallel between the

Hamletian Gregers Werle's 'murder' of Hedvig in Ibsen's *The Wild Duck* and the Student's 'murder' of the Young Lady.

27   Strindberg (1959) 279.

28   Buchwald, 151.

29   Strindberg (1962) xix, 116.

30   For further similarities between the two plays, see Törnqvist (1979).

31   It is not, as is often claimed, an Eddic poem.

32   See Lindström in Strindberg (1963) 84-86.

33   Ibid., 98-99.

34   Torsslow, 25-27.

Notes to One: Source text

1   Strindberg (1991a) 115, 119, 125, 143, 163.

2   Ibid., 122.

3   Ibid., 127.

4   Loc. cit.

5   Ibid., 116.

6   SgNM 3.22,4, quoted from Stockenström (1978) 136.

7   Stockenström (1978) 136.

8   Strindberg (1991a) 119.

9   See Landquist's text-critical commentary *SS* 45:342-45, and Törnqvist (1973b) 29.

10   The text-critical commentary of *SV* is yet to appear.

11   Strindberg (1998b) xxxvii. Unlike *SV 58*, neither Strindberg (1907) nor *SS* 45 distinguish between Strindberg's *points suspensifs* (...) and his triple dashes (---); only the former are used.

12   In his letter to Schering 7 April 1907, Strindberg speaks of the final "scene" of *The Ghost Sonata* but the context indicates that by this he simply means the end of the play.

13   This term is borrowed from Pfister (171). For a detailed survey of the sequence and character constellation of the configurations, see the chart in Appendix 1.

14   Falck, 81-82.

15   Lindström (1969) 66.

16   Rokem, 66.

17   Lindström (1969) 71.

18   The fact that the Milkmaid "*is dressed in summer clothes*" is not relevant, since she is a vision.

19   Szondi, 31.

20   Cf. Williams' declaration (103) that "the unifying consciousness is that of the Student."

21   Lindström (1964) 169.

22   Brandell (1981).

23   Szondi, 31.

24   Letter to director Victor Castegren 22 Oct. 1908, in Strindberg (1991) 151.

25   See Mays.

26 In his essay on *Hamlet,* Strindberg (1959, 75) compares this play to "a symphony, polyphonically developed with independent motifs, which are beautifully woven together; it is fugued." He speaks of "the andante of Act I," the "largo maestoso" of Act IV, "the gravediggers' scherzo" and "the presto of the finale."

27 Strindberg (1959) 19.

28 Steene (1982) 113.

29 Sprinchorn (1962) xx.

30 Berendsohn, 541-43.

31 Vowles, 175-76. According to him, the three instruments correspond to the three leadings parts: the Young Lady (violin), the Student (cello), the Old Man (piano). But Hummel's absence in Act III does not support this idea.

32 Jarvi, 79-83. For the musical aspect, see also Sondrup.

33 Falck, 53.

34 This interpretation agrees with Brandell's view (1989, 323) that the play is essentially about this life. For the view that Strindberg already when the play opens "lets us journey with him to the other side of the grave," see Sprinchorn (1978, 378-79) and (1982, 264). Stockenström (1978, 136-37, 144) more convincingly argues that Strindberg, judging from his manuscript notes, played with the idea of setting the play in the afterlife – the Mummy may be a remnant of this – but eventually changed his mind.

35 Bryant-Bertail, 307. Actually, he recites rather than sings.

36 Cf. Sjöstedt's (208) remark that "the main theme is [the] unmasking of men and society, which finally turns into the unmasking of human existence and its earthly conditions."

37 One is reminded of the contrasting couple Edgar-Edmund in *King Lear.*

38 Kjellin/Ramnefalk, 93-94.

39 Göran Lindström in Strindberg (1963, 81) combines it with the Finland-Swedish historian and Swedenborgian Johan Arckenholtz, whereas Hans Lindström (1979, 32) suggests the German historian Johann Wilhelm von Arckenholz. Both suggestions have the disadvantage that they do not illuminate the character and disregard the fact that either man would be known by very few recipients of the play.

40 Strindberg (1962) 226.

41 Northam, 41.

42 Frænkl, 53.

43 Delblanc, 94.

44 I differ from Ollén in *SV:58, 411* in his view that the Consul has two daughters.

45 Berendsohn, 541.

46 Strindberg (1998) 61.

47 Since we would expect the bedclothes on the balcony with the flag of the consulate to belong to the Consul, Strindberg actually fuses the idea of divorce with that of death. In either case the quilt concretizes the change from cohabitation to singleness.

48 Lamm (1942) 312.

49 Strindberg (1977) 251. The manuscript clearly shows that the Cook, not found in the list of characters, was added at a late stage.Cf. fig 2.

50 Wilkinson, 476.

51 Delblanc, 110.

52 Loc. cit.

53   Leifer, 181, 187.

54   Strindberg (1963) 76.

55   The correspondence between the women is indicated by their related Christian names: Beate (beautiful), Amalia (irreproachable), Adèle (noble).

56   Those who have passed their Swedish matriculation were and are allowed to wear a white student's cap from 1 May until 1 October.

57   Northam, 41.

58   Lunin (248), for example, sees the house as "the House of the World for all humanity," a kind of "Noah's arc" containing examples of various human species.

59   In the notes for the play, it says: "He must pass through the room of ordeals."

60   This according to the stage directions of Act III. Those of Act II present another picture. Here the hyacinth room seems to border on the hall.

61   Northam, 43.

62   Ibid., 47.

63   Cf. Ibsen's *The Wild Duck,* where Gina gets her husband a job, and an illegitimate child, after having been made pregnant by her boss, Werle.

64   Cf. Bentley's remark (172) that "the point is that servant and master are linked in one universal guilt."

65   Berendsohn, 539.

66   See the reproductions in Floerke, 36.

67   Similarly, the initial stage directions for the drama fragment *Toten-Insel,* written immediately after *The Ghost Sonata,* laconically state "*The backdrop: Böcklin's* Toten-Insel" (*SV* 63:329) – without any specification of version. In *SV* 58:416 the second version (1880), now in Metropolitan Museum, is reproduced, whereas in *SV* 63:5 the third version, now in Berlin, is reproduced. The indication is that these versions, too, may have inspired Strindberg.

68   The reproduction found on Strindberg's alternative title page for *The Ghost Sonata* (*SV* 58:402) – cf. fig.1 – concerns this version, in Strindberg's time owned by F.A. Simrock in Berlin (Floerke, 36), since 1920 in Kunstmuseum Basel (Zelger, 8).

69   While the laurel, as Ekman points out (191), here represents worldly honour and success – cf. the function of the Officer's laurel wreath in *A Dream Play* – the cypress is traditionally the tree of churchyards, of death.

70   For a discussion of this "experiment," as she prefers to call it, see Knape.

71   Northam, 41, 48.

72   Ekman, 169.

73   Cf. the note in Strindberg (1977a) 15 April 1907: "This is what I cannot understand: if you should cover up their wretchedness and flatter your fellow-men. I want to write positively and beautifully but am not allowed to; I take it as a horrible duty to be truthful, and life is incredibly ugly."

74   Strindberg (1959) 101-02.

75   Lindström in Strindberg (1963) 84.

76   Lindström (1964) 173-74.

77   Sprinchorn in Strindberg (1962) 227, note 13.

78   Cf. *Miss Julie,* where Jean holds a lilac twig under Julie's nose when he relates how he, as a boy, was crawling through the shit-hole of the outdoor lavatory.

79   Strindberg (1959) 98.

80 As Kennedy points out, the dialogue in this act "compresses a whole cycle of relationship – love, marriage, decline and death – within [-] one sustained encounter" (211).

81 Jolivet, 327.

82 Strindberg's manuscript has the following variety, used in *SV 58:220*, revealing the influence from E.T.A. Hoffmann: "It is the colouring bottle, the Devil's elixir with scorpion letters on it! It is the witch Mrs Soya [-]." – In August 1999, Swedish newspapers reported that various kinds of soya are dangerous to your health!

83 In that case his situation is similar to that of doctor Rank in *A Doll's House* and of Osvald in *Ghosts*.

84 In the manuscript, Strindberg had originally written: "a virgin with hereditary or acquired" (*SS 45:345*).

85 Leifer, 189.

86 Under the heading "Factors," Strindberg mentions in his notes for the play: "The state of Innocence = the tree of Knowledge=/[-]/the Marble statue=." Strindberg (1991a) 132-33.

87 According to Lindström (1979, 31-32), the references to *The Valkyrie* have a personal background. Christian Hammer's exlibris, found in a number of books in Strindberg's library, shows a valkyrie holding a hammer – Thor's attribute – driving a four-in-hand. Although this may well have served as a source of inspiration, Strindberg must have realized that such a private allusion would be spoilt on an audience.

88 Leifer, 179. For a more dubious Jungian approach to the *Valkyrie* motif, see Converse, 64-68.

Notes to Two: Target texts

1 German translations of *Spöksonaten* are discussed in Paul, French ones in Tidström.

2 Lindström's edition (Strindberg, 1963) may also have been of significance.

3 Unfortunately, the translators seldom inform their readers of which edition they have used. (13) and (15) are in this respect exceptional.

4 In the revised version (Strindberg, 1986a) this evaluative comparison is omitted.

5 French recipients may have a problem with this ritual, since in France it is customary to hang a black cloth above the entrance as a sign of decease (Tidström, 132).

6 *SV* contains extensive word explanations. Those concerning *Spöksonaten* are found in *SV 58:454-60*.

7 *SS 45:156* has the form "sportsman."

8 Cf. Ewbank in Strindberg (1997), 149, note 19, and Robinson in Strindberg (1998), 309.

9 Törnqvist (1976b), 13.

10 Schering in Strindberg (1908) renders it as "sieht aus, als sterbe sie."

11 Concerning this problem, see Törnqvist (1998).

12 Sprinchorn in Strindberg (1962) xiv-xv.

13 Tidström, 122.

14 So do Schering, Rémon, and Adamov/Bjurström. See Tidström, 124-25.

15 For a discussion of the biblical references, see Bandy, 200-202.

16   Cf. Lindström (1964) 170-76.
17   Robinson in Strindberg (1998) xxxvii-xxxviii.
18   This unwanted situation is clearly documented in Ollén's 1982 survey of the stage history of Strindberg's plays. We receive much information about directing, acting and scenography but very little about the translations used, obviously because the critics have been silent on this point.

Notes to Three: Stage productions

1   Bark, 87.
2   This according to Ollén (1982, 531), who bases his information on Michal. Falck's (358) number is fourteen.
3   Signature S. in *Nya Dagligt Allehanda* 22 Jan. 1908.
4   While Meyer (544) rightly points to this as one reason why some Strindberg productions were failures, his claim that some of "the new plays Strindberg wrote for the Intimate were not good," is an opinion few would share.
5   *Dagens Nyheter* 22 Jan. 1908.
6   Sven Söderman in *Stockholms Dagblad* 22 January 1908.
7   Bergman, op. cit.
8   Söderman, op. cit.
9   Sign. G.B. in *Svenska Dagbladet* 22 Jan. 1908.
10   Vera von Kraemer in *Social-Demokraten* 22 Jan. 1908.
11   Anna Branting in *Stockholms-Tidningen* 22 Jan. 1908.
12   Söderman, op. cit. and sign. G.B., op. cit.
13   Bergman, op. cit. Cf. Strindberg's letter to Svea Åhman 31 Jan. 1908: "I praised your 'Mummy' in *The Ghost Sonata*, and do so still." Strindberg (1992) 760.
14   Von Kraemer, op. cit.
15   Strindberg (1992) 761-62.
16   Strindberg (1918) 94.
17   Letter to August Falck 28 March 1908, in Strindberg (1992) 769.
18   Bergman (1966) 290.
19   Paul, 132.
20   All quotations in the following, unless otherwise indicated, are from Reinhardt's prompt book after Kvam, 71-86 or Bark, 104-16.
21   Bark (104) rightly remarks that the prompt book should be measured against the information provided in the reviews. This is, however, easier said than done, since the reviewers only comment on some of the aspects touched upon in the prompt book. Largely deprived of visual material, we cannot in other cases tell whether the intentions were effectuated or not.
22   Kvam, 78.
23   Ibid., 82-83.
24   Reinhardt placed lamps inside the flower pots to make them radiate a mysterious light (Bark, 113).
25   Kvam, 84.
26   Styan, 38.

27 Sign. René in *Social-Demokraten* 4 May 1917.
28 *Dagens Nyheter* 4 May 1917.
29 Abell, 33.
30 René, op. cit.
31 August Brunius in *Svenska Dagbladet* 4 May 1917.
32 Abell, 33.
33 René, op. cit.
34 Daniel Fallström in *Stockholms-Tidningen* 4 May 1917.
35 Birger Bæckström in *Göteborgs-Posten* 11 May 1917.
36 Sven Söderman in *Stockholms Dagblad* 4 May 1917.
37 Sign. c. in *Dagbladet* 10 Sep. 1953.
38 *Social-Demokraten* 17 Oct. 1942.
39 Strindberg had his entrance from Karlavägen 40, later 80. Molander lived at Karlaplan 6.
40 *Stockholms-Tidningen* 17 Oct. 1942.
41 Sigfrid Siwertz in *Vecko-Journalen*, No. 43, 1942.
42 The observation is Bark's, 142.
43 Erik Wettergren in *Afton-Tidningen* 17 Oct. 1942.
44 Agne Beijer in *Göteborgs Handels- och Sjöfartstidning* 19 Oct. 1942.
45 Wettergren, op. cit.
46 *Bonniers Litterära Magasin*, 11/9, 1942, 7.
47 Bark, 144.
48 Siwertz, op. cit.
49 Svensson, op. cit.
50 Beyer, op. cit.
51 Grevenius, op. cit.
52 P.G. Peterson in *Aftonbladet* 17 Oct. 1942.
53 Sten Selander in *Svenska Dagbladet* 17 Oct. 1942.
54 Beyer, op. cit.
55 Peterson, op. cit.
56 Wettergren, op. cit.
57 Beijer, op. cit.
58 Loc. cit.
59 The description is put together from various reviews.
60 Beyer, op. cit.
61 Grevenius, op. cit.
62 Beyer, op. cit.
63 *Ny Tid* 16 Sep. 1946.
64 Sign. Holl., 20 Feb. 1948.
65 Aud Thagaard in *Morgenposten* 9 Oct. 1953.
66 *Dagens Nyheter* 9 Oct. 1953.
67 Ebbe Linde in *Dagens Nyheter* 12 May 1962.
68 Ibid.
69 Theatre program for Bergman's *Ghost Sonata* production in Malmö, 5.
70 Steene (1998) 12, 18.
71 Malmö theatre program, loc. cit.
72 Ibid., 7.

73   Bergman (1992) 140. The Markers (1992, 76) claim that there were only four performances.
74   Marker (1992), 75.
75   Bergman (1992) 123. It remains a riddle how this rhymes with Bergman's statement, in his program note for his 1940 *Macbeth* production, that Shakespeare's play is "an anti-Nazi drama" (Billquist, 26).
76   Timm, 127.
77   Malmö program, 7.
78   Bergman in Timm, 127.
79   Sign. Lager in *Göteborgs Handels- och Sjöfartstidning* 19 March 1954.
80   Per Erik Wahlund in *Svenska Dagbladet* 6 March 1954.
81   Nils Beyer in *Morgon-Tidningen* 6 March 1954.
82   Hansingvar Hanson in *Stockholms-Tidningen* 6 March 1954. Cf. Steene's remark (1998, 29) that when Bergman started out as a director, "he brought with him a puppeteer master's view of a performance, someone pulling strings and expecting his marionettes to move at his will."
83   P.G. Peterson in *Aftonbladet* 6 March 1954.
84   *Expressen* 6 March 1954.
85   Wirmark, 79.
86   Ibid., 82.
87   Sjöman, 11.
88   Information by Erland Josephson, at the time head of Dramaten, on 24 Nov. 1972. In a very different Polish version (see production list), the two roles had been played by the same actress already in 1964.
89   Interview 5 Jan. 1973.
90   Fredrikshovsgatan 5 and the Oscar church respectively, both in Stockholm.
91   Törnqvist (1999b) 235-37.
92   Interview 5 Jan. 1973.
93   Bergman in interview 5 Jan. 1973.
94   Bergman: "I have only retained those sounds which are suggestive to an audience today." Interview 5 Jan. 1973.
95   The same double meaning is found in the nightmare sequence at the beginning of Bergman's film WILD STRAWBERRIES, where the tolling of church bells warns the guilty old Isaac Borg that he is soon to die.
96   Undated letter to Egil Törnqvist, received Jan. 1973.
97   Bergman has declared that since the making of his film THE SILENCE, first called "God's Silence," in 1963, he does not believe in a life after death.
98   Marik Vos had originally designed a realistic, blue uniform.
99   Interview 5 Jan. 1973. – Later Bergman (1989, 138-39) has revealed that the inspiration for this device was, at least partly, autobiographical. In the "young beauty" of Cecilia von Gotthard, whom he courted for a while when he had finished school, "glimpses of shades of her mother's behaviour could be seen. Later, this led me to the conclusion that the Mummy and the Young Lady [-] ought to be played by the same actress."
100   Bergman (1989) 123.
101   In accordance with Swedish habits of address, Bengtsson literally says "Company director Hummel."

102 For concrete examples, see Törnqvist (1973) 216-17.
103 *Dagens Nyheter* 14 Jan. 1973.
104 *Svenska Dagbladet* 14 Jan. 1973.
105 *Göteborgs-Posten* 14 Jan. 1973.
106 *Aftonbladet* 14 Jan. 1973.
107 Lars Ring (*Svenska Dagbladet* 13 Feb. 2000) rightly pointed to the parallel with the opening of *A Dream Play*, where Indra's Daughter descends to earth. However, where she, being a goddess, moves downwards, the Student, being a 'child,' crawls upwards.
108 In the program, the list of the cast is significantly inbscribed in the Red House, shadowing in the background.
109 Cf. the comment in Törnqvist (1995) 180-81 on the interiors of FANNY AND ALEXANDER.
110 Barbara Villiger Heilig in *Neue Zürcher Zeitung* 14 Feb. 2000.
111 Information from the scenographer, Göran Wassberg.
112 Leif Zern in *Dagens Nyheter* 13 Feb. 2000.
113 She was not unlike the crucifix in THE SEVENTH SEAL and WINTER LIGHT.
114 Ring, op. cit.
115 *Arbetet* 17 Feb. 2000.
116 Barbro Westling in *Aftonbladet* 13 Feb. 2000.
117 Sjögren, op. cit.
118 Leif Zern in *Dagens Nyheter* 13 Feb. 2000.
119 Carlhåkan Larsén in *Sydsvenska Dagbladet* 13 Feb. 2000.
      Gun Zanton-Ericsson in *Östgöta-Correspondenten* 14 Feb. 2000.
120 *Expressen* 13 Feb. 2000.

Notes to Four: Adaptations

1   Esslin (1980) 177.
2   Concerning the narrator as reporter in radio drama, see Hallingberg, 162-65, 260.
3   Esslin (1980) 183.
4   Finland-Swedish, spoken by about 5% of the population in Finland, differs less from the Swedish spoken in Sweden than Scottish from English. Yet it is easily recognized through its deviating intonation and pronunciation.
5   For a survey of formal differences between stage and screen reception, see Törnqvist (1999b) 12-25.
6   Bazin (92) defends the fixed camera, usually considered an undesirable 'theatrical' device, holding that it reveals "a reluctance to fragment things arbitrarily and a desire instead to show an image that is uniformly understandable and that compels the spectator to make his own choice."
7   He was to produce *A Dream Play*, very freely, for Swedish TV in 1980.
8   The actor, Allan Edwall, who had played the part of the Old Man in Verner-Carlsson's radio version did the part of the Student in Molander's production at Dramaten at about the same time. Ten years later he again did the part of the Old Man in Bergenstråhle's TV version. See production list.

Notes to Epilogue

1   Valency, 348-49.
2   *Nouvelles Littéraires*, 3 Feb. 1923. Quoted from Swerling, 9.
3   *Avenir*, 4 March 1933. Quoted from Swerling, 13.
4   Lindström in Strindberg (1963) 74.
5   See Diebold, 235-335, and Dahlström, 117-19.
6   Sokel, xiv.
7   Lagerkvist, 43.
8   Bergman (1928) 68.
9   Abell, 32, 34.
10   Bayerdörfer et al., 324.
11   "Strindberg and Our Theatre," 3 Jan. 1924, *Provincetown Playbill*. In a letter to Kenneth Macgowan (Bryer, 267), dated 8 Feb. 1951, O'Neill declares: "I wish I could see some Strindberg. I think back to *The Spook Sonata*." For Strindberg's influence on O'Neill, see Törnqvist (1981).
12   Sheaffer, 317.
13   Published in Artaud, 127-39.
14   Swerling, 68.
15   Alldahl, 35.
16   Artaud quoted from Innes, 73-74.
17   Ibid., 75.
18   Ibid., 74. Cf. Bergman's 2000 production.
19   Esslin (1961) 251.
20   Bair, 402. See also Heed.
21   Oster, passim; Meidal, 173, 178-79.
22   Knapp, 228.
23   *Théâtre Populaire*, No. 31, 1958. Quoted from Swerling, x.
24   Ward, 254. For Witkiewicz' interest in *The Ghost Sonata*, see Uggla, 121-22.
25   Törnqvist (1976a) 82, and Törnqvist (1999a) 64-69. The actress playing Anna was also the Milkmaid in Bergman's 1973 production of *The Ghost Sonata*.
26   Törnqvist (1976a) 81-82, 87-89.
27   Sjöman, 61.
28   Ibid., 24.
29   Ibid., 16-17, note 1.
30   Bergman (1970), 182. This passage is inaccurately translated in Bergman (1993), 168.
31   Blackwell, 53.
32   Bergman (1989) 150.
33   Quoted from Sjögren, 38.
34   Timm, 127.
35   Loc. cit.
36   Gertraude Wilhelm's summary of *Gespenstersonate* in Radler, 673.
37   "Strindberg and Our Theatre," 3 Jan. 1924.

Cited works

References to newspaper articles, including reviews, theatre programs etc. are found only in the notes.

Abell, Kjeld. 1962. *Teaterstrejf i påskevejr*. Copenhagen: Gyldendal.

Alldahl, Tomas. 1974. *Ett drömspel* och *Spöksonaten*: Det konkreta språkets teater, *Meddelanden från Strindbergssällskapet*, 53/54.

Artaud, Antonin. 1961. Projet de mise en scène pour *La Sonate des spectres* de Strindberg. In *Oeuvres complètes*, 2, Paris: Gallimard.

Aslan, Odette. 1988. *Roger Blin and Twentieth-Century Playwrights*, trans. Ruby Cohn, Cambridge: Cambridge UP.

Bair, Deirdre. 1990. *Samuel Beckett*, New York: Touchstone.

Bandy, Stephen C. 1968. Strindberg's Biblical Sources for The Ghost Sonata, *Scandinavian Studies*, 40/3.

Bark, Richard. 1981. *Strindbergs drömspelsteknik – i drama och teater*, Lund: Studentlitteratur.

Bayerdörfer, Hans-Peter, Hans Otto Horch, Georg-Michael Schulz (eds.). 1983. *Strindberg auf der deutschen Bühne: Eine exemplarische Rezeptions-geschichte der Moderne in Dokumenten (1890 bis 1925)*, Neumünster: Karl Wachholtz.

Bazin, André. 1967. *What is Cinema?*, 1, trans. Hugh Gray, Berkeley: U of California P.

Bentley, Eric. 1955. *The Playwright as Thinker*, New York: Meridian Books.

Berendsohn, Walter. 1965. *August Strindbergs skärgårds- och Stockholms-skildringar: Struktur- och stilstudier*, Stockholm: Rabén & Sjögren.

Bergman, Gösta M. 1928. *Pär Lagerkvists dramatik*, Stockholm: Norstedts.

– 1966. *Den moderna teaterns genombrott 1890-1925*, Stockholm: Bonniers.

Bergman, Ingmar. 1970. Stig Björkman, Torsten Manns, Jonas Sima, *Bergman om Bergman*, Stockholm: Norstedts.

– 1992. *The Magic Lantern: An Autobiography*, trans. Joan Tate, Harmondsworth: Penguin.

– 1993. Stig Björkman etc. *Bergman on Bergman: Interviews with Ingmar Bergman*, trans. Paul Britten Austin, New York: Da Capo.

Billquist, Fritiof. 1960. *Ingmar Bergman: Teatermannen och filmskaparen*, Stockholm: Natur och Kultur.

Blackwell, Marilyn Johns. 1981. The Chamber Plays and the Trilogy: A Re-valuation of the Case of Strindberg and Bergman. In Marilyn Johns

Blackwell (ed.), *Structures of Influence: A Comparative Approach to August Strindberg*, Chapel Hill: U of North Carolina P.

Brandell, Gunnar. 1981. Questions without Answers: On Strindberg's and Ibsen's Dialogue. In Marilyn Johns Blackwell (ed.), *Structures of Influence: A Comparative Approach to August Strindberg*, Chapel Hill: U of North Carolina P.

– 1989. *Strindberg – ett författarliv*, 4, Stockholm: Bonniers.

Bryant-Bertail, Sarah. 1988. The Tower of Babel: Space and Movement in *The Ghost Sonata*. In Göran Stockenström (ed.), *Strindberg's Dramaturgy*, Minneapolis: U of Minnesota P.

Bryer, Jackson R. 1982. *The Theatre we Worked for*. New Haven: Yale UP.

Buchwald, Reinhard. 1964. *Führer durch Goethes Faustdichtung*, Stuttgart: Kröner.

Converse, Terry John. 1999. *The Psychology of the Grotesque in August Strindberg's* The Ghost Sonata, Lewiston, NY: Edwin Mellen.

Dahlström, Carl. 1965. *Strindberg's Dramatic Expressionism*, 2nd ed. Ann Arbor: U of Michigan.

Delblanc, Sven. 1968. Kärlekens föda: Ett motiv i Strindbergs kammarspel – bakgrund och innebörd. In Egil Törnqvist (ed.), *Drama och teater*, Stockholm: Almqvist & Wiksell.

Diebold, Bernhard. 1928. *Anarchie im Drama: Kritik und Darstellung der modernen Dramatik*, Berlin: Heinrich Keller.

Ekman, Hans-Göran. 1997. *Villornas värld: Studier i Strindbergs kammarspel*, Stockholm: Gidlunds.

Esslin, Martin. 1961. *The Theatre of the Absurd*. Garden City, NY: Doubleday Anchor.

– 1980. *Mediations: Essays on Brecht, Beckett and the Media*, London: Methuen.

Falck, August. 1935. *Fem år med Strindberg*, Stockholm: Wahlström & Widstrand.

Floerke, Gustav. 1902. *Böcklin: Aufzeichnungen und Entwürfe*, 2nd ed., München: Bruckmann.

Frænkl, Pavel. 1966. *Strindbergs dramatiske fantasi i* Spöksonaten: *En stildramaturgisk undersøkelse*, Oslo: Universitetsforlaget.

Gado, Frank. 1986. *The Passion of Ingmar Bergman*, Durham: Duke UP.

Hallingberg, Gunnar. 1967. *Radiodramat: Svensk hörspelsdiktning – bakgrund, utveckling, formvärld*, Stockholm: Sveriges Radio.

Heed, Sven Åke. 1994. La Sonate des spectres et le théâtre d'avant-garde français. In Gunnel Engwall (ed.), *Strindberg et la France*, Stockholm: Almqvist & Wiksell International.

Innes, Christopher. 1993. *Avant Garde Theatre 1892-1992*, London/New York: Routledge.

Jarvi, Raymond. 1972. Strindberg's *The Ghost Sonata* and Sonata Form, *Mosaic*, 5/4.

Jolivet, Alfred. 1931. *Le Théâtre de Strindberg*, Paris: Bibliothèque de la Revue des cours et conferences.

Kjellin, Gösta/Marie-Louise Ramnefalk. 1971. *Modern dramatik: Tio analyser*, Stockholm: Bonniers.

Kennedy, Andrew K. 1983. *Dramatic Dialogue: The Duologue of Personal Encounter*, Cambridge: Cambridge UP.

Knape, Karen. 2000. *Toten-Insel*: Ett dramatiskt "experiment." In Birgitta Steene (ed.), *Strindbergiana*, 15, Stockholm: Atlantis.

Knapp, Gerhard P. 1981. From *lilla helvetet* to the Boxing Ring: Strindberg and Dürrenmatt. In Marilyn Johns Blackwell (ed.), *Structures of Influence: A Comparative Approach to August Strindberg*, Chapel Hill: U of North Carolina P.

Kvam, Kela. 1974. *Max Reinhardt og Strindbergs visionære dramatik*, København: Akademisk forlag.

Lagerkvist, Pär. 1918. Modern teater: Synpunkter och angrepp. In *Dramatik*, 1, Stockholm: Bonniers, 1956.

Lamm, Martin. 1926. *Strindbergs dramer*, 2, Stockholm: Bonniers.

– 1942. *August Strindberg*, 2, Stockholm: Bonniers.

Leifer, Leif. 1960. Den lutrende ild: En studie i symbolikken i Strindbergs kammerspil, *Samlaren*, 81, Uppsala: Svenska Litteratursällskapet.

Lindström, Göran. 1956. Strindberg contra Ibsen: Något om *Vildanden* och *Spöksonaten*, *Ibsen-årbok*, 1955-56, Skien: Oluf Rasmussen.

– 1964. Dialog och bildspråk i Strindbergs kammarspel. In Göran Lindström (ed.), *Strindbergs språk och stil*, Lund: Gleerups.

– 1969. *Att läsa dramatik*, Lund: Gleerups.

Lindström, Hans. 1977. *Strindberg och böckerna I: Biblioteken 1883, 1892 och 1912*, Uppsala: Svenska Litteratursällskapet.

– 1979. Mosaiken i Spöksonaten, *Svensk Litteraturtidskrift*, 42/3.

– 1990. *Strindberg och böckerna II: Boklån och läsning*, Uppsala: Svenska Litteratursällskapet.

Lunin, Hanno. 1962. *Strindbergs Dramen*, Emsdetten: Lechte.

Marker, Lise-Lone and Frederick J. Marker. 1992. *Ingmar Bergman: A Life in the Theater*, Cambridge: Cambridge UP.

– 1996. *A History of Scandinavian Theatre*, Cambridge: Cambridge UP.

Mays, Milton A. 1967. Strindberg's *Ghost Sonata*: Parodied Fairy Tale on Original Sin, *Modern Drama*, 10/2.

Meidal, Hannes. 1999. Gubben Hummel – Hamms anfader? Samuel Becketts
    Slutspel i ljuset av August Strindbergs *Spöksonaten*. In Birgitta Steene (ed.),
    Strindbergiana, 14, Stockholm: Atlantis.
Meyer, Michael. 1987. *Strindberg: A Biography*, Oxford/New York: Oxford
    UP.
Michal, E. 1981. *Tal- och sångpjeser uppförde å Stockholms samtliga teatrar
    och öfriga lokaler spelåren 1863-1913*, Teatervetenskap, 23, Solna.
Northam, John. 1966. Strindberg's *Spook Sonata*. In Carl Reinhold
    Smedmark (ed.), *Essays on Strindberg*, Stockholm: Strindberg Society.
Ollén, Gunnar. 1961. *Strindbergs dramatik*, Stockholm: Sveriges Radio.
– 1982. *Strindbergs dramatik*, Stockholm: Sveriges Radio.
Oster, Rose-Marie. 1969. Hamm and Hummel: Beckett and Strindberg on
    Human Condition, *Scandinavian Studies*, 41/4.
Paul, Fritz. 1990. "Innerlich und äusserlich schrecklich verwickelt."
    Übersetzer-Inszenierungen in Strindbergs *Gespenstersonate* und *Nach
    Damaskus II*. In Brigitte Schultze (ed.), *Literatur und Theater: Traditionen
    und Konventionen als Problem der Dramenübersetzung*, Tübingen:
    Gunter Narr.
Pfister, Manfred. 1991. *The Theory and Analysis of Drama*, trans. John
    Halliday, Cambridge: Cambridge UP.
Radler, Rudolf. 1985. *Knaurs grosser Schauspielführer*. München: Droemer
    Knaur.
Rokem, Freddie. 1986. *Theatrical Space in Ibsen, Chekhov and Strindberg:
    Public Forms of Privacy*, Ann Arbor: Umi Research.
Sheaffer, Louis. 1968. *O'Neill: Son and Playwright*, Boston: Little, Brown,
    and Co.
Sjögren, Henrik. 1968. *Ingmar Bergman på teatern*, Stockholm: Almqvist &
    Wiksell.
Sjöman, Vilgot. 1963. *L136: Dagbok med Ingmar Bergman*, Stockholm:
    Norstedts.
Sjöstedt, Nils Åke. 1981. *The Ghost Sonata*. In Oskar Bandle et al. (eds.),
    Strindbergs Dramen im Lichte neuerer Methodendiskussionen,
    Basel/Frankfurt am Main: Helbing & Lichtenhahn.
Sokel, Walter H. (ed.). 1963. Introduction to *An Anthology of German Ex-
    pressionist Drama*, Garden City, NY: Doubleday Anchor.
Sondrup, Stephen. 1981. Aspects of Musical Logic in Strindberg's
    Spöksonaten, *Scandinavian Studies*, 53/1.
Sprinchorn, Evert. 1976. Heine, Hummel, and the Hyacinth Girl,
    Meddelanden från Strindbergssällskapet, 56.
– 1978. Hell and Purgatory in Strindberg, *Scandinavian Studies*, 50/4.
– 1982. *Strindberg as Dramatist*, New Haven/London: Yale UP.

Steene, Birgitta. 1982. *August Strindberg: An Introduction to his Major Works*, Stockholm: Almqvist & Wiksell International/ Atlantic Highlands, NJ: Humanities Press Inc.

– 1998. Ingmar Bergman's First Meeting with Thalia, *Nordic Theatre Studies*, 11.

Stockenström, Göran. 1978. The Journey from the Isle of Life to the Isle of Death: The Idea of Reconciliation in *The Ghost Sonata*, *Scandinavian Studies*, 50/2.

– (ed.) 1988. *Strindberg's Dramaturgy*, Minneapolis: U of Minnesota P.

Strindberg, August. 1907. *Spök-sonaten: Kammarspel Opus III*, Stockholm: Ljus.

– 1908. *Gespenstersonate*, trans. Emil Schering. In *Strindbergs Werke: Deutsche Gesamtausgabe*, *1/9*, *Kammerspiele*, München/Leipzig: Georg Müller.

– 1912-21. John Landquist (ed.), *Samlade skrifter av August Strindberg*, Stockholm: Bonniers. [*Spök-sonaten* in SS 45, 1921, 147-211]

– 1916 (1). *The Spook Sonata*, trans. Edwin Björkman. In *Plays by August Strindberg*, Fourth Series, New York: Scribner's.

– 1918. August Falck (ed.), *Strindberg och teater*, Stockholm: Dahlbergs Förlag A.B.

– 1926. *La Sonate des spectres*, trans. Maurice Rémon, Paris: Stock.

– 1929 (2). *The Ghost Sonata*. In *Easter and Other Plays*, trans. Erik Palmstierna and James Bernard Fagan, London: Jonathan Cape.

– 1955 (3). *The Ghost Sonata*. In *Six Plays of Strindberg*, trans. Elizabeth Sprigge, Garden City, NY: Doubleday Anchor.

– 1959. *Open Letters to the Intimate Theater*, trans. and introd. Walter Johnson, Seattle and London: U of Washington P.

– 1960 (4). *The Ghost Sonata*, trans. Max Faber. In *Miss Julie and Other Plays*, London: Heinemann.

– 1961. *La Sonate des spectres*, trans. Arthur Adamov and Carl-Gustaf Bjurström. In *Théâtre 6: Pièces de chambre*, Paris: L'Arche.

– 1962 (5). *The Ghost Sonata*, in *The Chamber Plays*, trans. and introd. Evert Sprinchorn, New York: Dutton.

– 1963. *Spöksonaten*, ed. and introd. Göran Lindström, Lund: Gleerups.

– 1965 (6). *The Ghost Sonata*. In *Eight Expressionist Plays*, trans. Arvid Paulson, New York: New York UP.

– 1966 (7). *A Dream Play and The Ghost Sonata*, trans. Carl Richard Mueller, San Francisco: Chandler.

– 1973 (8). *The Ghost Sonata*. In *A Dream Play and Four Chamber Plays*. trans. Walter Johnson, Seattle: U of Washington P.

– 1976 (9). *The Ghost Sonata*. In *Plays: One*, trans. Michael Meyer, London: Methuen.

– 1976. Björn Meidal (ed.), *August Strindbergs Brev*, 15, Stockholm: Bonniers.

– 1977a. *Ockulta dagboken: 1896-1908*, Stockholm: Gidlunds.

– 1977b. (10) *Ghost Sonata* and *When We Dead Awaken*, trans. Thaddeus L. Torp, Arlington Heights, IL: AHM Publishing Corporation.

– 1981-. Lars Dahlbäck (chief ed.), *August Strindbergs Samlade Verk*, Stockholm: Almqvist & Wiksell/Norstedts. [*Spök-sonaten* in SV 58, 1991, ed. Gunnar Ollén, 159-225]

– 1981 (11). *The Ghost Sonata*. In *Five Plays*, trans. Harry G. Carlson, Berkeley: U of California P.

– 1986a. *The Ghost Sonata*. In *Selected Plays*, 2, trans. Evert Sprinchorn, Minneapolis: U of Minnesota P.

– 1986b. *La Sonate des spectres*, trans. Arthur Adamov and Carl-Gustaf Bjurström. In *Théâtre complet*, 6, Paris: L'Arche.

– 1991a. Barbro Ståhle Sjönell (ed.), *Katalog över "Gröna säcken": Strindbergs efterlämnade papper i Kungl. biblioteket*, SgNM 1-9, Stockholm: Kungl. biblioteket.

– 1991b. Björn Meidal (ed.), *August Strindbergs Brev*, 17, Stockholm: Bonniers.

– 1991c (12). *The Ghost Sonata*. In *The Chamber Plays*, trans. Eivor Martinus, London: Absolute Classics.

– 1992. Michael Robinson (ed.), *Strindberg's Letters*, 2, Chicago/London: U of Chicago P.

– 1997a (13). *The Ghost Sonata*. In *Three Chamber Plays*, trans. Inga-Stina Ewbank, Leeds: Alumnus.

– 1997b (14). *Strindberg – Other Sides: Seven Plays*, trans. Joe Martin, New York: Peter Lang.

– 1998 (15). *The Ghost Sonata*. In *Miss Julie and Other Plays*, trans. Michael Robinson, Oxford/New York: Oxford UP.

Styan, J.L. 1982. *Max Reinhardt*, Cambridge: Cambridge UP.

Swerling, Anthony. 1971. *Strindberg's Impact in France 1920-1960*, Cambridge: Trinity Lane.

Szondi, Peter. 1987. *Theory of the Modern Drama*, ed. and trans. Michael Hays, Cambridge: Polity.

Tidström, Karin. 1999. *Cette fameuse "Sonate des spectres...": Une pièce de chambre d'August Strindberg en France. Traduction et réception*, Cahiers de la recherche, 9, Stockholm: Stockholm University.

Timm, Mikael. 1994. *Ögats glädje: Texter om film*, Stockholm: Carlssons.

Torsslow, Stig. 1972/73. *Spöksonaten och Den polske juden*, Dramaten, 24.

Törnqvist, Egil. 1969. *Hamlet* and *The Ghost Sonata. Drama Survey*, 7/1-2.
– 1973. *Bergman och Strindberg*: Spöksonaten – *drama och iscensättning. Dramaten 1973*, Stockholm: Prisma.
– 1976a. Kammarspel på tre sätt. In Jan Stenkvist (ed.), *Från Snoilsky till Sonnevi: Litteraturvetenskapliga studier tillägnade Gunnar Brandell*, Stockholm: Natur och Kultur.
– 1976b. Att översätta Strindberg: *Spöksonaten* på engelska. *Svensk Litteraturtidskrift*, 2.
– 1979. *Faust* and *The Ghost Sonata*. In Wilhelm Friese (ed.), *Strindberg und die deutschsprachigen Länder: Beiträge zur nordischen Philologie*, 8, Basel/Stuttgart: Helbing & Lichtenhahn.
– 1981. Strindberg and O'Neill. In Marilyn Johns Blackwell (ed.), *Structures of Influence: A Comparative Approach to August Strindberg*, Chapel Hill: U of North Carolina P.
– 1995. *Between Stage and Screen: Ingmar Bergman Directs*, Amsterdam: Amsterdam UP.
– 1998. Translating Strindbergian Imagery for the Stage, *Tijdschrift voor Skandinavistiek*, 19/1.
– 1999a. Strindberg, Bergman and the Silent Character, *Tijdschrift voor Skandinavistiek*, 20/1.
– 1999b. *Ibsen, Strindberg and the Intimate Theatre: Studies in TV Presentation*, Amsterdam: Amsterdam UP.
Uggla, Andrzej. 1977. *Strindberg och den polska teatern 1890-1970: En studie i reception* [with a summary in English], Uppsala: Lundequistska.
Valency, Maurice. 1963. *The Flower and the Castle: An Introduction to Modern Drama*, New York: Grosset & Dunlap.
Vowles, Richard. 1967. Strindberg and Beethoven. In Gunnar Svanfeldt (ed.), *Växelverkan mellan skönlitteraturen och andra konstarter*, Uppsala: Litteraturhistoriska institutionen.
Ward, John. 1980. *The Social and Religious Plays of Strindberg*, London: Athlone.
Wilkinson, Lynn R. 1993. The Politics of the Interior: Strindberg's Chamber Plays, *Scandinavian Studies*, 65/4.
Williams, Raymond. 1973. *Drama from Ibsen to Brecht*, Harmondsworth: Penguin.
Wirmark, Margareta. 1999. Strindberg versus Bergman: The End of Spöksonaten, *Tijdschrift voor Skandinavistiek*, 20/1.
Zelger, Franz. 1991. *Die Toteninsel: Selbstheroisierung und Abgesang der abendländischen Kultur*, Frankfurt: Fischer.

List of illustrations

Cover photo: The Young Lady and the Student in Ingmar Bergman's 2000 production of *The Ghost Sonata*. Photo: Bengt Wanselius.

1 Title page of Strindberg's fair copy of *The Ghost Sonata*. Courtesy Strindbergsmuseet.

2 A page of the original manuscript of *The Ghost Sonata*. Courtesy Kungl. Biblioteket.

3 Front cover of the first edition of *The Ghost Sonata*.

4 The stage of Strindberg's and Falck's Intimate Theatre in Stockholm. Courtesy Strindbergsmuseet.

5 Program for the first production of *The Ghost Sonata*. Courtesy Kungl. Biblioteket.

6 The Old Man and the Mummy in Max Reinhardt's 1916 production. Drawing: Gerda Ploug-Sarp.

7 Act I in Olof Molander's 1942 production. Photo: Almberg & Preinitz. Courtesy Drottningholms teatermuseum.

8 Act II in Olof Molander's 1942 production. Photo: Almberg & Preinitz. Courtesy Drottningholms teatermuseum.

9 The Old Man and the Mummy in Act II of Olof Molander's 1942 production. Photo: Almberg & Preinitz. Courtesy Drottningholms teatermuseum.

10 Act III in Olof Molander's 1962 production. Photo: Beata Bergström. Courtesy Drottningholms teatermuseum.

11 Act I in Ingmar Bergman's 1941 production. Courtesy Drottningholms teatermuseum.

12 The ghost supper in Bergman's 1941 production. Courtesy Drottningholms teatermuseum.

13 The Student and the Milkmaid in Ingmar Bergman's 1954 production. Photo: Skånereportage, Malmö. Courtesy Malmö Dramatiska Teater.

14 The Old Man and the Mummy in Bergman's 1954 production. Photo: Skånereportage, Malmö. Courtesy Drottningholms teatermuseum.

15 The Student and the Young Lady in Bergman's 1954 production. Photo: Skånereportage, Malmö. Courtesy Drottningholms teatermuseum.

16 Act I in Ingmar Bergman's 1973 production. Photo: Beata Bergström. Courtesy Drottningholms teatermuseum.

17 The Milkmaid and the Student in Bergman's 1973 production. Photo: Beata Bergström. Courtesy Drottningholms teatermuseum.

18 The Old Man and the Student in Bergman's 1973 production. Photo: Beata Bergström. Courtesy Drottningholms teatermuseum.

19 The Young Lady in Act I of Bergman's 1973 production. Photo: Beata Bergström. Courtesy Drottningholms teatermuseum.

20 The Milkmaid drowning at the end of Act I in Bergman's 1973 production. Photo: Beata Bergström. Courtesy Drottningholms teatermuseum.

21 Act II in Bergman's 1973 production. Photo: Beata Bergström. Courtesy Drottningholms teatermuseum.

22 The Mummy in Act II of Bergman's 1973 production. Photo: Beata Bergström. Courtesy Drottningholms teatermuseum.

23 The Old Man unmasking the Colonel in Bergman's 1973 production. Photo: Beata Bergström. Courtesy Drottningholms teatermuseum.

24 Bengtsson unmasking the Old Man in Bergman's 1973 production. Photo: Beata Bergström. Courtesy Drottningholms teatermuseum.

25 Act III in Bergman's 1973 production. Photo: Beata Bergström. Courtesy Drottningholms teatermuseum.

26 The Cook in Bergman's 1973 production. Photo: Beata Bergström. Courtesy Drottningholms teatermuseum.

27 The Student 'raping' the Young Lady in Bergman's 1973 production. Photo: Beata Bergström. Courtesy Drottningholms teatermuseum.

28 The curled up Young Lady and the disillusioned Student in Bergman's 1973 production. Photo: Beata Bergström. Courtesy Drottingholms teatermuseum.

29 The ending in Bergman's 1973 production. Photo: Beata Bergström. Courtesy Drottningholms teatermuseum.

30 The Milkmaid drowning in Bergman's 2000 production. Photo: Bengt Wanselius.

31 The Mummy and the Old Man in Bergman's 2000 production. Photo: Bengt Wanselius.

32 The Student attacking the Young Lady in Bergman's 2000 production. Photo: Bengt Wanselius.

33 The Old Man and the Student in Johan Bergenstråhle's 1972 TV production. Photo: Lars Wiklund.

Index

Refers to pp. 7-170, 177-88 and 241-50. Pages containing illustrations are in italics.

CPSIA information can be obtained
at www.ICGtesting.com
Printed in the USA
LVOW05s1834210816
501252LV00026B/795/P